CHARACTERS OF SHAKESPEARE'S PLAYS

by WILLIAM HAZLITT

Prophets of Sensibility:
Precursors of Modern Cultural Thought
General Editor: Professor Harold Bloom,
Yale University

CHELSEA HOUSE
1983

This edition is a reprint of the 1901 edition
published by George Bell and Sons

Copyright © 1983 by Chelsea House Publishers
All rights reserved
Printed and bound in the United States of America

ISBN: 0-87754-332-1

PROPHETS OF SENSIBILITY: PRECURSORS OF MODERN CULTURAL THOUGHT

by Harold Bloom
Professor of the Humanities
Yale University

It was one of the peculiarities of literary Modernism, in the Age of Pound, Joyce and Eliot, and of their New Critical followers, to argue that the imaginative literature of the twentieth century had its true origins in seventeenth-century sensibility. In this polemical contention, Eliot could insist that his poetic and critical stance, or more simply his personal culture, had its sources in Lancelot Andrewes and John Donne, rather, say, than in Walter Pater and Matthew Arnold. Assertions of a remote ancestry have the special charm of escaping the immediate squalors of the family romance. We need not smile too ironically at the personal mythologies of an Eliot or a Pound when we reflect upon the even more formidable Sigmund Freud, who in *Beyond the Pleasure Principle* cheerfully proclaims his descent from Empedocles, safely distant at two millennia, while stubbornly denying his palpable precursor, Arthur Schopenhauer.

But the wry humor of these necessary stratagems of the spirit cannot be allowed to obscure the truth of intellectual and aesthetic genealogy. Wallace Stevens once remarked that genealogy is the art of correcting other genealogists' mistakes. One broad way of characterizing the Prophets of Sensibility series is to observe that it intends to correct Eliot's persuasive misreading of the family relationship between nineteenth- and twentieth-century thought and literature. A book like Walter Pater's early masterpiece, *The Renaissance,* reverberates endlessly in such characteristic modern creators as Yeats, Eliot, Joyce, Pound, Stevens, Woolf, Hart Crane, and even in a vitalistic heretic like D. H. Lawrence. None of them (except for Yeats) would have granted Pater's authority and fatherhood, yet he haunts them all (and many others) both in cadence and in concept. Pater, like Arnold, Ruskin, Carlyle, Butler, Hazlitt, De Quincey, and Coleridge is simply too close for the comfort of autonomy to assert itself.

Certainly the anxiety of influence is a crucial sorrow in the vexed story of the true heritage of Modernism. But, as an anxiety, it may conceal deeper continuities between Romantic and Victorian forerunners and their belated heirs. Prophecy, an ancient Hebraic mode of literature, became in the nineteenth century a new kind of vitalistic mode, one that erased the always wavering boundaries between criticism and creation. What, after all, is the literary genre of Pater's *The Renaissance?* The prose *Imaginary Conversations* of Landor and the verse monologues of Browning are no more radical as experiments than are these reveries of Walter Pater. Pater blends moral reflection, prose poetry, psychological portraiture, art and literary criticism, cultural history and a curious kind of mythopoeic fiction into an amalgam that defies conventional description, but that has the ultimate purpose of subverting Christian evaluations of the *agon* between the desires of this world and the work of the spirit. As a prophet, Pater restores to art the epiphanies appropriated by orthodox dualisms, whether of religion or of philosophy.

Pater's *The Renaissance* dramatizes the authentic burden of the Prophets of Sensibility. This burden is not so much secularization as it is the problematic transferences and descents of authority from earlier times, when it could be recognized and accepted, to the threshold of our age, where authority can be recognized precisely as what has vanished, and what could not be accepted if somehow it reappeared. Freud, who devised the clinical transference of the model of the taboo, attempted to make of psychoanalysis a modernist *praxis* that would reestablish the images of authority upon a supposedly scientific basis. Ruskin, Carlyle, Pater and the other Victorian prophets assumed, rather, that authority could be established again only upon an aesthetic basis. Had Freud (and Nietzsche) written in English, we would group them now with the Prophets of Sensibility. Science and philosophy, like religion, have yielded to the literary culture, and the pragmatic consequences of that yielding are at the center of Romantic and Victorian prophecy.

Prophecy, in the Hebraic sense, was moral truth-telling of the most violent kind, always following the formula of "The Word of God came to me . . ." The God Word that came to the nineteenth-century prophets mixed perception and sensation into a new kind of sensibility, one that is still with us today. Difficult to describe, this sensibility emphasizes a continuum haunted by intimations of mortality punctuated by brief bursts of radiance–privileged moments in which a peculiar vividness gives the illusion of redeeming life. It may be the stigma of the nineteenth-century Prophets of Sensibility that (except for Pater) they sought to combat this climate of the spirit but oddly fostered it implicitly (even as Pater did so overtly). The increasing internalization of the self depended upon an augmentation of estrangement from the object world, and what was intended as prophetic warning and lament as to this estrangement became instead a subtle suggestion of an inevitable movement in elite sensibility.

Today we have the strange anomaly that Nietzsche, the Continental version of the Prophets of Sensibility, is credited with fathering the future, while the

Prophets are neglected. But time's revenges work themselves out, and these writers will father the future again, even as they prophesied our current sensibility. They could not save or even preserve the post-Christian spirituality they sought to imbue in society, but they fostered in its place a pragmatic triumph of literary culture, beyond religion and beyond speculative philosophy. Psychoanalysis, despite its scientism, is only another form of that literary culture. So, in another way, are the textualist literary criticism and language-oriented "human sciences" that are vivid parts of Structuralist and post-Structuralist formulations. There are true and false prophets of sensibility, even as there were true and false prophets among the ancient Hebrews. The test for prophecy finally is canonization; the books that return from the dead certify themselves as inescapable, and so as a vital part of the truth. We can say of each of us in relation to the books in this Prophets of Sensibility series what Pater said of his hero in *Marius the Epicurean*. The experience of reading them

> . . . gave him a definitely ascertained measure of his moral or intellectual need, of the demand his soul must make upon the powers, whatsoever they might be, which had brought him, as he was, into the world at all. . . .

CONTENTS.

———

viii   *Contents.*

CHARACTERS

OF

SHAKESPEAR'S PLAYS.

——◦◦——

CYMBELINE.[1]

CYMBELINE is one of the most delightful of Shakespear's
historical plays. It may be considered as a dramatic
romance, in which the most striking parts of the story are
thrown into the form of a dialogue, and the intermediate
circumstances are explained by the different speakers, as
occasion renders it necessary. The action is less concen-
trated in consequence; but the interest becomes more
aërial and refined from the principle of perspective
introduced into the subject by the imaginary changes of
scene, as well as by the length of time it occupies. The
reading of this play is like going a journey with some
uncertain object at the end of it, and in which the
suspense is kept up and heightened by the long intervals
between each action. Though the events are scattered

[1] " First printed in the folio of 1623. Malone is probably not far
from the truth when he conjectures that 'Cymbeline' was written in
1609."—DYCE. This drama appears to have been one of the poet's
latest performances. No English work extant in Shakespear's day
has yet been found to which he is likely to have been indebted for
his materials. Mr. Dyce, in common with Steevens and Malone,
was unaware that 'Westward for Smelts' was not licensed for the
press till 1619.—ED.

over such an extent of surface, and relate to such a variety
of characters, yet the links which bind the different
interests of the story together are never entirely broken.
The most straggling and seemingly casual incidents are
contrived in such a manner as to lead at last to the most
complete development of the catastrophe. The ease and
conscious unconcern with which this is effected only
makes the skill more wonderful. The business of the
plot evidently thickens in the last act: the story moves
forward with increasing rapidity at every step; its various
ramifications are drawn from the most distant points to
the same centre; the principal characters are brought
together, and placed in very critical situations; and the
fate of almost every person in the drama is made to
depend on the solution of a single circumstance: the
answer of Iachimo to the question of Imogen respecting
the obtaining of the ring from Posthumus. Dr. Johnson
is of opinion that Shakespear was generally inattentive to
the winding-up of his plots. We think the contrary is
true: and we might cite in proof of this remark not only
the present play, but the conclusion of *Lear*, of *Romeo and
Juliet*, of *Macbeth*, of *Othello*, even of *Hamlet*, and of other
plays of less moment, in which the last act is crowded
with decisive events brought about by natural and striking
means.

The pathos in CYMBELINE is not violent or tragical, but
of the most pleasing and amiable kind. A certain tender
gloom overspreads the whole. Posthumus is the ostensible
hero of the piece, but its greatest charm is the character
of Imogen. Posthumus is only interesting from the
interest she takes in him; and she is only interesting
herself from her tenderness and constancy to her husband.
It is the peculiar excellence of Shakespear's heroines, that
they seem to exist only in their attachment to others.
They are pure abstractions of the affections. We think
as little of their persons as they do themselves, because

we are let into the secrets of their hearts, which are more
important. We are too much interested in their affairs to
stop to look at their faces, except by stealth and at
intervals. No one ever hit the true perfection of the
female character, the sense of weakness leaning on the
strength of its affections for support, so well as Shakespear:
no one ever so well painted natural tenderness free from
affectation and disguise: no one else ever so well showed
how delicacy and timidity, when driven to extremity
grow romantic and extravagant; for the romance of his
heroines (in which they abound) is only an excess of the
habitual prejudices of their sex, scrupulous of being false
to their vows, truant to their affections, and taught by the
force of feeling when to forego the forms of propriety for
the essence of it. His women were in this respect
exquisite logicians; for there is nothing so logical as
passion. They knew their own minds exactly; and only
followed up a favourite purpose, which they had sworn to
with their tongues, and which was engraven on their
hearts, into its untoward consequences. They were the
prettiest little set of martyrs and confessors on record.
Cibber, in speaking of the early English stage, accounts
for the want of prominence and theatrical display in
Shakespear's female characters from the circumstance,
that women in those days were not allowed to play the
parts of women, which made it necessary to keep them a
good deal in the background. Does not this state of
manners itself, which prevented their exhibiting themselves in public, and confined them to the relations and
charities of domestic life, afford a truer explanation of the
matter? His women are certainly very unlike stage-
heroines, the reverse of tragedy-queens.

We have almost as great an affection for Imogen as she
had for Posthumus; and she deserves it better. Of all
Shakespear's women she is perhaps the most tender and
the most artless. Her incredulity in the opening scene

with Iachimo, as to her husband's infidelity, is much the
same as Desdemona's backwardness to believe Othello's
jealousy.   Her answer to the most distressing part of the
picture is only, "My lord, I fear, has forgot Britain."[1]
Her readiness to pardon Iachimo's false imputations and
his designs against herself, is a good lesson to prudes;
and may show that where there is a real attachment to
virtue, it has no need to bolster itself up with an out-
rageous or affected antipathy to vice.   The scene[2] in
which Pisanio gives Imogen his master's letter, accusing
her of incontinency on the treacherous suggestions of
Iachimo, is as touching as it is possible for anything to
be :—

> " *Pisanio.* What cheer, Madam ?
>   *Imogen.* False to his bed !   What is it to be false ?
> To lie in watch there, and to think on him ?
> To weep 'twixt clock and clock ?   If sleep charge nature,
> To break it with a fearful dream of him,
> And cry myself awake ?   That's false to's bed, is it ?
>   *Pisanio.* Alas, good lady !
>   *Imogen.* I false ? thy conscience witness :—Iachimo,
> Thou didst accuse him of incontinency,
> Thou then look'dst like a villain : now, methinks,
> Thy favour's good enough.   Some jay of Italy,
> Whose mother was her painting, hath betray'd him :
> Poor I am stale, a garment out of fashion,
> And, for I'm richer than to hang by th' walls,
> I must be ript :—to pieces with me !   O,
> Men's vows are women's traitors.   All good seeming
> By thy revolt, O husband, shall be thought
> Put on for villainy : not born where't grows,
> But worn a bait for ladies.
>   *Pisanio.* Good Madam, hear me—
>   *Imogen.* Talk thy tongue weary: speak ;
> I've heard I am a strumpet, and mine ear,
> Therein false struck, can take no greater wound,
> Nor tent, to bottom that."———

When Pisanio, who had been charged to kill his
mistress, puts her in a way to live, she says,

[1 Act I, sc. 6]   [2 Act iii., sc. 4.]

" Why, good fellow,
What shall I do the while? Where bide? How live?
Or in my life what comfort, when I am
Dead to my husband?

Yet when he advises her to disguise herself in boy's
clothes, and suggests " a course pretty and full of view,"
by which she may " haply be near the residence of
Posthumus," she exclaims:

" O, for such means!
Though peril to my modesty, not death on't,
I would adventure."

And when Pisanio, enlarging on the consequences, tells
her she must change

——— " Fear and niceness,
The handmaids of all women, or more truly,
Woman its pretty self into a waggish courage,
Ready in gibes, quick-answer'd, saucy, and
As quarrellous as the weasel"———

she interrupts him hastily [1]—

" Nay, be brief;
I see into thy end, and am almost
A man already."

In her journey thus disguised to Milford Haven, she
loses her guide and her way; and unbosoming her complaints, says beautifully—

——— " My dear lord,
Thou'rt one o' the false ones: now I think on thee,
My hunger's gone; but even before I was
At point to sink for food." [2]

She afterwards finds, as she thinks, the dead body of
Posthumus, and engages herself as a footboy to serve a
Roman officer, when she has done all due obsequies to
him whom she calls her former master———

[1] Scarcely so; for he speaks six lines after this, before she breaks
in.—Ed.
[2 Act iii., sc. 6.]

—————— " And when
With wild wood-leaves and weeds I há' strew'd his grave,
And on it said a century of prayers,
Such as I can, twice o'er, I'll weep and sigh,
And leaving so his service, follow you,
So please you entertain me." [1]

Now this is the very religion of love. She all along
relies little on her personal charms, which she fears may
have been eclipsed by some painted jay of Italy; she
relies on her merit, and her merit is in the depth of her
love, her truth and constancy. Our admiration of her
beauty is excited with as little consciousness as possible
on her part. There are two delicious descriptions given
of her, one when she is asleep, and one when she is
supposed dead. Arviragus thus addresses her—

——————" With fairest flowers,
Whilst summer lasts, and I live here, Fidele,
I'll sweeten thy sad grave; thou shalt not lack
The flow'r that's like thy face, pale primrose; nor
The azur'd harebell, like thy veins; no, nor
The leaf of eglantine, which not to slander,
Out-sweeten'd not thy breath." [2]

The yellow Iachimo gives another thus, when he steals
into her bedchamber:—

——————" Cytherea,
How bravely thou becom'st thy bed! Fresh lily!
And whiter than the sheets! That I might touch!
But kiss; one kiss! 'Tis her breathing that
Perfumes the chamber thus: the flame o' the taper
Bows toward her, and would under-peep her lids
To see th' enclosèd lights now canopied
Under these windows, white and azure, laced
With blue of heaven's own tinct . . . . .
On her left breast
A mole cinque-spotted, like the crimson drops
I' the bottom of a cowslip." [3]

There is a moral sense in the proud beauty of this last

[¹ Act iv., sc. 2.]   [² *Ibid.*]   [³ Act ii., sc. 2.]

image, a rich surfeit of the fancy, as that well-known passage beginning, "Me of my lawful pleasure she restrained, and prayed me oft forbearance,"[1] sets a keener edge upon it by the inimitable picture of modesty and self-denial.

The character of Cloten, the conceited, booby lord, and rejected lover of Imogen, though not very agreeable in itself, and at present obsolete, is drawn with much humour and quaint extravagance. The description which Imogen gives of his unwelcome addresses to her : " Whose love-suit hath been to me as fearful as a siege :" is enough to cure the most ridiculous lover of his folly. It is remark-able that though Cloten makes so poor a figure in love, he is described as assuming an air of consequence as the Queen's son in a council of state; and with all the absurdity of his person and manners, he is not without shrewdness in his observations. So true is it that folly is as often owing to a want of proper sentiments as to a want of understanding! The exclamation of the ancient critic : " O, Menander and Nature, which of you copied from the other !" would not be misapplied to Shakespear.[2]

The other characters in this play are represented with great truth and accuracy, and as it happens in most of the author's works, there is not only the utmost keeping in each separate character; but in the casting of the different parts, and their relation to one another, there is an affinity and harmony, like what we may observe in the gradations of colour in a picture. The striking and powerful contrasts in which Shakespear abounds could not escape observation; but the use he makes of the principle of analogy to reconcile the greatest diversities

[1 Act ii., sc. 5.]
2 This is a question which at present we are scarcely com-petent to decide, as the comic dramas of Menander have come down to us, unfortunately, in a very imperfect, or rather fragmentary shape. In his own day, and even so late as the time of Ovid, they enjoyed, it seems, great popularity.—ED.

of character and to maintain a continuity of feeling throughout, has not been sufficiently attended to. In CYMBELINE, for instance, the principal interest arises out of the unalterable fidelity of Imogen to her husband under the most trying circumstances. Now the other parts of the picture are filled up with subordinate examples of the same feeling, variously modified by different situations, and applied to the purposes of virtue or vice. The plot is aided by the amorous importunities of Cloten, by the persevering determination of Iachimo to conceal the defeat of his project by a daring imposture: the faithful attachment of Pisanio to his mistress is an affecting accompaniment to the whole; the obstinate adherence to his purpose in Bellarius, who keeps the fate of the young princes so long a secret in resentment for the ungrateful return to his former services, the incorrigible wickedness of the Queen, and even the blind uxorious confidence of Cymbeline, are all so many lines of the same story, tending to the same point. The effect of this coincidence is rather felt than observed; and as the impression exists unconsciously in the mind of the reader, so it probably arose in the same manner in the mind of the author, not from design, but from the force of natural association, a particular train of thought suggesting different inflections of the same predominant feeling, melting into, and strengthening one another, like chords in music.

The characters of Bellarius, Guiderius, and Arviragus, and the romantic scenes in which they appear, are a fine relief to the intrigues and artificial refinements of the court from which they are banished. Nothing can surpass the wildness and simplicity of the descriptions of the mountain life they lead. They follow the business of huntsmen, not of shepherds; and this is in keeping with the spirit of adventure and uncertainty in the rest of the story, and with the scenes in which they are afterwards called on to act. How admirably the youthful fire and impatience to emerge from their obscurity in the young princes is opposed to the cooler calculations and prudent resignation of their more experienced counsellor! How well the disadvantages of knowledge and of ignorance, of solitude and society, are placed against each other!

> " *Guiderius.* Out of your proof you speak : we, poor unfledg'd,
> Have never wing'd from view o' the nest; nor know not
> What air's from home. Haply this life is best,
> If quiet life be best; sweeter to you
> That have a sharper known ; well corresponding
> With your stiff age : but unto us it is
> A cell of ignorance; travelling a-bed,
> A prison for a debtor, that not dares
> To stride a limit.
>   *Arviragus.* What should we speak of
> When we are old as you? When we shall hear
> The rain and wind beat dark December! How,
> In this our pinching cave, shall we discourse
> The freezing hours away? We have seen nothing.
> We are beastly; subtle as the fox for prey,
> Like warlike as the wolf for what we eat :
> Our valour is to chase what flies; our cage
> We make a quire, as doth the prison'd bird,
> And sing our bondage freely." [1]

The answer of Bellarius to this expostulation is hardly satisfactory ; for nothing can be an answer to hope, or the passion of the mind for unknown good, but experience. The forest of Arden in *As you like it* can alone compare with the mountain scenes in CYMBELINE : yet how different the contemplative quiet of the one from the enterprising boldness and precarious mode of subsistence in the other! Shakespear not only lets us into the minds of his characters, but gives a tone and colour to the scenes he describes from the feelings of their supposed inhabitants He at the same time preserves the utmost propriety of action and passion, and gives all their local accompaniments. If he was equal to the greatest things, he was not above an attention to the smallest. Thus the gallant

[1] Act iii., sc. 3.]

sportsmen in CYMBELINE have to encounter the abrupt declivities of hill and valley: Touchstone and Audrey jog along a level path. The deer in CYMBELINE are only regarded as objects of prey, "The game's a-foot," &c.— with Jacques they are fine subjects to moralize upon at leisure, "under the shade of melancholy boughs."

We cannot take leave of this play, which is a favourite with us, without noticing some occasional touches of natural piety and morality. We may allude here to the opening of the scene in which Bellarius instructs the young princes to pay their orisons to heaven:

> ————"Stoop, boys! this gate
> Instructs you how t' adore the heavens; and bows you
> To morning's holy office. . . . .
>> *Guiderius.* Hail, heaven!
>> *Arviragus.* Hail, heaven!
>> *Bellarius.* Now for our mountain-sport, up to yond hill."[1]

What a grace and unaffected spirit of piety breathes in this passage! In like manner, one of the brothers says to the other, when about to perform the funeral rites to Fidele,

> "Nay, Cadwal, we must lay his head to th' east;[2]
> My Father hath a reason for't"—[3]

—as if some allusion to the doctrines of the Christian faith had been casually dropped in conversation by the old man, and had been no farther inquired into.

Shakespear's morality is introduced in the same simple, unobtrusive manner. Imogen will not let her companions stay away from the chase to attend her when sick, and gives her reason for it—

> "Stick to your journal course; *the breach of custom
> Is breach of all.*"[4]

When the Queen attempts to disguise her motives for

[1] Act iii., sc. 3.]
[2] See 'Popular Antiquities of Great Britain,' 1869, ii., 217, 18 where this passage (among others) is quoted.—ED.
[3] Act iv., sc. 2.]   [4] *Ibid.*]

procuring the poison from Cornelius, by saying she means to try its effects on " creatures as we count not worth the hanging," his answer conveys at once a tacit reproof of her hypocrisy, and a useful lesson of humanity—

———————" Your highness
Shall from this practice but make hard your heart"—[1]

———◆———

MACBETH.[2]

"The poet's eye in a fine frenzy rolling
Doth glance from heaven to earth, from earth to heaven;
And as imagination bodies forth
The forms of things unknown, the poet's pen
Turns them to shape, and gives to airy nothing
A local habitation and a name."
[*Midsummer Night's Dream*, v. 1.]

MACBETH and *Lear*, *Othello* and *Hamlet*, are usually reck-oned Shakespear's four principal tragedies. *Lear* stands first for the profound intensity of the passion ; *Macbeth* for the wildness of the imagination and the rapidity of the action; *Othello* for the progressive interest and powerful alternations of feeling ; *Hamlet* for the refined develop-ment of thought and sentiment. If the force of genius shown in each of these works is astonishing, their variety is not less so. They are like different creations of the same mind, not one of which has the slightest reference to the rest. This distinctness and originality is indeed the necessary consequence of truth and nature. Shake-spear's genius alone appeared to possess the resources of nature. He is "your only *tragedy-maker.*" His plays

[1 Act i., sc. 6.]
2 "First printed in the folio of 1623."—DYCE. Macbeth is sup-posed to have been written in 1605, and represented in the following year. Dr. Simon Forman saw it represented at the Globe in 1610. The present paper may be compared with one in *A View of the English Stage*, 1818, pp. 58–66.—ED.

have the force of things upon the mind. What he repre-
sents is brought home to the bosom as a part of our experience, implanted in the memory as if we had known
the places, persons, and things of which he treats. MACBETH
is like a record of a preternatural and tragical event. It
has the rugged severity of an old chronicle with all that
the imagination of the poet can engraft upon traditional
belief. The castle of Macbeth, round which " the air
smells wooingly," and where " the temple-haunting martlet
builds," has a real subsistence in the mind; the Weird
Sisters meet us in person on "the blasted heath;" the
" air-drawn dagger " moves slowly before our eyes; the
" gracious Duncan," the " blood-boltered Banquo "[1] stand
before us : all that passed through the mind of Macbeth
passes, without the loss of a tittle, through ours. All
that could actually take place, and all that is only possible
to be conceived, what was said and what was done, the
workings of passion, the spells of magic, are brought
before us with the same absolute truth and vividness.
Shakespear excelled in the openings of his plays : that
of MACBETH is the most striking of any. The wildness of
the scenery, the sudden shifting of the situations and
characters, the bustle, the expectations excited, are equally
extraordinary. From the first entrance of the Witches
and the description of them when they meet Macbeth,

> ————————" What are these
> So wither'd, and so wild in their attire,
> That look not like th' inhabitants o' th' earth
> And yet are on't ?"[2]

the mind is prepared for all that follows.

This tragedy is alike distinguished for the lofty imagination it displays, and for the tumultuous vehemence of
the action; and the one is made the moving principle of
the other. The overwhelming pressure of preternatural
agency urges on the tide of human passion with redoubled

[1 Act iv., sc. 1.]   [2 Act i., sc. 3.]

force. Macbeth himself appears driven along by the
violence of his fate like a vessel drifting before a storm :
he reels to and fro like a drunken man ; he staggers
under the weight of his own purposes and the suggestions
of others ; he stands at bay with his situation ; and from
the superstitious awe and breathless suspense into which
the communications of the Weird Sisters throw him, is
hurried on with daring impatience to verify their predictions, and with impious and bloody hand to tear aside the
veil which hides the uncertainty of the future. He is not
equal to the struggle with fate and conscience. He now
" bends up each corporal agent to this terrible feat ;"[1] at
other times his heart misgives him, and he is cowed and
abashed by his success. " The attempt, and not the deed,
confounds us." His mind is assailed by the stings of
remorse, and full of " preternatural solicitings." His
speeches and soliloquies are dark riddles on human life,
baffling solution, and entangling him in their labyrinths.
In thought he is absent and perplexed, sudden and desperate in act, from a distrust of his own resolution. His
energy springs from the anxiety and agitation of his mind.
His blindly rushing forward on the objects of his ambition and revenge, or his recoiling from them, equally
betrays the harassed state of his feelings. This part of
his character is admirably set off by being brought in
connection with that of Lady Macbeth, whose obdurate
strength of will and masculine firmness give her the
ascendancy over her husband's faltering virtue. She at
once seizes on the opportunity that offers for the accom-
plishment of all their wished-for greatness, and never
flinches from her object till all is over. The magnitude
of her resolution almost covers the magnitude of her
guilt. She is a great bad woman, whom we hate, but
whom we fear more than we hate. She does not excite
our loathing and abhorrence like Regan and Goneril.

[1] Act i., sc. 7.]

She is only wicked to gain a great end, and is perhaps more distinguished by her commanding presence of mind and inexorable self-will, which do not suffer her to be diverted from a bad purpose, when once formed, by weak and womanly regrets, than by the hardness of her heart or want of natural affections. The impression which her lofty determination of character makes on the mind of Macbeth is well described where he exclaims,

> " Bring forth men-children only;
> For thy undaunted mettle should compose
> Nothing but males !"[1]

Nor do the pains she is at to "screw his courage to the sticking-place," the reproach to him, not to be "lost so poorly in himself," the assurance that "a little water clears them of this deed," show anything but her greater consistency in depravity. Her strong-nerved ambition furnishes ribs of steel to "the sides of his intent;" and she is herself wound up to the execution of her baneful project with the same unshrinking fortitude in crime, that in other circumstances she would probably have shown patience in suffering. The deliberate sacrifice of all other considerations to the gaining " for their future days and nights sole sovereign sway and masterdom," by the murder of Duncan, is gorgeously expressed in her invocation on hearing of "his fatal entrance under her battlements :"—

> " Come, you spirits
> That tend on mortal thoughts, unsex me here :
> And fill me, from the crown to the toe, top-full
> Of direst cruelty ! make thick my blood,
> Stop up th' access and passage to remorse,
> That no compunctious visitings of nature
> Shake my fell purpose, nor keep peace between
> Th' effect and it. Come to my woman's breasts,
> And take my milk for gall, you murdering ministers,
> Wherever in your sightless substances

[1 Act i., sc. 7.]

> You wait on nature's mischief! Come, thick night!
> And pall thee in the dunnest smoke of hell,
> That my keen knife see not the wound it makes,
> Nor heav'n peep through the blanket of the dark,
> To cry, Hold, hold!—[1]

When she first hears that "the king [Duncan] comes here to-night,"[2] she is so overcome by the news, which is beyond her utmost expectations, that she answers the messenger, "Thou'rt mad to say it:" and on receiving her husband's account of the predictions of the Witches, conscious of his instability of purpose, and that her presence is necessary to goad him on to the consummation of his promised greatness, she exclaims—

> ————"Hie thee hither,
> That I may pour my spirits in thine ear,
> And chastise with the valour of my tongue
> All that impedes thee from the golden round,
> Which fate and metaphysical aid doth seem
> To have thee crown'd withal."[3]

This swelling exultation and keen spirit of triumph, this uncontrollable eagerness of anticipation, which seems to dilate her form and take possession of all her faculties, this solid, substantial flesh-and-blood display of passion, exhibit a striking contrast to the cold, abstracted, gratuitous, servile malignity of the Witches, who are equally instrumental in urging Macbeth to his fate for the mere love of mischief, and from a disinterested delight in deformity and cruelty. They are hags of mischief, obscene panders to inquity, malicious from their impotence of enjoyment, enamoured of destruction, because they are themselves unreal, abortive, half-existences: who become sublime from their exemption from all human sympathies and contempt for all human affairs, as Lady Macbeth does by the force of passion! Her fault seemt to have been an excess of that strong principle of self-interest and family aggrandisement, not amenable to the

[1 Act i., sc. 5.]   [2 Ibid.]   [3 Ibid.]

common feelings of compassion and justice, which is so marked a feature in barbarous nations and times. A passing reflection of this kind, on the resemblance of the sleeping king to her father, alone prevents her from slaying Duncan with her own hand.

In speaking of the character of Lady Macbeth, we ought not to pass over Mrs. Siddons's manner of acting that part.[1] We can conceive of nothing grander. It was something above nature. It seemed almost as if a being of a superior order had dropped from a higher sphere to awe the world with the majesty of her appearance. Power was seated on her brow, passion emanated from her breast as from a shrine ; she was tragedy personified. In coming on in the sleeping-scene, her eyes were open, but their sense was shut. She was like a person bewildered and unconscious of what she did. Her lips moved involuntarily : all her gestures were involuntary and mechanical. She glided on and off the stage like an apparition. To have seen her in that character was an event in every one's life, not to be forgotten.

The dramatic beauty of the character of Duncan, which excites the respect and pity even of his murderers, has been often pointed out. It forms a picture of itself. An instance of the author's power of giving a striking effect to a common reflection, by the manner of introducing it, occurs in a speech of Duncan, complaining of his having been deceived in his opinion of the Thane of Cawdor, at the very moment that he is expressing the most unbounded confidence in the loyalty and services of Macbeth.

> "There's no art
> To find the mind's construction in the face :
> He was a gentleman, on whom I built
> An absolute trust . . . . .

---

[1] Mrs. Siddons performed in this part at Covent Garden, June 7, 1817. See this part of the subject treated more at length in *A View of the English Stage*, 1818, pp. 446-8.—ED.

O worthiest cousin,   (*addressing himself tc Macbeth*)
The sin of my ingratitude even now
Was heavy upon me," &c.[1]

Another passage to show that Shakespear lost sight of
nothing that could in any way give relief or heightening
to his subject, is the conversation which takes place
between Banquo and Fleance immediately before the
murder-scene of Duncan.

"*Banquo.* How goes the night, boy?
Fleance. The moon is down : I have not heard the clock.
Banquo. And she goes down at twelve.
Fleance.   I take't, 'tis later, Sir.
Banquo. Hold, take my sword :—There's husbandry in heaven,
    Their candles are all out : take thee that too :
    A heavy summons lies like lead upon me,
    And yet I would not sleep : Merciful Powers,
    Restrain in me the cursed thoughts that nature
    Gives way to in repose !"[2]

In like manner, a fine idea is given of the gloomy
coming on of evening, just as Banquo is going to be assas-
sinated.

"Light thickens and the crow
Makes wing to the rooky wood."
        *   *   *   *   *
"Now spurs the lated traveller apace
To gain the timely inn."[3]

' Macbeth ' (generally speaking) is done upon a stronger
and more systematic principle of contrast than any other
of Shakespear's plays. It moves upon the verge of an
abyss, and is a constant struggle between life and death.
The action is desperate and the reaction is dreadful. It
is a huddling together of fierce extremes, a war of opposite
natures which of them shall destroy the other. There is
nothing but what has a violent end or violent beginnings.
The lights and shades are laid on with a determined
hand ; the transitions from triumph to despair, from the
height of terror to the repose of death, are sudden and

[¹ Act i., sc. 4.]   [² Act ii., sc. 1.]   [³ Act iii., sc. 2–3.]

startling; every passion brings in its-fellow-contrary, and the thoughts pitch and jostle against each other as in the dark. The whole play is an unruly chaos of strange and forbidden things, where the ground rocks under our feet. Shakespear's genius here took its full swing, and trod upon the farthest bounds of nature and passion. This circumstance will account for the abruptness and violent antitheses of the style, the throes and labour which run through the expression, and from defects will turn them into beauties. " So fair and foul a day I have not seen," &c " Such welcome and unwelcome news together." " Good men's lives expire before the flowers in their caps, dying or e'er they sicken."[1] " Look like the innocent flower, but be the serpent under 't."[2] The scene before the castle-gate follows the appearance of the Witches on the heath, and is followed by a midnight murder. Duncan is cut off betimes by treason leagued with witchcraft, and Macduff is ripped untimely from his mother's womb to avenge his death. Macbeth, after the death of Banquo, wishes for his presence in extravagant terms, " To him and all we thirst," and when his ghost appears, cries out, " Avaunt and quit my sight," and being gone, he is " himself again." Macbeth resolves to get rid of Macduff, that " he may sleep in spite of thunder;" and cheers his wife on the doubtful intelligence of Banquo's taking-off with the encouragement—

> " *Macbeth.* Then be thou jocund: ere the bat hath flown
> His cloister'd flight; ere to black Hecate's summons
> The shard-borne beetle with his drowsy hums
> Hath rung night's yawning peal, there shall be done
> A deed of dreadful note——"[3]

In Lady Macbeth's speech " Had he not resembled my father as he slept, I had done 't," there is murder and filial piety together; and in urging him to fulfil his vengeance against the defenceless king, her thoughts spare

[1 Act iv., sc. 3.]   [2 Act i., sc. 5.]   [3 Act iii., sc. 2.]

the blood neither of infants nor old age. The description of the Witches is full of the same contradictory principle; they "rejoice when good kings bleed," they are neither of the earth nor the air, but both; "they should be women, but their beards forbid it;" they take all the pains possible to lead Macbeth on to the height of his ambition, only to betray him "in deeper consequence," and after showing him all the pomp of their art, discover their malignant delight in his disappointed hopes, by that bitter taunt, "Why stands Macbeth thus amazedly?" We might multiply such instances everywhere.

The leading features in the character of Macbeth are striking enough, and they form what may be thought at first only a bold, rude, Gothic outline. By comparing it with other characters of the same author we shall perceive the absolute truth and identity which is observed in the midst of the giddy whirl and rapid career of events. Macbeth in Shakespear no more loses his identity of character in the fluctuations of fortune or the storm of passion, than Macbeth in himself would have lost the identity of his person. Thus he is as distinct a being from Richard III. as it is possible to imagine, though these two characters in common hands, and indeed in the hands of any other poet, would have been a repetition of the same general idea, more or less exaggerated. For both are tyrants, usurpers, murderers, both aspiring and ambitious, both courageous, cruel, treacherous. But Richard is cruel from nature and constitution. Macbeth becomes so from accidental circumstances. Richard is from his birth deformed in body and mind, and naturally incapable of good. Macbeth is full of "the milk of human kindness," is frank, sociable, generous. He is tempted to the commission of guilt by golden opportunities, by the instigations of his wife, and by prophetic warnings. Fate and metaphysical aid conspire against his virtue and his loyalty. Richard on the contrary needs no prompter, but wades through a series of crimes to the height of his ambition from the ungovern-able violence of his temper and a reckless love of mischief. He is never gay but in the prospect or in the success of his villainies : Macbeth is full of horror at the thoughts of the murder of Duncan, which he is with difficulty prevailed on to commit, and of remorse after its perpetration. Richard has no mixture of common humanity in his composition, no regard to kindred or posterity, he owns no fellowship with others, he is "himself alone." Macbeth is not destitute of feelings of sympathy, is accessible to pity, is even made in some measure the dupe of his uxoriousness, ranks the loss of friends, of the cordial love of his followers, and of his good name, among the causes which have made him weary of life, and regrets that he has ever seized the crown by unjust means, since he cannot transmit it to his posterity—[1]

> " For Banquo's issue have I fil'd my mind ;
> For them the gracious Duncan have I murder'd, . . .
> To make them kings, the seed of Banquo kings."

In the agitation of his mind, he envies those whom he has sent to peace—

> ————" Duncan is in his grave ;
> After life's fitful fever he sleeps well."[2]

It is true, he becomes more callous as he plunges deeper in guilt.

> ————" 1 have supp'd full with horrors ;
> Direness, familiar to my slaughterous thoughts,
> Cannot once start me "—[3]

And he in the end anticipates his wife in the boldness and bloodiness of his enterprises, while she for want of the same stimulus of action, " is troubled with thick-coming fancies that keep her from her rest,"[4] goes mad and dies. Macbeth endeavours to escape from reflection on his crimes by repelling their consequences, and banishes remorse for

[1 Act iii., sc. 1.] [2 Act iii., sc. 2.] [3 Act v., sc. 5.] [4 Act v. sc. 3.]

the past by the meditation of future mischief. This is not the principle of Richard's cruelty, which displays the wanton malice of a fiend as much as the frailty of human passion. Macbeth is goaded on to acts of violence and retaliation by necessity; to Richard, blood is a pastime. There are other decisive differences inherent in the two characters. Richard may be regarded as a man of the world, a plotting, hardened knave, wholly regardless of everything but his own ends, and the means to secure them. Not so Macbeth. The superstitions of the age, the rude state of society, the local scenery and customs, all give a wildness and imaginary grandeur to his character. From the strangeness of the events that surround him, he is full of amazement and fear; and stands in doubt between the world of reality and the world of fancy. He sees sights not shown to mortal eye, and hears unearthly music. All is tumult and disorder within and without his mind; his purposes recoil upon himself, are broken and disjointed; he is the double thrall of his passions and his evil destiny. Richard is not a character either of imagination or pathos, but of pure self-will. There is no conflict of opposite feelings in his breast. The apparitions which he sees only haunt him in his sleep; nor does he live like Macbeth in a waking dream. Macbeth has considerable energy and manliness of character; but then he is "subject to all the skyey influences." He is sure of nothing but the present moment. Richard in the busy turbulence of his projects never loses his self-possession, and makes use of every circumstance that happens as an instrument of his long-reaching designs. In his last extremity we can only regard him as a wild beast taken in the toils: while we never entirely lose our concern for Macbeth; and he calls back all our sympathy by that fine close of thoughtful melancholy,

———————"My way of life
Is fallen into the sear, the yellow leaf;

And that which should accompany old age,
As honour, love, obedience, troops of friends,
I must not look to have; but in their stead
Curses not loud but deep, mouth-honour, breath,
Which the poor heart would fain deny, and dare not." [1]

We can conceive a common actor to play Richard
tolerably well; we can conceive no one to play Macbeth
properly, or to look like a man that had encountered the
Weird Sisters. All the actors that we have ever seen,
appear as if they had encountered them on the boards of
Covent-garden or Drury-lane, but not on the heath at
Fores, and as if they did not believe what they had seen.
The Witches of 'Macbeth' indeed are ridiculous on the
modern stage, and we doubt if the Furies of Æschylus
would be more respected. The progress of manners and
knowledge has an influence on the stage, and will in time
perhaps destroy both tragedy and comedy. Filch's pick-
ing pockets in the 'Beggar's Opera' is not so good a jest
as it used to be: by the force of the police and of philosophy, Lillo's murders and the ghosts in Shakespear will
become obsolete. At last, there will be nothing left,
good nor bad, to be desired or dreaded, on the theatre or in
real life. A question has been started with respect to
the originality of Shakespear's witches, which has been
well answered by Mr. Lamb in his notes to the 'Specimens of the Early Dramatic Poets.'

"Though some resemblance may be traced between the
charms in 'Macbeth,' and the incantations in this play
(the 'Witch of Middleton'), which is supposed to have
preceded it, this coincidence will not detract much from
the originality of Shakespear. His Witches are distinguished from the Witches of Middleton by essential
differences. These are creatures to whom man or woman
plotting some dire mischief might resort for occasional
consultation. Those originate deeds of blood, and begin

[¹ Act v., sc. 3.]

bad impulses to men. From the moment that their eyes
first meet with Macbeth's, he is spell-bound. That meeting sways his destiny. He can never break the fascina-
tion. These Witches can hurt the body; those have
power over the soul. Hecate in Middleton has a son, a
low buffoon : the hags of Shakespear have neither child of
their own, nor seem to be descended from any parent.
They are foul anomalies, of whom we know not whence
they are sprung, nor whether they have beginning or
ending. As they are without human passions, so they
seem to be without human relations. They come with
thunder and lightning, and vanish to airy music. This is
all we know of them. Except Hecate, they have no
names, which heightens their mysteriousness. The
names, and some of the properties which Middleton has
given to his hags, excite smiles. The Weird Sisters are
serious things. Their presence cannot co-exist with
mirth. But, in a lesser degree, the Witches of Middleton
are fine creations. Their power too is, in some measure,
over the mind. They raise jars, jealousies, strifes, *like a
thick scurf o'er life.*"

JULIUS CÆSAR.[1]

'JULIUS CÆSAR' was one of three principal plays by
different authors, pitched upon by the celebrated Earl of
Halifax to be brought out in a splendid manner by sub-
scription, in the year 1707. The other two were the
'King and No King' of [Beaumont and] Fletcher, and
Dryden's 'Maiden Queen.' There perhaps might be political
reasons for this selection, as far as regards our author.
Otherwise, Shakespear's 'Julius Cæsar' is not equal as a

[1] Not printed, till was included in the collected volume of 1623;
but the drama is supposed to have been in existence in, if not
before, 1601. See Dyce's ed. 1868, vi., 613.—ED.

whole, to either of his other plays taken from the Roman history. It is inferior in interest to 'Coriolanus,' and both in interest and power to 'Antony and Cleopatra.' It however abounds in admirable and affecting passages, and is remarkable for the profound knowledge of character, in which Shakespear could scarcely fail. If there is any exception to this remark, it is in the hero of the piece himself. We do not much admire the representation here given of Julius Cæsar, nor do we think it answers to the portrait given of him in his Commentaries. He makes several vapouring and rather pedantic speeches, and does nothing. Indeed, he has nothing to do. So far, the fault of the character is the fault of the plot.

The spirit with which the poet has entered at once into the manners of the common people, and the jealousies and heart-burnings of the different factions, is shown in the first scene, where Flavius and Marullus, tribunes of the people, and some citizens of Rome, appear upon the stage.

" *Flavius.* Thou art a cobbler, art thou?

Sec. Cit. Truly, Sir, *all* that I live by, is the *awl:* I meddle with no tradesman's matters, nor women's matters, but *with awl.* I am indeed, Sir, a surgeon to old shoes; when they are in great danger, I re-cover them. . .

Flavius. But wherefore art not in thy shop to-day?
Why dost thou lead these men about the streets?

Sec. Cit. Truly, Sir, to wear out their shoes, to get myself into more work. But indeed, Sir, we make holiday, to see Cæsar, and to rejoice in his triumph." [1]

To this specimen of quaint low humour immediately follows that unexpected and animated burst of indignant eloquence, put into the mouth of one of the angry tribunes.[2]

" *Marullus.* Wherefore rejoice! What conquest brings he home?
What tributaries follow him to Rome,
To grace in captive-bonds his chariot-wheels?

[1 Act i., sc. 1.] [2 *Ibid.*]

You blocks, you stones, you worse than senseless things!
O you hard hearts, you cruel men of Rome!
Knew you not Pompey? Many a time and oft
Have you climb'd up to walls and battlements,
To towers and windows, yea, to chimney-tops,
Your infants in your arms, and there have sat
The live-long day with patient expectation,
To see great Pompey pass the streets of Rome:
And when you saw his chariot but appear,
Have you not made an universal shout,
That Tiber trembled underneath her banks
To hear the replication of your sounds,
Made in her concave shores?
And do you now put on your best attire?
And do you now cull out an holiday?
And do you now strew flowers in his way
That comes in triumph over Pompey's blood?
Be gone!
Run to your houses, fall upon your knees,
Pray to the Gods to intermit the plague,
That needs must light on this ingratitude."

The well-known dialogue between Brutus and Cassius,
in which the latter breaks the design of the conspiracy to
the former, and partly gains him over to it, is a noble
piece of high-minded declamation. Cassius's insisting on
the pretended effeminacy of Cæsar's character, and his
description of their swimming across the Tiber together
"once upon a raw and gusty day," are among the finest
strokes in it. But perhaps the whole is not equal to the
short scene which follows, when Cæsar enters with his
train:—

" *Brutus.* The games are done, and Cæsar is returning.
   Cassius. As they pass by, pluck Casca by the sleeve,
And he will, after his sour fashion, tell you
What has proceeded worthy note to-day.
               (*Re-enter Cæsar and his train.)*
   Brutus. I will do so; but look you, Cassius,
The angry spot doth glow on Cæsar's brow,
And all the rest look like a chidden train.
Calphurnia's cheek is pale; and Cicero
Looks with such ferret and such fiery eyes,

As we have seen him in the Capitol,
Being cross'd in conference by some senator.
　Cassius. Casca will tell us what the matter is.
　Cæsar. Antonius——
　Antony. Cæsar?
　Cæsar. Let me have men about me that are fat,
Sleek-headed men, and such as sleep o' nights:
Yon Cassius has a lean and hungry look,
He thinks too much; such men are dangerous.
　Antony. Fear him not, Cæsar; he's not dangerous
He is a noble Roman, and well given.
　Cæsar. Would he were fatter! but I fear him not:
Yet if my name were liable to fear,
I do not know the man I should avoid
So soon as that spare Cassius. He reads much;
He is a great observer, and he looks
Quite through the deeds of men; he loves no plays,
As thou dost, Antony; he hears no music:
Seldom he smiles, and smiles in such a sort,
As if he mock'd himself, and scorn'd his spirit,
That could be mov'd to smile at anything.
Such men as he be never at heart's ease,
Whilst they behold a greater than themselves;
And therefore are they very dangerous.
I rather tell thee what is to be fear'd
Than what I fear; for always I am Cæsar.
Come on my right hand, for this ear is deaf,
And tell me truly what thou think'st of him." [1]

We know hardly any passage more expressive of the
genius of Shakespear than this. It is as if he had been
actually present, had known the different characters and
what they thought of one another, and had taken down
what he heard and saw, their looks, words, and gestures,
just as they happened.

The character of Mark Antony is farther speculated
upon where the conspirators deliberate whether he shall
fall with Cæsar. Brutus is against it—

" And for Mark Antony, think not of him:
For he can do no more than Cæsar's arm,

<hr>

Act i., sc. 2.]

When Cæsar's head is off.
    Cassius.   Yet I fear him:
For in th ingrafted love he bears to Cæsar—
    Brutus. Alas, good Cassius, do not think of him:
If he love Cæsar, all that he can do
Is to himself, take thought, and die for Cæsar:
And that were much, he should; for he is given
To sports, to wildness, and much company.
    Trebonius. There is no fear in him; let him not die:
For he will live, and laugh at this hereafter."[1]

They were in the wrong; and Cassius was right.

The honest manliness of Brutus is however sufficient to find out the unfitness of Cicero to be included in their enterprise, from his affected egotism and literary vanity.

> " O, name him not: let us not break with him ;
> For he will never follow anything
> That other men begin."[2]

His [Cicero's] scepticism as to prodigies and his moralising on the weather—" This disturbed sky is not to walk in" are in the same spirit of refined imbecility.

Shakespear has in this play and elsewhere shown the same penetration into political character and the springs of public events as into those of every-day life. For instance, the whole design of the conspirators to liberate their country fails from the generous temper and overweening confidence of Brutus in the goodness of their cause and the assistance of others. Thus it has always been. Those who mean well themselves think well of others, and fall a prey to their security. That humanity and honesty which dispose men to resist injustice and tyranny, render them unfit to cope with the cunning and power of those who are opposed to them. The friends of liberty trust to the professions of others, because they are themselves sincere, and endeavour to reconcile the public good with the least possible hurt to its enemies, who have no regard to anything but their own unprincipled ends, and stick at nothing to accomplish them. Cassius was

        [1 Act ii., sc. 1.]   [2 *Ibid.*]

better cut out for a conspirator. His heart prompted his
head. His watchful jealousy made him fear the worst
that might happen, and his irritability of temper added to
his inveteracy of purpose, and sharpened his patriotism.
The mixed nature of his motives made him fitter to con-
tend with bad men. The vices are never so well employed
as in combating one another. Tyranny and servility are
to be dealt with after their own fashion: otherwise, they
will triumph over those who spare them, and finally pro-
nounce their funeral panegyric, as Antony did that of
Brutus:

> " All the conspirators, save only he,
> Did that they did in envy of great Cæsar:
> He only in a general honest thought
> And common good to all, made one of them." [1]

The quarrel between Brutus and Cassius is managed in a
masterly way. The dramatic fluctuation of passion, the
calmness of Brutus, the heat of Cassius, are admirably
described; and the exclamation of Cassius on hearing of
the death of Portia, which he does not learn till after their
reconciliation, "How 'scaped I killing when I cross'd you
so?"[2] gives double force to all that has gone before. The
scene between Brutus and Portia, where she endeavours to
extort the secret of the conspiracy from him, is conceived
in the most heroical spirit, and the burst of tenderness in
Brutus—

> " You are my true and honourable wife;
> As dear to me as are the ruddy drops
> That visit my sad heart "—[3]

is justified by her whole behaviour. Portia's breathless
impatience to learn the event of the conspiracy, in the
dialogue with Lucius, is full of passion. The interest
which Portia takes in Brutus and that which Calphurnia
takes in the fate of Cæsar are discriminated with the
nicest precision. Mark Antony's speech over the dead

[1 Act v., sc. 5.]   [2 Act iv., sc. 3.]   [3 Act ii., sc 1.]

body of Cæsar has been justly admired for the mixture of pathos and artifice in it : that of Brutus certainly is not so good.

The entrance of the conspirators to the house of Brutus at midnight is rendered very impressive. In the midst of this scene, we meet with one of those careless and natural digressions which occur so frequently and beautifully in Shakespear. After Cassius has introduced his friends one by one, Brutus says—

> " They are all welcome.
> What watchful cares do interpose themselves
> Betwixt your eyes and night ?
>> *Cassius.* Shall I entreat a word ?
>>> (*Brutus and Cassius whisper.)*
>> *Decius.* Here lies the east : doth not the day break here ?
>> *Casca.* No.
>> *Cinna.* O pardon, Sir, it doth ; and yon gray lines,
> That fret the clouds, are messengers of day.
>> *Casca.* You shall confess that you are both deceiv'd :
> Here, as I point my sword, the sun arises ;
> Which is a great way growing on the south,
> Weighing the youthful season of the year.
> Some two months hence, up higher toward the north
> He first presents his fire, and the high east
> Stands, as the Capitol, directly here." [1]

We cannot help thinking this graceful familiarity better than all the fustian in the world.—The truth of history in 'Julius Cæsar' is very ably worked up with dramatic effect. The councils of generals, the doubtful turns of battles, are represented to the life. The death of Brutus is worthy of him : it has the dignity of the Roman senator with the firmness of the Stoic philosopher. But what is perhaps better than either, is the little incident of his boy, Lucius, falling asleep over his instrument, as he is playing to his master in his tent, the night before the battle. Nature had played him the same forgetful trick once before, on

[1 Act ii., sc. 1.]

the night of the conspiracy.   The humanity of **Brutus is the** same on both occasions.

> ————————" It is no matter :
> Enjoy the heavy honey-dew of slumber.
> Thou hast no figures nor no fantasies,
> Which busy care draws in the brains of men.
> Therefore thou sleep'st so sound." [1]

OTHELLO. [2]

It has been said that tragedy purifies the affections by terror and pity. That is, it substitutes imaginary sym pathy for mere selfishness. It gives us a high and permanent interest, beyond ourselves, in humanity as such. It raises the great, the remote, and the possible to an equality with the real, the little, and the near. It makes man a partaker with his kind. It subdues and softens the stubbornness of his will. It teaches him that there are and have been others like himself, by showing him as in a glass what they have felt, thought, and done. It opens the chambers of the human heart. It leaves nothing indifferent to us that can affect our common nature.   It excites our sensibility by exhibiting the passions wound up to the utmost pitch by the power of imagination or the temptation of circumstances; and corrects their fatal excesses in ourselves by pointing to the greater extent of sufferings and of crimes to which they have led others. Tragedy creates a balance of the affections.   It makes us thoughtful spectators in the lists of life.   It is the refiner of the species; a discipline of humanity. The habitual study of poetry and works of

[1] Act ii., sc. 1.]
[2] First printed in 1622, but supposed to have been written in or before 1600. The exact date however, has yet to be ascertained, it seems.—Ed.

Imagination is one chief part of a well-grounded education. A taste for liberal art is necessary to complete the character of a gentleman. Science alone is hard and mechanical. It exercises the understanding upon things out of ourselves, while it leaves the affections unemployed, or engrossed with our own immediate, narrow interests. —'Othello' furnishes an illustration of these remarks. It excites our sympathy in an extraordinary degree. The moral it conveys has a closer application to the concerns of human life than that of almost any other of Shakespear's plays. "It comes directly home to the bosoms and business of men." The pathos in 'Lear' is indeed more dreadful and overpowering; but it is less natural, and less of every day's occurrence. We have not the same degree of sympathy with the passions described in 'Macbeth.' The interest in 'Hamlet' is more remote and reflex. That of 'Othello' is at once equally profound and affecting.

The picturesque contrasts of character in this play are almost as remarkable as the depth of the passion.[1] The Moor Othello, the gentle Desdemona, the villain Iago, the good-natured Cassio, the fool Roderigo, present a range and variety of character as striking and palpable as that produced by the opposition of costume in a picture. Their distinguishing qualities stand out to the mind's eye, so that even when we are not thinking of their actions or sentiments, the idea of their persons is still as present to us as ever. These characters and the images they stamp upon the mind are the farthest asunder possible, the distance between them is immense: yet the compass of knowledge and invention which the poet has

[1] This and what follows is stated a little differently, and more at length, in a paper contributed to the 'Examiner' newspaper for 1816 (p. 299), by the present writer under the signature L. C. The paper formed one of the 'Round Table' series, which was not ro printed in the two little volumes published in 1817.—ED.

shown in embodying these extreme creations of his genius
is only greater than the truth and felicity with which he
has identified each character with itself, or blended their
different qualities together in the same story. What a
contrast the character of Othello forms to that of Iago!
at the same time, the force of conception with which these
two figures are opposed to each other is rendered still
more intense by the complete consistency with which the
traits of each character are brought out in a state of the
highest finishing. The making one black and the other
white, the one unprincipled, the other unfortunate in the
extreme, would have answered the common purposes of
effect, and satisfied the ambition of an ordinary painter of
character. Shakespear has laboured the finer shades of
difference in both with as much care and skill as if he
had had to depend on the execution alone for the success
of his design. On the other hand, Desdemona and Æmilia
are not meant to be opposed with anything like strong
contrast to each other. Both are, to outward appearance,
characters of common life, not more distinguished than
women usually are, by difference of rank and situation.
The difference of their thoughts and sentiments is however laid open, their minds are separated from each other
by signs as plain and as little to be mistaken as the com-
plexions of their husbands.

The movement of the passion in Othello is exceedingly
different from that of Macbeth. In Macbeth there is a
violent struggle between opposite feelings, between ambition and the stings of conscience, almost from first to
last: in Othello, the doubtful conflict between contrary
passions, though dreadful, continues only for a short
time, and the chief interest is excited by the alternate
ascendency of different passions, by the entire and un-
foreseen change from the fondest love and most unbounded
confidence to the tortures of jealousy and the madness of
hatred. The revenge of Othello, after it has once taken

thorough possession of his mind, never quits it, but grows stronger and stronger at every moment of its delay. The nature of the Moor is noble, confiding, tender, and generous; but his blood is of the most inflammable kind; and being once roused by a sense of his wrongs, he is stopped by no considerations of remorse or pity till he has given a loose to all the dictates of his rage and his despair. It is in working his noble nature up to this extremity through rapid but gradual transitions, in raising passion to its height from the smallest beginnings and in spite of all obstacles, in painting the expiring conflict between love and hatred, tenderness and resentment, jealousy and remorse, in unfolding the strength and the weakness of our nature, in uniting sublimity of thought with the anguish of the keenest woe, in putting in motion the various impulses that agitate this our mortal being, and at last blending them in that noble tide of deep and sustained passion, impetuous but majestic, that "flows on to the Propontic, and knows no ebb," that Shakespear has shown the mastery of his genius and of his power over the human heart. The third act of 'OTHELLO' is his finest display, not of knowledge or passion separately, but of the two combined, of the knowledge of character with the expression of passion, of consummate art in the keeping up of appearances with the profound workings of nature, and the convulsive movements of uncontrollable agony, of the power of inflicting torture and of suffering it. Not only is the tumult of passion in Othello's mind heaved up from the very bottom of the soul, but every the slightest undulation of feeling is seen on the surface, as it arises from the impulses of imagination or the malicious suggestions of Iago. The progressive preparation for the catastrophe is wonderfully managed from the Moor's first gallant recital of the story of his love, of " the spells and witchcraft he had used," from his unlooked-for and romantic success, the fond satisfaction with which he dotes

on his own happiness, the unreserved tenderness of Desdemona and her innocent importunities in favour of
Cassio, irritating the suspicions instilled into her husband's mind by the perfidy of Iago, and rankling there to
poison, till he loses all command of himself, and his rage
can only be appeased by blood. She is introduced, just
before Iago begins to put his scheme in practice, pleading
for Cassio with all the thoughtless gaiety of friendship
and winning confidence in the love of Othello.

> " What ! Michael Cassio ?
> That came a wooing with you, and so many a time,
> When I have spoke of you dispraisingly,
> Hath ta'en your part, to have so much to do
> To bring him in? . . . Why this is not a boon :
> 'Tis as I should intreat you wear your gloves,
> Or feed on nourishing dishes, or keep you warm ;
> Or sue to you to do peculiar profit
> To your own person : nay, when I have a suit,
> Wherein I mean to touch your love indeed,
> It shall be full of poise and difficult weight,
> And fearful to be granted."[1]

Othello's confidence, at first only staggered by broken
hints and insinuations, recovers itself at sight of Desdemona ; and he exclaims

> " If she be false, O, then Heaven mocks itself:
> I'll not believe 't."

But presently after, on brooding over his suspicions by
himself, and yielding to his apprehensions of the worst,
his smothered jealousy breaks out into open fury, and he
returns to demand satisfaction of Iago like a wild beast
stung with the envenomed shaft of the hunters. " Look
where he comes," &c. In this state of exasperation and
violence, after the first paroxysms of his grief and tenderness have had their vent in that passionate apostrophe,
"I felt not Cassio's kisses on her lips," Iago, by false
aspersions, and by presenting the most revolting images

[1 Act iii., sc. 3.]

to his mind,[1] easily turns the storm of passion from himself against Desdemona, and works him up into a trembling agony of doubt and fear, in which he abandon♦ all his love and hopes in a breath.

> " Now do I see 'tis true. Look here, Iago,
> All my fond love thus do I blow to Heaven.
> 'Tis gone.—
> Arise, black vengeance, from the hollow hell!
> Yield up, O love, thy crown and hearted throne
> To tyrannous hate! Swell, bosom, with thy fraught;
> For 'tis of aspics' tongues."[2]

From this time, his raging thoughts "ne'er look back, ne'er ebb to humble love," till his revenge is sure of its object, the painful regrets and involuntary recollections of past circumstances which cross his mind amidst the dim trances of passion, aggravating the sense of his wrongs, but not shaking his purpose. Once indeed, where Iago shows him Cassio with the handkerchief in his hand, and making sport (as he thinks) of his mis‑ fortunes, the intolerable bitterness of his feelings, the extreme sense of shame, makes him fall to praising her accomplishments and relapse into a momentary fit of weakness, "Yet, O the pity of it, Iago, the pity of it!" This returning fondness however only serves, as it is managed by Iago, to whet his revenge, and set his heart more against her. In his conversations with Desdemona, the persuasion of her guilt and the immediate proofs of her duplicity seem to irritate his resentment and aversion to her; but in the scene immediately preceding her death, the recollection of his love returns upon him in all its tenderness and force; and after her death, he all at once forgets his wrongs in the sudden and irreparable sense of his loss:

[1] See the passage, beginning—" It is impossible you should see this, were they as prime as goats,' &c. [Act iii., sc. 3,]

[2] *Ubi supra.*]

" My wife ! My wife ! What wife ? I have no wife.
　Oh insupportable ! Oh heavy hour !"

This happens before he is assured of her innocence;
but afterwards his remorse is as dreadful as his revenge
has been, and yields only to fixed and death-like despair.
His farewell speech, before he kills himself, in which he
conveys his reasons to the senate for the murder of his
wife, is equal to the first speech in which he gave them
an account of his courtship of her, and "his whole
course of love." Such an ending was alone worthy of
such a commencement.

If anything could add to the force of our sympathy
with Othello, or compassion for his fate, it would be the
frankness and generosity of his nature, which so little
deserve it. When Iago first begins to practise upon his
unsuspecting friendship, he answers—

　　　　——" 'Tis not to make me jealous,
To say my wife is fair, feeds well, loves company,
Is free of speech, sings, plays, and dances well;
Where virtue is, these are more virtuous.
Nor from my own weak merits will I draw
The smallest fear or doubt of her revolt,
For she had eyes and chose me—" [1]

This character is beautifully (and with affecting simplicity) confirmed by what Desdemona herself says of
him to Æmilia after she has lost the handkerchief, the
first pledge of his love to her.

" Believe me, I had rather have lost my purse
Full of crusadoes; and, but my noble Moor
Is true of mind, and made of no such baseness,
As jealous creatures are, it were enough
To put him to ill thinking.
　　Æmilia.　　　　　　Is he not jealous?
　　Desdemona. Who, he? I think the sun where he was born
Drew all such humours from him." [2]

In a short speech of Æmilia's, there occurs one of
those side-intimations of the fluctuations of passion which

[1 Act iii., sc. 3.]　　　　　[2 Act iii., sc. 4.]

we seldom meet with but in Shakespear. After Othello
has resolved upon the death of his wife, and bids her
dismiss her attendant for the night, she answers,

> " I will, my lord.
>   *Æmilia.* How goes it now? *He looks gentler than he did."*

Shakespear has here put into half a line what some
authors would have spun out into ten set speeches.

The character of Desdemona is inimitable both in
itself, and as it appears in contrast with Othello's groundless jealousy, and with the foul conspiracy of which she is
the innocent victim. Her beauty and external graces are
only indirectly glanced at : we see "her visage in her
mind ;" her character everywhere predominates over her
person.

> ————" A maiden never bold ;
> Of spirit so still and quiet, that her motion
> Blush'd at herself." [1]

There is one fine compliment paid to her by Cassio,
who exclaims triumphantly when she comes ashore at
Cyprus after the storm,

> " Tempests themselves, high seas, and howling winds,
>   The gutter'd rocks, and congregated sands,—
>   Traitors ensteep'd to clog the guiltless keel—
>   As having sense of beauty, do omit
>   Their mortal natures, letting go safely by
>   The divine Desdemona." [2]

In general, as is the case with most of Shakespear's
females, we lose sight of her personal charms in her
attachment and devotedness to her husband.

> ————" My heart's subdu'd
> Even to the very quality of my lord.
>   *   *   *   *
> And to his honours and his valiant parts
> Did I my soul and fortunes consecrate." [3]

The lady protests so much herself, and she is as good as
her word. The truth of conception, with which timidity

[1 Act i., sc. 3.]   [2 Act ii., sc. 1.]   [3 Act i., sc. 3.]

and boldness are united in the same character, is marvel‧
lous. The extravagance of her resolutions, the pertinacity
of her affections, may be said to arise out of the gentleness
of her nature. They imply an unreserved reliance on the
purity of her own intentions, an entire surrender of her
fears to her love, a knitting of herself (heart and soul) to
the fate of another. Bating the commencement of her
passion, which is a little fantastical and headstrong
(though even that may perhaps be consistently accounted
for from her inability to resist a rising inclination[1]),
her whole character consists in having no will of her
own, no prompter but her obedience. Her romantic turn
is only a consequence of the domestic and practical part
of her disposition; and instead of following Othello to
the wars, she would gladly have "remained at home a
moth of peace," if her husband could have stayed with her.
Her resignation and angelic sweetness of temper do not
desert her at the last. The scenes in which she laments
and tries to account for Othello's estrangement from her
are exquisitely beautiful. After he has struck her, and
called her names, she says,

> ————" Alas, Iago,
> What shall I do to win my lord again?
> Good friend, go to him; for by this light of heaven,
> I know not how I lost him. Here I kneel :—
> If e'er my will did trespass 'gainst his love,
> Either in discourse of thought, or actual deed,
> Or that mine eyes, mine ears, or any sense,
> Delignted them in any other form;
> Or that I do not, and ever did,
> And ever will—though he do shake me off
> To beggarly divorcement—love him dearly,
> Comfort forswear me! Unkindness may do much,
> And his unkindness may defeat my life,
> But never taint my love. . . .
>   *Iago.* I pray you, be content: 'tis but his humour.

---

[1] " *Iago.* Ay, too gentle.
     Othello. Nay, that's certain." [Act iv., sc. 1.]

The business of the state does him offence.
  Desdemona. If 'twere no other !"—[1]

The scene which follows with Æmilia and the song of
the Willow, are equally beautiful, and show the author's
extreme power of varying the expression of passion, in all
its moods and in all circumstances.

" *Æmilia.* I would you had never seen him.
  Desdemona. So would not I : my love doth so approve him,
That even his stubbornness, his checks, his frowns—
Prythee unpin me—have grace and favour in them," &c. [2]

Not the unjust suspicions of Othello, not Iago's un-
provoked treachery, place Desdemona in a more amiable
or interesting light than the conversation (half earnest,
half jest) between her and Æmilia on the common behaviour of women to their husbands. This dialogue
takes place just before the last fatal scene. If Othello
had overheard it, it would have prevented the whole
catastrophe ; but then it would have spoiled the play.

The character of Iago is one of the supererogations of
Shakespear's genius. Some persons, more nice than wise,
have thought this whole character unnatural, because his
villainy is *without a sufficient motive.* Shakespear, who
was as good a philosopher as he was a poet, thought
otherwise. He knew that the love of power, which is
another name for the love of mischief, is natural to man.
He would know this as well or better than if it had been
demonstrated to him by a logical diagram, merely from
seeing children paddle in the dirt or kill flies for sport.
Iago in fact belongs to a class of character, common to
Shakespear and at the same time peculiar to him ; whose
heads are as acute and active as their hearts are hard and
callous. Iago is to be sure an extreme instance of the
kind ; that is to say, of diseased intellectual activity,
with the most perfect indifference to moral good or evil,
or rather with a decided preference of the latter, because

[1 Act iv., sc. 2.]   [2 Act iv., sc. 3.]

it fails more readily in with his favourite propensity
gives greater zest to his thoughts and scope to his actions.
He is quite or nearly as indifferent to his own fate as to
that of others; he runs all risks for a trifling and doubtful advantage; and is himself the dupe and victim of his
ruling passion—an insatiable craving after action of the
most difficult and dangerous kind. "Our ancient" is a
philosopher, who fancies that a lie that kills has more
point in it than an alliteration or an antithesis; who
thinks a fatal experiment on the peace of a family a better
thing than watching the palpitations in the heart of a flea
in a microscope; who plots the ruin of his friends as an
exercise for his ingenuity, and stabs men in the dark to
prevent *ennui*. His gaiety, such as it is, arises from the
success of his treachery; his ease from the torture he has
inflicted on others. He is an amateur of tragedy in real
life; and instead of employing his invention on imaginary
characters, or long-forgotten incidents, he takes the
bolder and more desperate course of getting up his plot
at home, casts the principal parts among his nearest
friends and connections, and rehearses it in downright
earnest, with steady nerves and unabated resolution. We
will just give an illustration or two.

One of his most characteristic speeches is that immediately after the marriage of Othello.

> "*Roderigo.* What a full fortune does the thick-lips owe,
> If he can carry 't thus !
>   *Iago.*   Call up her father:
> Rouse him (*Othello*); make after him, poison his delight,
> Proclaim him in the streets, incense her kinsmen,
> And tho' he in a fertile climate dwell,
> Plague him with flies : though that his joy be joy,
> Yet throw such changes of vexation on 't,
> As it may lose some colour." [1]

In the next passage, his imagination runs riot in the

[1 Act i., sc. 1.]

mischief he is plotting, and breaks out into the wildness
and impetuosity of real enthusiasm.

> " *Roderigo.* Here is her father's house: I'll call aloud.
> *Iago.* Do; with like timorous accent and dire yell
> As when, by night and negligence, the fire
> Is spied in populous cities."

One of his most favourite topics, on which he is rich
indeed, and in descanting on which his spleen serves him
for a Muse, is the disproportionate match between Desdemona and the Moor. This is a clue to the character of
the lady which he is by no means ready to part with. It
is brought forward in the first scene, and he recurs to it,
when in answer to his insinuations against Desdemona,
Roderigo says,

> "I cannot believe that in her—she's full of most blest con-
> ditions."[1]
> *Iago.* Blessed fig's end! The wine she drinks is made of grapes.
> If she had been blest, she would never have loved the Moor."[2]

And again with still more spirit and fatal effect afterwards, when he turns this very suggestion arising in
Othello's own breast to her prejudice.

> " *Othello.* And yet how nature erring from itself—
> *Iago.* Ay, there's the point;—as—to be bold with you—
> Not to affect many proposed matches
> Of her own clime, complexion, and degree," &c.[3]

This is probing to the quick. Iago here turns the
character of poor Desdemona, as it were, inside out. It is
certain that nothing but the genius of Shakespear could
have preserved the entire interest and delicacy of the
part, and have even drawn an additional elegance and
dignity from the peculiar circumstances in which she is
placed. The habitual licentiousness of Iago's conversation is not to be traced to the pleasure he takes in gross
or lascivious images, but to his desire of finding out the

---

[1] Mr. Dyce reads " condition."—Ed.
[2] Act ii., sc. 1.]   [3] Act iii., sc. 3.]

worst side of everything, and of proving himself an over-
match for appearances. He has none of "the milk of
human kindness" in his composition. His imagination
rejects everything that has not a strong infusion of the
most unpalatable ingredients; his mind digests only
poisons. Virtue or goodness or whatever has the least
"relish of salvation in it," is, to his depraved appetite,
sickly and insipid : and he even resents the good opinion
entertained of his own integrity, as if it were an affront
cast on the masculine sense and spirit of his character.
Thus at the meeting between Othello and Desdemona, he
exclaims :

> ————" O, you are well tun'd now !
> But I'll set down the pegs that make this music,
> As honest as I am "— [1]

his character of *bonhommie* not sitting at all easy upon
him. In the scenes where he tries to work Othello to
his purpose, he is proportionably guarded, insidious,
dark, and deliberate. We believe nothing ever came up to
the profound dissimulation and dexterous artifice of the
well-known dialogue in the third act, where he first enters
upon the execution of his design.

> " *Iago.* My noble lord.—
>   *Othello.*   What dost thou say, Iago ?
>   *Iago.* Did Michael Cassio, when you woo'd my lady,
> Know of your love ?
>   *Othello.* He did from first to last. Why dost thou ask ?
>   *Iago.* But for a satisfaction of my thought ;
> No further harm.
>   *Othello.*   Why of thy thought, Iago ?
>   *Iago.* I did not think he had been acquainted with her.
>   *Othello.* O yes, and went between us very oft—
>   *Iago.* Indeed !
>   *Othello.* Indeed ? Ay, indeed. Discern'st thou aught in that ?
> Is he not honest ?

---

[1] Act ii., sc. 1.]

Iago. Honest, my lord?
Othello. Honest? Ay, honest.
Iago. My lord, for aught I know
Othello. What dost thou think?
Iaga.   Think, my lord!
Othello.   Think, my lord
By heaven, he echoes me,
As if there was some monster in his thought
Too hideous to be shown."—¹

The stops and breaks, the deep workings of treachery
under the mask of love and honesty, the anxious watch-
fulness, the cool earnestness, and if we may so say, the
passion of hypocrisy, marked in every line, receive their
last finishing in that inconceivable burst of pretended
indignation at Othello's doubts of his sincerity:

————" O grace! O Heaven forgive me!
Are you a man? Have you a soul or sense?
God be wi' you! take mine office.—O wretched fool,
That liv'st to make thine honesty a vice!—
O monstrous world! Take note, take note, O world!
To be direct and honest is not safe.—
I thank you for this profit, and from hence
I'll love no friend, since love breeds such offence." ²

If Iago is detestable enough when he has business on
his hands and all his engines at work, he is still worse
when he has nothing to do, and we only see into the
hollowness of his heart. His indifference when Othello
falls into a swoon, is perfectly diabolical:

" *Iago.* How is it, General? Have you not hurt your head?
Othello. Dost thou mock me?
Iago. I mock you! No, by Heaven," &c.³

The part indeed would hardly be tolerated, even as a
foil to the virtue and generosity of the other characters in
the play, but for its indefatigable industry and inex
haustible resources, which divert the attention of the
spectator (as well as his own) from the end he has in

[¹ Act iii., sc. 3.]   [² *Ibid.*]   [³ Act iv., sc. 1.]

view to the means by which it must be accomplished.
Edmund the Bastard in 'Lear' is something of the same
character, placed in less prominent circumstances. Zanga[1]
is a vulgar caricature of it.

— ◆ —

TIMON OF ATHENS.[2]

'TIMON OF ATHENS' always appeared to us to be written
with as intense a feeling of his subject as any one play
of Shakespear. It is one of the few in which he seems to
be in earnest throughout, never to trifle nor go out of his
way. He does not relax in his efforts, nor lose sight of
the unity of his design. It is the only play of our author
in which spleen is the predominant feeling of the mind.
It is as much a satire as a play : and contains some of the
finest pieces of invective possible to be conceived, both
in the snarling, captious answers of the cynic Apemantus,
and in the impassioned and more terrible imprecations of
Timon. The latter remind the classical reader of the
force and swelling impetuosity of the moral declamations
in Juvenal, while the former have all the keenness and
caustic severity of the old Stoic philosophers. The soul
of Diogenes appears to have been seated on the lips of
Apemantus. The churlish profession of misanthropy in
the cynic is contrasted with the profound feeling of it in
Timon, and also with the soldier-like and determined
resentment of Alcibiades against his countrymen, who

[1] The hero of ' The Revenge,' a tragedy by Edward Young, Lond.
1721, 8vo.—ED.

[2] First printed in the folio of 1623. There is a second drama on
the same subject from an anonymous pen, of uncertain date, but
conjectured to have been written about 1590. One or two of the
incidents are similar to incidents in Shakespear's drama, the composition of which is assigned to 1610 or thereabout. The story
itself is in Painter's ' Palace of Pleasure,' 1566, and in North's
Plutarch,' 1579.—ED.

have banished him, though this forms only an incidental episode in the tragedy.

The fable consists of a single event;—of the transition from the highest pomp and profusion of artificial refinement to the most abject state of savage life, and privation of all social intercourse. The change is as rapid as it is complete ; nor is the description of the rich and generous Timon, banqueting in gilded palaces, pampered by every luxury, prodigal of his hospitality, courted by crowds of flatterers, poets, painters, lords, ladies, who—

> " Follow his strides, his lobbies fill with tendance,
> Rain sacrificial whisperings in his ear ;
> Make sacred even his stirrup, and through him
> Drink the free air"—[1]

more striking than that of the sudden falling off of his friends and fortune, and his naked exposure in a wild forest digging roots from the earth for his sustenance, with a lofty spirit of self-denial, and bitter scorn of the world, which raise him higher in our esteem than the dazzling gloss of prosperity could do. He grudges himself the means of life, and is only busy in preparing his grave. How forcibly is the difference between what he was, and what he is, described in Apemantus's taunting questions, when he comes to reproach him with the change in his way of life !

> ————" What, think'st
> That the bleak air, thy boisterous chamberlain,
> Will put thy shirt on warm ? will these moss'd trees
> That have outlived the eagle, page thy heels,
> And skip where thou point'st out ? will the cold brook,
> Candied with ice, caudle thy morning taste
> To cure thy o'er-night's surfeit ? Call the creatures,
> Whose naked natures live in all the spite
> Of wreakful heaven, whose bare unhoused trunks,
> To the conflicting elements expos'd,
> Answer mere nature—bid them flatter thee." [2]

The manners are everywhere preserved with distinct

[1 Act i., sc. 1.]   [2 Act iv., sc. 3.]

truth. The poet and painter are very skilfully played off against one another, both affecting great attention to the other, and each taken up with his own vanity, and the superiority of his own art. Shakespear has put into the mouth of the former a very lively description of the genius of poetry and of his own in particular.

> —————" A thing slipt idly from me
> Our poesy is as a gum, which oozes
> From whence 'tis nourish'd. The fire i' th' flint
> Shows not till it be struck: our gentle flame
> Provokes itself, and like the current flies
> Each bound it chafes." [1]

The hollow friendship and shuffling evasions of the Athenian lords, their smooth professions and pitiful ingratitude, are very satisfactorily exposed, as well as the different disguises to which the meanness of self-love resorts in such cases to hide a want of generosity and good faith. The lurking selfishness of Apemantus does not pass undetected amidst the grossness of his sarcasms and his contempt for the pretensions of others. Even the two courtezans who accompany Alcibiades to the cave of Timon are very characteristically sketched; and the thieves who come to visit him are also " true men" in their way.—An exception to this general picture of selfish depravity is found in the old and honest steward Flavius, to whom Timon pays a full tribute of tenderness. Shakespear was unwilling to draw a picture "*ugly all over with hypocrisy.*" He owed this character to the good-natured solicitations of his Muse. His mind might well have been said to be the " sphere of humanity."

The moral sententiousness of this play equals that of Bacon's Treatise on the Wisdom of the Ancients, and is indeed seasoned with greater variety. Every topic of contempt or indignation is here exhausted; but while the sordid licentiousness of Apemantus, which turns everything to gall and bitterness, shows only the natural virulence of his temper and antipathy to good or evil alike, Timon does not utter an imprecation without betraying the extravagant workings of disappointed passion. of love altered to hate. Apemantus sees nothing good in any object, and exaggerates whatever is disgusting: Timon is tormented with the perpetual contrast between things and appearances, between the fresh, tempting outside and the rottenness within, and invokes mischiefs on the heads of mankind proportioned to the sense of his wrongs and of their treacheries. He impatiently cries out, when he finds the gold,

> " This yellow slave
> Will knit and break religions ; bless th' accursed ;
> Make the hoar leprosy ador'd ; place thieves,
> And give them title, knee, and approbation,
> With senators on the bench ; this is it,
> That makes the wappen'd widow wed again ;
> She, whom the spital-house and ulcerous sores
> Would cast the gorge at, *this embalms and spices*
> *To th' April day again.*" [1]

One of his most dreadful imprecations is that which occurs immediately on his leaving Athens.

> "Let me look back upon thee, O thou wall,
> That girdlest in those wolves, dive in the earth,
> And fence not Athens ! Matrons, turn incontinent !
> Obedience fail in children ! slaves and fools
> Pluck the grave wrinkled senate from the bench,
> And minister in their steads !—to general filths
> Convert o' th' instant green virginity !—
> Do't in your parents' eyes ! bankrupts, hold fast ;
> Rather than render back, out with your knives,
> And cut your trusters' throats ! Bound servants, steal ;
> Large-handed robbers your grave masters are
> And pill by law ! Maid, to thy master's bed :
> Thy mistress is o' th' brothel ! Son of sixteen,
> Pluck the lin'd crutch from thy old limping sire,
> With it beat out his brains ! piety and fear,

[1 Act iv., sc. 3.]

Religion to the Gods, peace, justice, truth,
Domestic awe, night-rest, and neighbourhood,
Instructions, manners, mysteries and trades,
Degrees, observances, customs and laws,
Decline to your confounding contraries ;
And let confusion live !—Plagues, incident to men,
Your potent and infectious fevers heap
On Athens, ripe for stroke ! Thou cold sciatica,
Cripple our senators, that their limbs may halt
As lamely as their manners ! Lust and liberty
Creep in the minds and marrows of our youth,
That 'gainst the stream of virtue they may strive,
And drown themselves in riot ! Itches, blains,
Sow all th' Athenian bosoms ; and their crop
Be general leprosy ! breath infect breath,
That their society (as their friendship) may
Be merely poison !" [1]

Timon is here just as ideal in his passion for ill as he
had been before in his belief of good. Apemantus was
satisfied with the mischief existing in the world, and with
his own ill-nature. One of the most decisive intimations
of Timon's morbid jealousy of appearances is in his
answer to Apemantus, who asks him,

" What things in the world canst thou nearest compare to thy
flatterers ?
Timon. Women nearest: but men, men are the things themselves." [2]

Apemantus, it is said, " loved few things better than to
abhor himself." This is not the case with Timon, who
neither loves to abhor himself nor others. All his vehement misanthropy is forced, up-hill work. From the
slippery turns of fortune, from the turmoils of passion
and adversity, he wishes to sink into the quiet of the
grave. On that subject his thoughts are intent, on that
he finds time and place to grow romantic. He digs his
own grave by the sea-shore ; contrives his funeral ceremonies amidst the pomp of desolation, and builds his
mausoleum of the elements.

[1 Act iv., sc. 1.]   [2 Act iv., sc. 3.]

" Come not to me again; but say to Athens,
Timon hath made his everlasting mansion
Upon the beachèd verge of the salt flood;
Which once a-day with his embossèd froth
The turbulent surge shall cover.—Thither come,
And let my grave-stone be your oracle." [1]

And again, Alcibiades, after reading his epitaph, says
of him,

" These well express in thee thy latter spirits:
Though thou abhorred'st in us our human griefs,
Scorn'd'st our brains' flow, and those our droplets which
From niggard nature fall; yet rich conceit
Taught thee to make vast Neptune weep for aye
On thy low grave "——[2]

thus making the winds his funeral dirge, his mourner
the murmuring ocean ; and seeking in the everlasting
solemnities of nature oblivion of the transitory splendour
of his life-time.

———◦◦◦———

CORIOLANUS.[3]

SHAKESPEAR has in this play shown himself well versed in
history and state affairs. ' Coriolanus' is a storehouse of
political commonplaces. Any one who studies it may
save himself the trouble of reading Burke's Reflections,
or Paine's Rights of Man, or the Debates in both Houses
of Parliament since the French Revolution or our own.
The arguments for and against aristocracy or democracy,
on the privileges of the few and the claims of the many,
on liberty and slavery, power and the abuse of it, peace
and war, are here very ably handled, with the spirit of a

[¹ Act v., sc. 1.]   [² Act v., sc. 4.]
³ "First printed in the folio of 1623. It is proved by the style to
have been one of the author's latest compositions: according to
Malone, it was written in 1610. North's ' Plutarch ' (translated from
the French of Amiot) supplied Shakespear with the incidents, and
indeed with much of the wording, of this tragedy."—*Dyce.*—ED.

poet and the acuteness of a philosopher. Shakespear himself seems to have had a leaning to the arbitrary side of
the question, perhaps from some feeling of contempt for
his own origin; and to have spared no occasion of· bating
the rabble. What he says of them is very true: what he
says of their betters is also very true, though he dwells
less upon it. The cause of the people is indeed but
little calculated as a subject for poetry : it admits of
rhetoric, which goes into argument and explanation, but
it presents no immediate or distinct images to the mind,

"———— no jutty, frieze,
Buttress, nor coign of vantage"[1]

for poetry " to make its pendent bed and procreant cradle "
in. The language of poetry naturally falls in with the
language of power. The imagination is an exaggerating
and exclusive faculty : it takes from one thing to add to
another : it accumulates circumstances together to give
the greatest possible effect to a favourite object. The
understanding is a dividing and measuring faculty : it
judges of things not according to their immediate impression on the mind, but according to their relations to one
another. The one is a monopolising faculty, which seeks
the greatest quantity of present excitement by inequality
and disproportion; the other is a distributive faculty,
which seeks the greatest quantity of ultimate good, by
justice and proportion. The one is an aristocratical, the
other a republican faculty. The principle of poetry is a
very anti-levelling principle. It aims at effect, it exists
by contrast. It admits of no medium. It is everything
by excess. It rises above the ordinary standard of sufferings and crimes. It presents a dazzling appearance.
It shows its head turretted, crowned, and crested. Its
front is gilt and blood-stained. Before it "it carries
noise, and behind it leaves tears." It has its altars and
its victims, sacrifices, human sacrifices. Kings, priests,

[1 'Macbeth,' act i., sc. 6.]

nobles, are its train-bearers, tyrants and slaves its execu-
tioners.—" Carnage is its daughter." Poetry is right-
royal. It puts the individual for the species, the one
above the infinite many, might before right. A lion
hunting a flock of sheep or a herd of wild asses is a more
poetical object than they ; and we even take part with the
lordly beast, because our vanity or some other feeling
makes us disposed to place ourselves in the situation of
the strongest party. So we feel some concern for the poor
citizens of Rome when they meet together to compare
their wants and grievances, till Coriolanus comes in and
with blows and big words drives this set of " poor rats,"
this rascal scum, to their homes and beggary before him.
There is nothing heroical in a multitude of miserable
rogues not wishing to be starved, or complaining that
they are like to be so: but when a single man comes
forward to brave their cries and to make them submit to
the last indignities, from mere pride and self-will, our
admiration of his prowess is immediately converted into
contempt for their pusillanimity. The insolence of power
is stronger than the plea of necessity. The tame submission to usurped authority or even the natural resistance to it, has nothing to excite or flatter the imagination :
it is the assumption of a right to insult or oppress others
that carries an imposing air of superiority with it. We
had rather be the oppressor than the oppressed. The
love of power in ourselves and the admiration of it in
others are both natural to man : the one makes him a
tyrant, the other a slave. Wrong dressed out in pride,
pomp, and circumstance, has more attraction than abstract
right. Coriolanus complains of the fickleness of the
people : yet, the instant he cannot gratify his pride and
obstinacy at their expense, he turns his arms against
his country. If his country was not worth defending,
why did he build his pride on its defence ? He is a
conqueror and a hero ; he conquers other countries, and

makes this a plea for enslaving his own ; and when he is prevented from doing so, he leagues with its enemies to destroy his country. He rates the people " as if he were a God to punish, and not a man of their infirmity." He scoffs at one of their tribunes for maintaining their rights and franchises : " Mark you his absolute *shall ?*" not marking his own absolute *will* to take everything from them, his impatience of the slightest opposition to his own pretensions being in proportion to their arrogance and absurdity. If the great and powerful had the bene-ficence and wisdom of Gods, then all this would have been well : if with a greater knowledge of what is good for the people, they had as great a care for their interest as they have themselves, if they were seated above the world, sympathising with the welfare, but not feeling the passions of men, receiving neither good nor hurt from them, but bestowing their benefits as free gifts on them, they might then rule over them like another Providence. But this is not the case. Coriolanus is unwilling that the senate should show their " cares " for the people, lest their " cares " should be construed into " fears," to the subversion of all due authority ; and he is no sooner disappointed in his schemes to deprive the people not only of the cares of the state, but of all power to redress themselves, than Volumnia is made madly to exclaim,

" Now the red pestilence strike all trades in Rome,
And occupations perish." [1]

This is but natural : it is but natural for a mother to have more regard for her son than for a whole city; but then the city should be left to take some care of itself. The care of the state cannot, we here see, be safely entrusted to maternal affection, or to the domestic charities of high life. The great have private feelings of their own, to which the interests of humanity and justice must courtesy. Their interests are so far from being the same

[[1] Act iv., sc. 1.]

as those of the community, that they are in direct and necessary opposition to them; their power is at the ex- pense of *our* weakness; their riches of *our* poverty; their pride of *our* degradation; their splendour of *our* wretchedness; their tyranny of *our* servitude. If they had the superior knowledge ascribed to them (which they have not) it would only render them so much more for- midable; and from Gods would convert them into Devils. The whole dramatic moral of ' Coriolanus ' is that those who have little shall have less, and that those who have much shall take all that others have left. The people are poor; therefore they ought to be starved. They are slaves; therefore they ought to be beaten. They work hard; therefore they ought to be treated like beasts of burden. They are ignorant; therefore they ought not to be allowed to feel that they want food, or clothing, or rest—that they are enslaved, oppressed, and miserable. This is the logic of the imagination and the passions; which seek to aggrandize what excites admiration and to heap contempt on misery, to raise power into tyranny, and to make tyranny absolute; to thrust down that which is low still lower, and to make wretches desperate : to exalt magistrates into kings, kings into gods; to degrade sub- jects to the rank of slaves, and slaves to the condition of brutes. The history of mankind is a romance, a mask, a tragedy, constructed upon the principles of *poetical justice;* it is a noble or royal hunt, in which what is sport to the few is death to the many, and in which the spectators halloo and encourage the strong to set upon the weak, and cry havoc in the chase though they do not share in the spoil. We may depend upon it that what men delight to read in books, they will put in practice in reality.

One of the most natural traits in this play is the dif- ference of the interest taken in the success of Coriolanus by his wife and mother. The one is only anxious for his honour; the other is fearful for his life.

> " *Volumnia.*   Methinks I hear hither your husband's drum
> I see him pluck Aufidius down by th' hair,
> As children from a bear, the Volsces shunning him :
> Methinks I see him stamp thus, and call thus—
> Come on, you cowards ; you were got in fear
> Though you were born in Rome ; his bloody brow
> With his mail'd hand then wiping, forth he goes
> Like to a harvest man, that's task'd to mow
> Or all, or lose his hire.
>   *Virgilia.*   His bloody brow !   O Jupiter, no blood !
>   *Volumnia.*   Away, you fool ! it more becomes a man
> Than gilt his trophy.   The breast of Hecuba,
> When she did suckle Hector, look'd not lovelier
> Than Hector's forehead, when it spit forth blood
> At Grecian swords, contemning." [1]

When she hears the trumpets that proclaim her son's
return, she says, in the true spirit of a Roman matron,

> " These are the ushers of Martius : before him
> He carries noise, and behind him he leaves tears.
> Death, that dark spirit, in's nervy arm doth lie,
> Which, being advanc'd, declines, and then men die." [2]

Coriolanus himself is a complete character : his love
of reputation, his contempt of popular opinion, his pride
and modesty, are consequences of each other.   His pride
consists in the inflexible sternness of his will ; his love
of glory is a determined desire to bear down all opposition, and to extort the admiration both of friends and
foes.   His contempt for popular favour, his unwillingness
to hear his own praises, spring from the same source.
He cannot contradict the praises that are bestowed upon
him ;   therefore he is impatient at hearing them.   He
would enforce the good opinion of others by his actions,
but does not want their acknowledgments in words.

> " Pray now, no more : my mother,
> Who has a charter to extol her blood,
> When she does praise me, grieves me." [3]

His magnanimity is of the same kind.   He admires in

[1 Act i., sc. 3.]   [2 Act ii., sc. 1.]   [3 Act i., sc. 9.]

an enemy that courage which he honours in himself; he places himself on the hearth of Aufidius with the same confidence that he would have met him in the field, and feels that by putting himself in his power, he takes from him all temptation for using it against him.

In the title-page of ' Coriolanus,' it is said at the bottom of the Dramatis Personæ, " The whole history exactly followed, and many of the principal speeches copied from the life of Coriolanus in Plutarch." It will be interesting to our readers to see how far this is the case. Two of the principal scenes, those between Coriolanus and Aufidius and between Coriolanus and his mother, are thus given in Sir Thomas North's Translation of Plutarch, dedicated to Queen Elizabeth, 1579. The first is as follows : —

"It was even twilight when he entered the city of Antium, and many people met him in the streets, but no man knew him. So he went directly to Tullus Aufidius' house, and when he came thither, he got him up straight to the chimney-hearth, and sat him down, and spake not a word to any man, his face all muffled over. They of the house spying him, wondered what he should be, and yet they durst not bid him rise. For ill-favouredly muffled and disguised as he was, yet there appeared a certain majesty in his countenance and in his silence: whereupon they went to Tullus, who was at supper, to tell him of the strange disguising of this man. Tullus rose presently from the board, and coming towards him, asked him what he was, and wherefore he came. Then Martius unmuffled himself, and after he had paused awhile, making no answer, he said unto him, ' If ' thou knowest me not yet, Tullus, and seeing me, dost not perhaps ' believe me to be the man I am indeed, I must of necessity betray ' myself to be that I am. I am Caius Martius, who hath done to ' thyself particularly, and to all the Volces generally, great hurt ' and mischief, which I cannot deny for my surname of Coriolanus ' that I bear. For I never had other benefit nor recompence of the ' true and painful service I have done, and the extreme dangers ' I have been in, but this only surname: a good memory and witness ' of the malice and displeasure thou shouldest bear me. Indeed the ' name only remaineth with me; for the rest, the envy and cruelty of ' the people of Rome have taken from me, by the sufferance of the dastardly nobility and magistrates, who have forsaken me, and let

' me be banished by the people. This extremity hath now driven
' me to come as a poor suitor, to take thy chimney-hearth, not of
any hope I have to save my life thereby. For if I had feared
death, I would not have come hither to have put myself in hazard;
' but pricked forward with desire to be revenged of them that thus
' have banished me, which now I do begin, in putting my person
' into the hands of their enemies. Wherefore if thou hast any heart
' to be wrecked of the injuries thy enemies have done thee, speed
' thee now, and let my misery serve thy turn, and so use it as my
' service may be a benefit to the Volces: promising thee, that I will
' fight with better good will for all you, than I did when I was
' against you, knowing that they fight more valiantly who know the
' force of the enemy, than such as have never proved it. And if it
' be so that thou dare not, and that thou art weary to prove fortune
' any more: then am I also weary to live any longer. And it were
' no wisdom in thee to save the life of him who hath been heretofore
' thy mortal enemy, and whose service now can nothing help, nor
' pleasure thee.' Tullus hearing what he said, was a marvellous
glad man, and taking him by the hand, he said unto him : 'Stand
up, O Martius, and be of good cheer, for in proffering thyself unto
us, thou dost us great honour: and by this means thou mayest
' hope also of greater things at all the Volces' hands.' So he feasted
him for that time, and entertained him in the honourablest manner
he could, talking with him of no other matters at that present: but
within few days after, they fell to consultation together in what sort
they should begin their wars." [1]

The meeting between Coriolanus and his mother is
also nearly the same as in the play :—[2]

"Now was Martius set then in his chair of state, with all the
honours of a general, and when he had spied the women coming
afar off, he marvelled what the matter meant: but afterwards
knowing his wife which came foremost, he determined at the first
to persist in his obstinate and inflexible rancour. But overcome in
the end with natural affection, and being altogether altered to see
them, his heart would not serve him to tarry their coming to his
chair, but coming down in haste, he went to meet them, and first
he kissed his mother, and embraced her a pretty while, then his
wife and little children. And nature so wrought with him, that
the tears fell from his eyes, and he could not keep himself from

[1] Plutarch's ' Lives,' translated by North, 1579, ed 1603, pp. 232,
233.—Ed.

[2] *Ibid.*, pp. 238, 239.—Ed.

making much of them, but yielded to the affection of his blood, as
if he had been violently carried with the fury of a most swift-
running stream. After he had thus lovingly received them, and
perceiving that his mother Volumnia would begin to speak to him,
he called the chiefest of the council of the Volces to hear what she
would say. Then she spake in this sort: ' If we held our peace,
' my son, and determined not to speak, the state of our poor bodies,
' and present sight of our raiment, would easily betray to thee what
  life we have led at home, since thy exile and abode abroad ; but
' think now with thyself, how much more unfortunate than all the
' women living, we are come hither, considering that the sight which
' should be most pleasant to all others to behold, spiteful fortune
' had made most fearful to us : making myself to see my son, and
' my daughter here her husband, besieging the walls of his native
' country : so as that which is the only comfort to all others in their
' adversity and misery, to pray unto the Gods, and to call to them
' for aid, is the only thing which plungeth us into most deep per-
' plexity. For we cannot, alas, together pray, both for victory for
' our country, and for safety of thy life also : but a world of grievous
' curses, yea more than any mortal enemy can heap upon us, are
' forcibly wrapped up in our prayers. For the bitter sop of most
' hard choice is offered thy wife and children, to forego one of the
' two : either to lose the person of thyself, or the nurse of their
' native country. For myself, my son, I am determined not to tarry
' till fortune in my lifetime do make an end of this war. For if I
  cannot persuade thee rather to do good unto both parties, than to
' overthrow and destroy the one, preferring love and nature before
' the malice and calamity of wars, thou shalt see, my son, and trust
' unto it, thou shalt no sooner march forward to assault thy country,
' but thy foot shall tread upon thy mother's womb, that brought
' thee first into this world. And I may not defer to see the day,
' either that my son be led prisoner in triumph by his natural
  countrymen, or that he himself do triumph of them, and of his
' natural country. For if it were so, that my request tended to
' save thy country, in destroying the Volces, I must confess, thou
  wouldest hardly and doubtfully resolve on that. For as to destroy
' thy natural country, it is altogether unmeet and unlawful, so were
' it not just and less honourable to betray those that put their trust
' in thee. But my only demand consisteth, to make a goal delivery
' of all evils, which delivereth equal benefit and safety, both to the
' one and the other, but most honourable for the Volces. For it shall
' appear, that having victory in their hands, they have of special
' favour granted us singular graces, peace and amity, albeit them-
' selves have no less part of both than we. Of which good, if so it

came to pass, thyself is the only author, and so hast thou the only
' honour. But if it fail, and fall out contrary, thyself alone de·
' servedly shalt carry the shameful reproach and burthen of either
' party. So, though the end of war be uncertain, yet this notwith-
' standing is most certain, that if it be thy chance to conquer, this
' benefit shalt thou reap of thy goodly conquest, to be chronicled
' the plague and destroyer of thy country. And if fortune also
overthrow thee, then the world will say, that through desire to
' revenge thy private injuries, thou hast for ever undone thy good
' friends, who did most lovingly and courteously receive thee.'
Martius gave good ear unto his mother's words, without interrupting
her speech at all, and after she had said what she would, he held his
peace a pretty while, and answered not a word. Hereupon she
began again to speak unto him, and said : ' My son, why dost thou
' not answer me ? Dost thou think it good altogether to give place
' unto thy choler and desire of revenge, and thinkest thou it not
' honesty for thee to grant thy mother's request in so weighty a
' cause ? Dost thou take it honourable for a noble man to remember
' the wrongs and injuries done him, and dost not in like case think
' it an honest noble man's part to be thankful for the goodness that
' parents do show to their children, acknowledging the duty and
' reverence they ought to bear unto them ? No man living is more
' bound to show himself thankful in all parts and respects than
' thyself; who so unnaturally showest all ingratitude. Moreover,
' my son, thou hast sorely taken of thy country, exacting grievous
' payments upon them, in revenge of the injuries offered thee ;
' besides, thou hast not hitherto showed thy poor mother any
' courtesy. And therefore, it is not only honest but due unto me,
' that without compulsion I should obtain my so just and reasonable
' request of thee. But since by reason I cannot persuade thee to
' it, to what purpose do I defer my last hope ?' And with these
words, herself, his wife and children, fell down upon their knees
before him : Martius seeing that, could refrain no longer, but went
straight and lifted her up, crying out, ' Oh mother, what have you
' done to me ?' And holding her hard by the right hand, ' Oh
' mother,' said he, ' you have won a happy victory for your country,
' but mortal and unhappy for your son: for I see myself vanquished
' by you alone.' These words being spoken openly, he spake a
little apart with his mother and wife, and then let them return
again to Rome, for so they did request him ; and so remaining in
camp that night, the next morning he dislodged, and marched
homeward into the Volces country again."

Shakespear has, in giving a dramatic form to this

passage, adhered very closely and properly to the text. He did not think it necessary to improve upon the truth of nature. Several of the scenes in 'Julius Cæsar,' particularly Portia's appeal to the confidence of her husband by showing him the wound she had given herself, and the appearance of the ghost of Cæsar to Brutus, are in like manner taken from the history.

TROILUS AND CRESSIDA.[1]

THIS is one of the most loose and desultory of our author's plays: it rambles on just as it happens, but it overtakes, together with some indifferent matter, a prodigious number of fine things in its way. Troilus himself is no character: he is merely a common lover: but Cressida and her uncle Pandarus are hit off with proverbial truth. By the speeches given to the leaders of the Grecian host, Nestor, Ulysses, Agamemnon, Achilles, Shakespear seems to have known them as well as if he had been a spy sent by the Trojans into the enemy's camp—to say nothing of their affording very lofty examples of didactic eloquence. The following is a very stately and spirited declamation:

> " *Ulysses.* Troy, yet upon his basis, had been down,
> And the great Hector's sword had lack'd a master,
> But for these instances.
> The specialty of rule hath been neglected.
> *   *   *   *   *   *
> The heavens themselves, the planets, and this centre,
> Observe degree, priority, and place,
> Insisture, course, proportion, season, form,
> Office, and custom, in all line of order:

---

[1] Printed twice in 1609, and again in the folio of 1623. There was an earlier drama on this subject by Thomas Decker and Henry Chettle, mentioned in Henslowe's Diary under 1599. The latter was the piece, probably, which we find licensed to James Roberts in 1602-3. But nothing is now known of it.—ED.

And therefore is the glorious planet Sol,
In noble eminence, enthron'd and spher'd
Amidst the other, whose med'cinable eye
Corrects the ill aspécts of planets evil,
And posts, like the commandment of a king,
Sans check, to good and bad. But when the planets
In evil mixture, to disorder wander,
What plagues, and what portents, what mutiny,
What raging of the sea, shaking of earth,
Commotion in the winds, frights, changes, horrors,
Divert and crack, rend and deracinate
The unity and married calm of states
Quite from their fixure! O, when degree is shak'd
(Which is the ladder to all high designs),
Then enterprise is sick! How could communities,
Degrees in schools, and brotherhoods in cities,
Peaceful commérce from dividable shores,
The primogenity and due of birth,
Prerogative of age, crowns, sceptres, laurels,
But by degree stand in authentic place?
Take but degree away, untune that string,
And hark, what discord follows! each thing meets
In mere oppugnancy: the bounded waters
Should lift their bosoms higher than the shores,
And make a sop of all this solid globe:
Strength should be lord of imbecility,
And the rude son should strike his father dead:
Force should be right, or rather, right and wrong
Between whose endless jar Justice resides—
Should lose their names, and so should Justice too.
Then everything includes itself in power,
Power into will, will into appetite;
And appetite, an universal wolf,
So doubly seconded with will and power,
Must make perforce an universal prey,
And last eat up himself. Great Agamemnon,
This chaos, when degree is suffocate,
Follows the choking:
And this neglection of degree it is,
That by a pace goes backward, with a purpose
It hath to climb. The general's disdained
By him one step below; he, by the next;
That next, by him beneath: so every step,
Exampled by the first pace that is sick

Of his superior, grows to an envious fever
Of pale and bloodless emulation;
And 'tis this fever that keeps Troy on foot,
Not her own sinews.   To end a tale of length,
Troy in our weakness stands, not in her strength." [1]

It cannot be said of Shakespear, as was said of some
one, that he was " without o'erflowing full."   He was full,
even to o'erflowing.   He gave heaped measure, running
over.   This was his greatest fault.   He was only in
danger " of losing distinction in his thoughts " (to borrow
his own expression)

> " As doth a battle, when they charge on heaps
> The enemy flying." [2]

There is another passage, the speech of Ulysses to Achilles,
showing him the thankless nature of popularity, which
has a still greater depth of moral observation and richness
of illustration than the former.   It is long, but worth the
quoting.   The sometimes giving an entire argument from
the unacted plays of our author may with one class of
readers have almost the use of restoring a lost passage;
and may serve to convince another class of critics, that
the poet's genius was not confined to the production of
stage effect by preternatural means.

> " *Ulysses.* Time hath, my lord, a wallet at his back,
> Wherein he puts alms for Oblivion ;
> A great-siz'd monster of ingratitudes:
> Those scraps are good deeds past, which are devour'd
> As fast as they are made, forgot as soon
> As they are done.   Perseverance, dear my lord,
> Keeps Honour bright : to have done, is to hang
> Quite out of fashion, like a rusty mail
> In monumental mockery.   Take th' instant way;
> For Honour travels in a strait so narrow,
> Where one but goes abreast; keep then the path,
> For Emulation hath a thousand sons,
> That one by one pursue; if you give way,
> Or hedge aside from the direct forthright,

[1 Act i., sc. 3.]   [2 Act iii., sc. 2.]

Like to an enter'd tide, they all rush by,
And leave you hindmost;
Or, like a gallant horse fall'n in first rank,
O'er-run and trampled on : then what they do in present,
Tho' less than yours in past must o'ertop yours:
For Time is like a fashionable host,
That slightly shakes his parting guest by th' hand,
And with his arms outstretch'd, as he would fly,
Grasps-in the comer : welcome ever smiles,
And farewell goes out sighing. O, let not virtue seek
Remuneration for the thing it was;
For beauty, wit,
High birth, vigour of bone, desert in service,
Love, friendship, charity, are subjects all
To envious and calumniating time.
One touch of nature makes the whole world kin ;
That all with one consent praise new-born gawds,
Tho' they are made and moulded of things past.
And give to dust, that is a little gilt,
More laud than gilt o'er-dusted.
The present eye praises the present object.
Then marvel not, thou great and complete man,
That all the Greeks begin to worship Ajax ;
Since things in motion sooner catch the eye,
Than what not stirs. The cry went once on thee,
And still it might, and yet it may again,
If thou would'st not entomb thyself alive,
And case thy reputation in thy tent." [1]

The throng of images in the above lines is prodigious;
and though they sometimes jostle against one another,
they everywhere raise and carry on the feeling, which is
intrinsically true and profound. The debates between
the Trojan chiefs on the restoring of Helen are full of
knowledge of human motives and character. Troilus
enters well into the philosophy of war, when he says in
answer to something that falls from Hector,

" Why, there you touch'd the life of our design .
Were it not glory that we more affected,
Than the performance of our heaving spleens,
I would not wish a drop of Trojan blood

[1 Act iii., sc. 3.]

Spent more in her defence. But, worthy Hector,
She is a theme of honour and renown,
A spur to valiant and magnanimous deeds." [1]

The character of Hector, in a few slight indications which appear of it, is made very amiable. His death is sublime, and shows in a striking light the mixture of barbarity and heroism of the age. The threats of Achilles are fatal; they carry their own means of execution with them:

"Come here about me, you my Myrmidons,
Mark what I say. Attend me where I wheel:
Strike not a stroke, but keep yourselves in breath;
And when I have the bloody Hector found,
Empale him with your weapons round about,
In fellest manner execute your aims.
Follow me, sirs, and my proceedings eye." [2]

He then finds Hector and slays him, as if he had been hunting down a wild beast. There is something revolting as well as terrific in the ferocious coolness with which he singles out his prey : nor does the splendour of the achievement reconcile us to the cruelty of the means.

The characters of Cressida and Pandarus are very amusing and instructive. The disinterested willingness of Pandarus to serve his friend in an affair which lies next his heart is immediately brought forward. "Go thy way, Troilus, go thy way; had I a sister were a grace, or a daughter a goddess, he should take his choice. O admirable man ! Paris, Paris is dirt to him, and I warrant Helen, to change, would give an eye to boot." [3] This is the language he addresses to his niece : nor is she much behindhand in coming into the plot. Her head is as light and fluttering as her heart. "It is the prettiest villain, she fetches her breath so short as a new-ta'en sparrow." Both characters are originals, and quite different from what they are in Chaucer. In Chaucer, Cressida is

[1 Act ii., sc. 2.] [2 Act v., sc. 7.] [3 Act i., sc. 2.] [4 Act iii., sc. 2.]

represented as a grave, sober, considerate personage (a widow—he cannot tell her age, nor whether she has children or no), who has an alternate eye to her character, her interest, and her pleasure : Shakespear's Cressida is a giddy girl, an unpractised jilt, who falls in love with Troilus, as she afterwards deserts him, from mere levity and thoughtlessness of temper. She may be wooed and won to anything and from anything, at a moment's warning ; the other knows very well what she would be at, and sticks to it, and is more governed by substantial reasons than by caprice or vanity. Pandarus again, in Chaucer's story, is a friendly sort of go-between, tolerably busy, officious, and forward in bringing matters to bear : but in Shakespear he has " a stamp exclusive and professional :" he wears the badge of his trade ; he is a regular knight of the game. The difference of the manner in which the subject is treated arises perhaps less from intention, than from the different genius of the two poets. There is no *double entendre* in the characters of Chaucer : they are either quite serious or quite comic. In Shakespear the ludicrous and the ironical are constantly blended with the stately and the impassioned. We see Chaucer's characters as they saw themselves, not as they appeared to others or might have appeared to the poet. He is as deeply implicated in the affairs of his personages as they could be themselves. He had to go a long journey with each of them, and became a kind of necessary confidant. There is little relief or light and shade in his pictures. The conscious smile is not seen lurking under the brow of grief or impatience. Everything with him is intense and continuous—a working out of what went before. Shakespear never committed himself to his characters. He trifled, laughed, or wept with them as he chose. He has no prejudices for or against them ; and it seems a matter of perfect indifference whether he shall be in jest or earnest. According to him " the web of our lives is of

a mingled yarn, good and ill together."[1]   His genius was
dramatic, as Chaucer's was historical.   He saw both sides
of a question, the different views taken of it according to
the different interests of the parties concerned, and he
was at once an actor and spectator in the scene.   If anything, he is too various and flexible : too full of transitions, of glancing lights, of salient points.   If Chaucer
followed up his subject too doggedly, perhaps Shakespear
was too volatile and heedless.   The Muse's wing too
often lifted him from off his feet.   He made infinite ex-
cursions to the right and the left :

> ———— "Who hath done to-day
> Mad and fantastic execution ;
> Engaging and redeeming of himself,
> With such a careless force and forceless care,
> As if that luck, in very spite of cunning
> Bade him win all."[2]

Chaucer attended chiefly to the real and natural, that
is, to the involuntary and inevitable impressions on the
mind in given circumstances ; Shakespear exhibited also
the possible and the fantastical,—not only what things
are in themselves, but whatever they might seem to be,
their different reflections, their endless combinations.   He
lent his fancy, wit, invention, to others, and borrowed
their feelings in return.   Chaucer excelled in the force of
habitual sentiment ; Shakespear added to it every variety
of passion, every suggestion of thought or accident.
Chaucer described external objects with the eye of a
painter, or he might be said to have embodied them with
the hand of a sculptor, every part is so thoroughly made
out and tangible :—Shakespear's imagination threw over
them a lustre

> "Prouder than blue Iris bends."

Everything in Chaucer has a downright reality.   A
simile or a sentiment is as if it were given in upon evi-

[1 'All's Well that ends Well' iv 3.]   [2 Act v., sc. 5.]

dence. In Shakespear the commonest matter-of-fact has
a romantic grace about it; or seems to float with the
breath of imagination in a freer element. No one could
have more depth of feeling or observation than Chaucer
but he wanted resources of invention to lay open the
stores of nature or the human heart with the same radiant
light that Shakespear has done. However fine or profound the thought, we know what is coming, whereas the
effect of reading Shakespear is "like vassalage at un-
awares encountering the eye of majesty."[1] Chaucer's
mind was consecutive, rather than discursive. He arrived
at truth through a certain process; Shakespear saw everything by intuition. Chaucer had a great variety of
power, but he could do only one thing at once. He set
himself to work on a particular subject. His ideas were
kept separate, labelled, ticketed, and parcelled out in a set
form, in pews and compartments by themselves. They
did not play into one another's hands. They did not
react upon one another, as the blower's breath moulds
the yielding glass. There is something hard and dry in
them. What is the most wonderful thing in Shakespear's
faculties is their excessive sociability, and how they gos-
siped and compared notes together.

We must conclude this criticism; and we will do it
with a quotation or two. One of the most beautiful passages in Chaucer's tale is the description of Cresseide's
first avowal of her love.

> " And as the newe abasched nightyngale,
> That stynteth firste whanne sche begynneth singe,
> Whanne that sche heereth any heerdis tale,
> Or in heggis any wight steringe ;
> And aftir, siker, doth her vois out ring :
> Right so Cryseide, whanne hir drede stint,
> Opened hir herte, and tolde him hir entent."[2]

See also the two next stanzas, and particularly that
divine one beginning—

[1] Act iii., sc. 2.]   [2] Bell's 'Chaucer, v. 158.]

" Her armes small, her back both straight and soft," &c.

Compare this with the following speech of Troilus to Cressida in the play :—

> "O, that I thought it could be in a woman—
> As, if it can, I will presume in you—
> To feed for aye her lamp and flames of love,
> To keep her constancy in plight and youth,
> Outliving beauties outward, with a mind
> That doth renew swifter than blood decays!
> Or, that persuasion could but thus convince me,
> That my integrity and truth to you
> Might be affronted with the match and weight
> Of such a winnow'd purity in love;
> How were I then uplifted !   But alas !
> I am as true as Truth's simplicity,
> And simpler than the infancy of Truth." [1]

These passages may not seem very characteristic at first sight, though we think they are so. We will give two, that cannot be mistaken. Patroclus says to Achilles,

> " Sweet, rouse yourself ; and the weak wanton Cupid
> Shall from your neck unloose his amorous fold,
> And like a dew-drop from the lion's mane,
> Be shook to air."

Troilus, addressing the God of Day on the approach of the morning that parts him from Cressida, says with much scorn,

> " What ! profrist thou thi light here for to selle ?
> Go selle it hem that smale seelis grave." [2]

If nobody but Shakespear could have written the former, nobody but Chaucer would have thought of the latter. Chaucer was the most literal of poets, as Richardson was of prose-writers.

[1 Act iii.. sc. 2.]   [2 Chaucer, *ubi supra*, p. 167.]

ANTONY AND CLEOPATRA.[1]

THIS is a very noble play. Though not in the first class
of Shakespear's productions, it stands next to them, and is,
we think, the finest of his historical plays, that is, of those
in which he made poetry the organ of history, and assumed
a certain tone of character and sentiment, in conformity
to known facts, instead of trusting to his observations of
general nature or to the unlimited indulgence of his own
fancy. What he has added to the actual story is upon a
par with it. His genius was, as it were, a match for
history as well as nature, and could grapple at will with
either. The play is full of that pervading comprehensive
power by which the poet could always make himself
master of time and circumstances. It presents a fine
picture of Roman pride and Eastern magnificence: and in
the struggle between the two, the empire of the world
seems suspended, like

> ————" The swan's down-feather,
> That stands upon the swell at full of tide,
> And neither way inclines." [2]

The characters breathe, move, and live. Shakespear does
not stand reasoning on what his characters would do or
say, but at once *becomes* them, and speaks and acts for
them. He does not present us with groups of stage-

---

[1] First printed, so far as is at present known, in the folio of 1623 ;
but in 1608, May 20, a play with this title, and almost unquestionably the same, was entered at Stationers' Hall. Shakespear has
derived his material from North's translation of Amiot's French
version of Plutarch.—ED.

[2 Act iii., sc. 2.]

puppets, of poetical machines making set speeches on human life, and acting from a calculation of problematical motives, but he brings living men and women on the scene, who speak and act from real feelings, according to the ebbs and flows of passion, without the least tincture of pedantry of logic or rhetoric. Nothing is made out by inference and analogy, by climax and antithesis, but everything takes place just as it would have done in reality, according to the occasion. The character of Cleopatra is a master-piece. What an extreme contrast it affords to Imogen! One would think it almost impossible for the same person to have drawn both. She is voluptuous, ostentatious, conscious, boastful of her charms, haughty, tyrannical, fickle. The luxurious pomp and gorgeous extravagance of the Egyptian queen are displayed in all their force and lustre, as well as the irregular grandeur of the soul of Mark Antony. Take only the first four lines that they speak as an example of the regal style of love-making :

> " *Cleopatra.* If it be love indeed, tell me how much?
> *Antony.* There's beggary in the love that can be reckon'd.
> *Cleopatra.* I'll set a bourn how far to be belov'd.
> *Antony.* Then must thou needs find out new heaven, new earth." [1]

The rich and poetical description of her person beginning—

> " The barge she sat in, like a burnish'd throne,
> Burn'd on the water; the poop was beaten gold,
> Purple the sails, and so perfumed that
> The winds were love-sick with them "—

seems to prepare the way for, and almost to justify the subsequent infatuation of Antony when in the sea-fight at Actium he leaves the battle, and " like a doating mallard " follows her flying sails.

Few things in Shakespear (and we know of nothing in

[1 Act i., sc. 1.]

any other author like them) have more of that local truth of imagination and character than the passage in which Cleopatra is represented conjecturing what were the employments of Antony in his absence—"He's speaking now, or murmuring—*Where's my serpent of old Nile?*"[1] Or again, when she says to Antony, after the defeat at Actium, and his summoning up resolution to risk another fight:

> " *Cleo.* ————— It is my birth-day;
> I had thought t' have held it poor; but since my lord
> Is Antony again, I will be Cleopatra." [2]

Perhaps the finest burst of all is Antony's rage after his final defeat when he comes in, and surprises the messenger of Cæsar kissing her hand:

> " To let a fellow that will take rewards,
> And say, God quit you! be familiar with
> My play-fellow, your hand; this kingly seal
> And plighter of high hearts!" [3]

It is no wonder that he orders him to be whipped; but his low condition is not the true reason: there is another feeling which lies deeper, though Antony's pride would not let him show it, except by his rage; he suspects the fellow to be Cæsar's proxy.

Cleopatra's whole character is the triumph of the voluptuous, of the love of pleasure and the power of giving it, over every other consideration. Octavia is a dull foil to her, and Fulvia a shrew and shrill-tongued. What a picture do those lines give of her—

> "Age cannot wither her, nor custom stale
> Her infinite variety; other women cloy
> The appetites they feed; but she makes hungry
> Where most she satisfies." [4]

What a spirit and fire in her conversation with Antony's messenger who brings her the unwelcome news of his marriage with Octavia! How all the pride of beauty and of high rank breaks out in her promised reward to him—

[1 Act i., sc. 5.] [2 Act iii., sc 13.] [3 *Ibid.*] [4 Act ii., sc. 2.]

"If thou so yield him, there is gold, and here
My bluest veins to kiss!"—[1]

She had great and unpardonable faults, but the
grandeur of her death almost redeems them. She learns
from the depth of despair the strength of her affections.
She keeps her queen-like state in the last disgrace, and
her sense of the pleasurable in the last moments of her
life. She tastes a luxury in death. After applying the
asp, she says with fondness—

" Dost thou not see my baby at my breast,
That sucks the nurse asleep? . . .
As sweet as balm, as soft as air, as gentle.
O Antony!"[2]

It is worth while to observe that Shakespear has contrasted the extreme magnificence of the descriptions in
this play with pictures of extreme suffering and physical
horror, not less striking, partly perhaps to place the
effeminate character of Mark Antony in a more favourable
light, and at the same time to preserve a certain balance
of feeling in the mind. Cæsar says, hearing of his rival'
conduct at the court of Cleopatra :

—————" Antony,
Leave thy lascivious wassails. When thou once
Wert beaten from Modena, where thou slew'st
Hirtius and Pansa, consuls, at thy heel
Did famine follow, whom thou fought'st against,
Though daintily brought up, with patience more
Than savages could suffer. Thou didst drink
The stale of horses, and the gilded puddle
Which beast would cough at : thy palate then did deign
The roughest berry on the rudest hedge ;
Yea, like the stag, when snow the pasture sheets,
The barks of trees thou browsed'st; on the Alps,
It is reported, thou didst eat strange flesh,
Which some did die to look on : and all this—
It wounds thine honour that I speak it now—
Was borne so like a soldier, that thy cheek
So much as lank'd not."[3]

[1 Act ii., sc. 5.]   [2 Act v., sc. 2.]   [3 Act i., sc. 4.]

The passage after Antony's defeat by Augustus, where he is made to say :

> " Yes, my lord, yes; he at Philippi kept
> His sword e'en like a dancer; while I struck
> The lean and wrinkled Cassius, and 'twas I
> That the mad Brutus ended "— [1]

is one of those fine retrospections which show us the winding and eventful march of human life. The jealous attention which has been paid to the unities both of time and place has taken away the principle of perspective in the drama, and all the interest which objects derive from distance, from contrast, from privation, from change of fortune, from long-cherished passion; and contrasts our view of life from a strange and romantic dream, long, obscure, and infinite, into a smartly-contested, three hours' inaugural disputation on its merits by the different candidates for theatrical applause.

The latter scenes of ' Antony and Cleopatra' are full of the changes of accident and passion. Success and defeat follow one another with startling rapidity. Fortune sits upon her wheel more blind and giddy than usual. This precarious state and the approaching dissolution of his greatness are strikingly displayed in the dialogue of Antony with Eros :

> " *Antony.* Eros, thou yet behold'st me?
> *Eros.*   Ay, noble lord.
> *Antony.* Sometime we see a cloud that's dragonish,
> A vapour sometime like a bear or lion,
> A tower'd citadel, a pendent rock,
> A forked mountain, or blue promontory
> With trees upon't, that nod unto the world,
> And mock our eyes with air: thou hast seen these signs;
> They are black vesper's pageants.
> *Eros.*   Ay, my lord.
> *Antony.* That which is now a horse, even with a thought
> The rack dislimns, and makes it indistinct
> As water is in water.

------

[1] Act iii., sc. 11.]

Eros.   It does, my lord.
Antony. My good knave, Eros, now thy captain is
Even such a body," &c.[1]

This is, without doubt, one of the finest pieces of
poetry in Shakespear. The splendour of the imagery, the
semblance of reality, the lofty range of picturesque objects
hanging over the world, their evanescent nature, the total
uncertainty of what is left behind, are just like the
mouldering schemes of human greatness. It is finer than
Cleopatra's passionate lamentation over his fallen grandeur,
because it is more dim, unstable, unsubstantial. Antony's
headstrong presumption and infatuated determination to
yield to Cleopatra's wishes to fight by sea instead of land,
meet a merited punishment; and the extravagance of his
resolutions, increasing with the desperateness of his circumstances, is well commented upon by Œnobarbus :

> ————————" I see men's judgments are
> A parcel of their fortunes, and things outward
> Do draw the inward quality after them
> To suffer all alike." [2]

The repentance of Œnobarbus after his treachery to his
master is the most affecting part of the play. He cannot
recover from the blow which Antony's generosity gives him,
and he dies broken-hearted, "a master-leaver and a fugitive."

Shakespear's genius has spread over the whole play a
richness like the overflowing of the Nile.

———•◦•———

HAMLET.[3]

This is that Hamlet the Dane whom we read of in our
youth, and whom we may be said almost to remember in

[1 Act iv., sc. 14.]   [2 Act iii., sc. 13.]

[3] Printed (from an imperfect MS., but one containing some good
readings) in 1603, then more completely in 1604, of which last
edition the 4to of 1605 appears to be a mere reissue. It was, of
course, included in the collected works in 1623.—ED.

our after-years; he who made that famous soliloquy on life, who gave the advice to the players, who thought " this goodly frame, the earth," a sterile promontory, and " this brave o'er-hanging firmament, the air, this majestical roof fretted with golden fire," " a foul and pestilent congregation of vapours;" whom "man delighted not, nor woman neither ;" he who talked with the grave-diggers, and moralised on Yorick's skull; the school-fellow of Rosencraus and Guildenstern at Wittenberg ; the friend of Horatio; the lover of Ophelia; he that was mad and sent to England; the slow avenger of his father's death ; who lived at the court of Horwendillus five hundred years before we were born, but all whose thoughts we seem to know as well as we do our own, because we have read them in Shakespear.

Hamlet is a name ; his speeches and sayings but the idle coinage of the poet's brain. What then, are they not real ? They are as real as our own thoughts. Their reality is in the reader's mind. It is *we* who are Hamlet. This play has a prophetic truth, which is above that of history. Whoever has become thoughtful and melancholy through his own mishaps or those of others ; whoever has borne about with him the clouded brow of reflection, and thought himself " too much i' th' sun ;" whoever has seen the golden lamp of day dimmed by envious mists rising in his own breast, and could find in the world before him only a dull blank with nothing left remarkable in it; whoever has known " the pangs of despised love, the insolence of office, or the spurns which patient merit of the unworthy takes ;" he who has felt his mind sink within him, and sadness cling to his heart like a malady, who has had his hopes blighted and his youth staggered by the apparitions of strange things ; who cannot be well at ease, while he sees evil hovering near him like a spectre; whose powers of action have been eaten up by thought, he to whom the universe seems infinite, and himself nothing ; whose kitterness of soul makes him careless of consequences, and who goes to a play as his best resource to shove off, to a second remove, the evils of life by a mock representation of them—this is the true Hamlet.

We have been so used to this tragedy that we hardly know how to criticise it any more than we should know how to describe our own faces. But we must make such observations as we can. It is the one of Shakespear's plays that we think of the oftenest, because it abounds most in striking reflections on human life, and because the distresses of Hamlet are transferred, by the turn of his mind, to the general account of humanity. Whatever happens to him we apply to ourselves, because he applies it so himself as a means of general reasoning. He is a great moraliser; and what makes him worth attending to is, that he moralises on his own feelings and experience. He is not a common-place pedant. If ' Lear ' is distinguished by the greatest depth of passion, ' Hamlet' is the most remarkable for the ingenuity, originality, and unstudied development of character. Shakespear had more magnanimity than any other poet, and he has shown more of it in this play than in any other. There is no attempt to force an interest : everything is left for time and circumstances to unfold. The attention is excited without effort, the incidents succeed each other as matters of course, the characters think and speak and act just as they might do if left entirely to themselves. There is no set purpose, no straining at a point. The observations are suggested by the passing scene—the gusts of passion come and go like sounds of music borne on the wind. The whole play is an exact transcript of what might be supposed to have taken place at the court of Denmark, at the remote period of time fixed upon, before the modern refinements in morals and manners were heard of. It would have been interesting enough to have been admitted as a bystander in such a scene, at such a time, to have heard and witnessed something of what was going on. But here we are more than spectators. We have not only "the outward pageants and the signs of grief;" but "we have that within which passes show." We read the thoughts of the heart, we catch the passions living as they rise. Other dramatic writers give us very fine versions and paraphrases of nature; but Shakespear, together with his own comments, gives us the original text, that we may judge for ourselves. This is a very great advantage.

The character of Hamlet stands quite by itself. It is not a character marked by strength of will or even of passion, but by refinement of thought and sentiment. Hamlet is as little of the hero as a man can well be: but he is a young and princely novice, full of high enthusiasm and quick sensibility—the sport of circumstances, questioning with fortune and refining on his own feelings, and forced from the natural bias of his disposition by the strangeness of his situation. He seems incapable of deliberate action, and is only hurried into extremities on the spur of the occasion, when he has no time to reflect, as in the scene where he kills Polonius, and again, where he alters the letters which Rosencraus and Guildenstern are taking with them to England, purporting his death. At other times, when he is most bound to act, he remains puzzled, undecided, and sceptical, dallies with his purposes, till the occasion is lost, and finds out some pretence to relapse into indolence and thoughtfulness again. For this reason he refuses to kill the King when he is at his prayers, and by a refinement in malice, which is in truth only an excuse for his own want of resolution, defers his revenge to a more fatal opportunity, when he shall be engaged in some act "that has no relish of salvation in it."

> "Now might I do it pat, now he is praying;
> And now I'll do 't;—and so he goes to heaven;
> And so am I reveng'd?—that would be scanned:
> A villain kills my father; and for that

I, his sole son, do this same villain send
To heaven.
O, this is hire and salary, not revenge. . . .
Up sword ; and know thou a more horrid hent,
When he is drunk asleep, or in his rage." [1]

He is the prince of philosophical speculators ; and because he cannot have his revenge perfect, according to the
most refined idea his wish can form, he declines it altogether. So he scruples to trust the suggestions of the
ghost, contrives the scene of the play to have surer proof
of his uncle's guilt, and then rests satisfied with this con-
firmation of his suspicions, and the success of his experiment, instead of acting upon it. Yet he is sensible of his
own weakness, taxes himself with it, and tries to reason
himself out of it :

" How all occasions do inform against me,
And spur my dull revenge! What is a man,
If his chief good and market of his time
Be but to sleep and feed ? A beast ; no more.
Sure he that made us with such large discourse,
Looking before and after, gave us not
That capability and god-like reason
To fust in us unus'd. Now whether it be
Bestial oblivion, or some craven scruple
Of thinking too precisely on th' event,—
A thought which, quarter'd, hath but one part wisdom,
And ever three parts coward,—I do not know
Why yet I live to say, This thing's to do;
Sith I have cause, and will, and strength, and means
To do 't. Examples, gross as earth, exhort me :
Witness this army of such mass and charge,
Led by a delicate and tender prince,
Whose spirit with divine ambition puff'd,
Makes mouths at the invisible event,
Exposing what is mortal and unsure
To all that fortune, death, and danger dare,
Even for an egg-shell. Rightly to be great
Is not to stir without great argument ;
But greatly to find quarrel in a straw,

[1 Act iii., sc. 8.]

> When honour's at the stake. How stand I, then,
> That have a father kill'd, a mother stain'd,
> Excitements of my reason and my blood,
> And let all sleep? while, to my shame, I see
> The imminent death of twenty thousand men,
> That for a fantasy and trick of fame,
> Go to their graves like beds, fight for a plot
> Whereon the numbers cannot try the cause,
> Which is not tomb enough and continent
> To hide the slain?—O, from this time forth,
> My thoughts be bloody, or be nothing worth." [1]

Still he does nothing ; and this very speculation on his
own infirmity only affords him another occasion for in-
dulging it.   It is not from any want of attachment to his
father or of abhorrence of his murder that Hamlet is thus
dilatory ; but it is more to his taste to indulge his imagination in reflecting upon the enormity of the crime and
refining on his schemes of vengeance, than to put them
into immediate practice.   His ruling passion is to think,
not to act: and any vague pretext that flatters this propensity instantly diverts him from his previous purposes.

The moral perfection of this character has been called
in question, we think, by those who did not understand it.
It is more interesting than according to rules; amiable,
though not faultless.   The ethical delineations of " that
noble and liberal casuist" (as Shakespear has been well
called) do not exhibit the drab-coloured quakerism of
morality.   His plays are not copied either from the
' Whole Duty of Man,' or from ' The Academy of Compli-
ments !' [2]   We confess we are a little shocked at the want
of refinement in those who are shocked at the want of refinement in Hamlet.   The neglect of punctilious exactness
in his behaviour either partakes of the " licence of the
time," or else belongs to the very excess of intellectual

[1] Act iv., sc. 4.]
[2] An heterogeneous collection of anecdotes, stories, precepts for
good conduct, copies of love-letters, and other interesting particulars
it was first published before 1640.—ED.

refinement in the character, which makes the common rules of life, as well as his own purposes, sit loose upon him. He may be said to be amenable only to the tribunal of his own thoughts, and is too much taken up with the airy world of contemplation to lay as much stress as he ought on the practical consequences of things. His habitual principles of action are unhinged and out of joint with the time. His conduct to Ophelia is quite natural in his circumstances. It is that of assumed severity only. It is the effect of disappointed hope, of bitter regrets, of affection suspended, not obliterated, by the distractions of the scene around him! Amidst the natural and preternatural horrors of his situation, he might be excused in delicacy from carrying on a regular courtship. When "his father's spirit was in arms," it was not a time for the son to make love in. He could neither marry Ophelia, nor wound her mind by explaining the cause of his alienation, which he durst hardly trust himself to think of. It would have taken him years to have come to a direct explanation on the point. In the harassed state of his mind, he could not have done much otherwise than he did. His conduct does not contradict what he says when he sees her funeral,

> "I loved Ophelia : forty thousand brothers
> Could not with all their quantity of love
> Make up my sum."—[1]

Nothing can be more affecting or beautiful than the Queen's apostrophe to Ophelia on throwing the flowers into the grave.

> "Sweets to the sweet, farewell.   [*Scattering flowers.*
> I hop'd thou should'st have been my Hamlet's wife
> I thought thy bride-bed to have deck'd, sweet maid,
> And not have strew'd thy grave." [2]

Shakespear was thoroughly a master of the mixed motives of human character, and he here shows us the Queen, who was so criminal in some respects, not without sensi-

[1 Act v., sc. 1.]   [2 *Ibid*]

bility and affection in other relations of life.—Ophelia is
a character almost too exquisitely touching to be dwelt
upon.   Oh rose of May, oh flower too soon faded !   Her
love, her madness, her death, are described with the truest
touches of tenderness and pathos.   It is a character which
nobody but Shakespear could have drawn in the way that
he has done, and to the conception of which there is not
even the smallest approach, except in some of the old romantic ballads.[1]   Her brother, Laertes, is a character we
do not like so well : he is too hot and choleric, and somewhat rhodomontade.   Polonius is a perfect character in its
kind; nor is there any foundation for the objections which
have been made to the consistency of this part.   It is said
that he acts very foolishly and talks very sensibly.   There
is no inconsistency in that.   Again, that he talks wisely
at one time and foolishly at another; that his advice to
Laertes is very excellent, and his advice to the King and
Queen on the subject of Hamlet's madness very ridiculous.
But he gives the one as a father, and is sincere in it ; he
gives the other as a mere courtier, a busy-body, and is accordingly officious, garrulous, and impertinent.   In short,
Shakespear has been accused of inconsistency in this and
other characters, only because he has kept up the distinction which there is in nature, between the understandings
and the moral habits of men, between the absurdity of their
ideas and the absurdity of their motives.   Polonius is not
a fool, but he makes himself so.   His folly, whether in his
actions or speeches, comes under the head of 'impropriety
of intention.

   We do not like to see our author's plays acted, and least

[1] In the account of her death, a friend has pointed out an instance
of the poet's exact observation of nature :—

> " There is a willow growing o'er a brook,
> That shows its hoary leaves i' th' glassy stream."

The inside of the leaves of the willow, next the water, is of a whitish
colour, and the reflection would therefore be " hoary. '

of all, ' Hamlet. There is no play that suffers so much in being transferred to the stage. Hamlet himself seems hardly capable of being acted. Mr. Kemble unavoidably fails in this character from a want of ease and variety. The character of Hamlet is made up of undulating lines ; it has the yielding flexibility of " a wave o' th' sea." Mr. Kemble plays it like a man in armour, with a determined inveteracy of purpose, in one undeviating straight line, which is as remote from the natural grace and refined susceptibility of the character, as the sharp angles and abrupt starts which Mr. Kean introduces into the part. Mr. Kean's Hamlet is as much too splenetic and rash as Mr. Kemble's is too deliberate and formal. His manner is too strong and pointed. He throws a severity, approaching to virulence, into the common observations and answers. There is nothing of this in Hamlet. He is, as it were, wrapped up in his reflections, and only *thinks aloud.* There should therefore be no attempt to impress what he says upon others by a studied exaggeration of emphasis or manner; no *talking at* his hearers. There should be as much of the gentleman and scholar as possible infused into the part, and as little of the actor. A pensive air of sadness should sit reluctantly upon his brow, but no appearance of fixed and sullen gloom. He is full of weakness and melancholy, but there is no harshness in his nature. He is the most amiable of misanthropes.

THE TEMPEST.[1]

THERE can be little doubt that Shakespear was the most universal genius that ever lived. " Either for tragedy, comedy, history, pastoral, pastoral-comical, historical-pas-

----

[1] First printed in the folio of 1623. It is supposed to be one of the latest of Shakespear's productions. The exact original, if had one, has not been met with.—ED.

toral, scene individable or poem unlimited, he is the only
man. Seneca cannot be too heavy, nor Plautus too light
for him." He has not only the same absolute command
over our laughter and our tears, all the resources of passion, of wit, of thought, of observation, but he has the most
unbounded range of fanciful invention, whether terrible
or playful, the same insight into the world of imagination
that he has into the world of reality; and over all there
presides the same truth of character and nature, and the
same spirit of humanity. His ideal beings are as true and
natural as his real characters; that is, as consistent with
themselves, or if we suppose such beings to exist at all,
they could not act, speak, or feel otherwise than as he
makes them. He has invented for them a language, manners, and sentiments of their own, from the tremendous
imprecations of the Witches in 'Macbeth,' when they do " a
deed without a name," to the sylph-like expressions of
Ariel, who "does his spiriting gently;" the mischievous
tricks and gossiping of Robin Goodfellow, or the uncouth
gabbling and emphatic gesticulations of Caliban in this
play.

The 'Tempest' is one of the most original and perfect of
Shakespear's productions, and he has shown in it all the
variety of his powers. It is full of grace and grandeur.
The human and imaginary characters, the dramatic and
the grotesque, are blended together with the greatest art,
and without any appearance of it. Though he has here
given "to airy nothing a local habitation and a name," yet
that part which is only the fantastic creation of his mind
has the same palpable texture, and coheres " semblably "
with the rest. As the preternatural part has the air of
reality, and almost haunts the imagination with a sense of
truth, the real characters and events partake of the wildness of a dream. The stately magician, Prospero, driven
from his dukedom, but around whom (so potent is his art)
airy spirits throng numberless to do his bidding; his

daughter Miranda (" worthy of that name "), to whom all
the power of his art points, and who seems the goddess of
the isle ; the princely Ferdinand, cast by fate upon the
haven of his happiness in this idol of his love ; the delicate Ariel ; the savage Caliban, half brute, half demon ;
the drunken ship's crew—are all connected parts of the
story, and can hardly be spared from the place they fill.
Even the local scenery is of a piece and character with the
subject.   Prospero's enchanted island seems to have risen
up out of the sea ; the airy music, the tempest-tossed
vessel, the turbulent waves, all have the effect of the land-
scape back-ground of some fine picture.   Shakespear's
pencil is (to use an allusion of his own) "like the dyer's
hand, subdued to what it works in."   Everything in him,
though it partakes of "the liberty of wit," is also subjected to "the law" of the understanding.   For instance,
even the drunken sailors, who are made reeling-ripe, share,
in the disorder of their minds and bodies, in the tumult
of the elements, and seem on shore to be as much at the
mercy of chance as they were before at the mercy of the
winds and waves.   These fellows with their sea-wit are
the least to our taste of any part of the play : but they are
as like drunken sailors as they can be, and are an indirect
foil to Caliban, whose figure acquires a classical dignity in
the comparison.

The character of Caliban is generally thought (and justly
so) to be one of the author's masterpieces.   It is not indeed pleasant to see this character on the stage any more
than it is to see the god Pan personated there.   But in
itself it is one of the wildest and most abstracted of all
Shakespear's characters, whose deformity whether of body
or mind is redeemed by the power and truth of the imagination displayed in it.   It is the essence of grossness, but
there is not a particle of vulgarity in it.   Shakespear has
described the brutal mind of Caliban in contact with the
pure and original forms of nature; the character grows

out of the soil where it is rooted, uncontrolled, uncouth,
and wild, uncramped by any of the meannesses of custom.
It is "of the earth, earthy." It seems almost to have been
dug out of the ground, with a soul instinctively superadded
to it answering to its wants and origin. Vulgarity is not
natural coarseness, but conventional coarseness, learned
from others, contrary to, or without an entire conformity
of natural power and disposition; as fashion is the common-place affectation of what is elegant and refined without
any feeling of the essence of it. Schlegel, the admirable
German critic on Shakespear, observes that Caliban is a
poetical character, and "always speaks in blank verse."
He first comes in thus:

> "*Caliban.* As wicked dew as e'er my mother brush'd
> With raven's feather from unwholesome fen,
> Drop on you both! a south-west blow on ye,
> And blister you all o'er!
>   *Prospero.* For this, be sure, to-night thou shalt have cramps,
> Side-stitches that shall pen thy breath up; urchins
> Shall for that vast of night that they may work,
> All exercise on thee: thou shalt be pinch'd
> As thick as honey-comb, each pinch more stinging
> Than bees that made 'em.
>   *Caliban.*   I must eat my dinner.
> This island's mine, by Sycorax my mother,
> Which thou tak'st from me. When thou cam'st first,
> Thou strok'dst me, and mad'st much of me; would'st give me
> Water with berries in't; and teach me how
> To name the bigger light, and how the less,
> That burn by day and night; and then I lov'd thee,
> And show'd thee all the qualities o' th' isle,
> The fresh springs, brine-pits, barren place and fertile:
> Cursèd be I that I did so! All the charms
> Of Sycorax, toads, beetles, bats, light on you!
> For I am all the subjects that you have,
> Which first was mine own king; and here you sty me
> In this hard rock, whiles you do keep from me
> The rest o' th' island."[1]

[1 Act i., sc. 2.]

And again, he promises Trinculo his services thus, if he
will free him from his drudgery :

> " I'll show thee the best springs; I'll pluck thee berries,
> I'll fish for thee, and get thee wood enough. . . .
> I prithee, let me bring thee where crabs grow,
> And I with my long nails will dig thee pig-nuts :
> Show thee a jay's nest, and instruct thee how
> To snare the nimble marmozet : I'll bring thee
> To clust'ring filberds ; and sometimes I'll get thee
> Young scamels from the rock." [1]

In conducting Stephano and Trinculo to Prospero's cell,
Caliban shows the superiority of natural capacity over
greater knowledge and greater folly ; and in a former
scene, when Ariel frightens them with his music, Caliban
to encourage them accounts for it in the eloquent poetry
of the senses :

> " Be not afeard ; the isle is full of noises,
> Sounds, and sweet airs, that give delight and hurt not.
> Sometime a thousand twangling instruments
> Will hum about mine ears, and sometime voices,
> That if I then had waked after long sleep,
> Would make me sleep again; and then, in dreaming,
> The clouds methought would open, and show riches
> Ready to drop upon me : that, when I wak'd,
> I cried to dream again." [2]

This is not more beautiful that it is true. The poet
here shows us the savage with the simplicity of a child,
and makes the strange monster amiable. Shakespear had
to paint the human animal rude and without choice in its
pleasures, but not without the sense of pleasure or some
germ of the affections. Master Barnardine in 'Measure
for Measure,' the savage of civilised life, is an admirable
philosophical counterpart to Caliban.

Shakespear has, as it were by design, drawn off from
Caliban the elements of whatever is ethereal and refined, to
compound them in the unearthly mould of Ariel. Nothing
was ever more finely conceived than this contrast between

[1 Act iii, sc. 2.]   [2 Act iii, sc. 2.]

the material and the spiritual, the gross and delicate.
Ariel is imaginary power, the swiftness of thought personified.   When told to make good speed by Prospero, he
says, "I drink the air before me."   This is something like
Puck's boast on a similar occasion, "I'll put a girdle round
about the earth in forty minutes."   But Ariel differs from
Puck in having a fellow-feeling in the interests of those
he is employed about.   How exquisite is the following
dialogue between him and Prospero !

> "*Ariel.*   Your charm so strongly works 'em,
> That if you now beheld them, your affections
> Would become tender.
>   *Prospero.*   Dost thou think so, spirit?
>   *Ariel.*   Mine would, sir, were I human.
>   *Prospero.*   And mine shall.
> Hast thou, which art but air, a touch, a feeling
> Of their afflictions, and shall not myself,
> One of their kind, that relish all as sharply
> Passion as they, be kindlier moved than thou art?" [1]

It has been observed that there is a peculiar charm in
the songs introduced in Shakespear, which, without conveying any distinct images, seem to recall all the feelings
connected with them, like snatches of half-forgotten music
heard indistinctly and at intervals.   There is this effect
produced by Ariel's songs, which (as we are told) seem to
sound in the air, and as if the person playing them were
invisible.   We shall give one instance out of many of this
general power :

> " *Enter* FERDINAND ; *and* ARIEL, *invisible, playing and*
> *singing :* FERDINAND *following.*

> ARIEL'S SONG.

> Come unto these yellow sands,
> And then take hands;
> Court'sied when you have, and kiss'd,—
> The wild waves whist;—

[1 Act v., sc. 1.]

Foot it featly here and there;
And sweet sprites the burden bear.
Hark, Hark!

[*Burden dispersedly within:* Bow, wow ͺ

The watch-dogs bark:

[*Burden dispersedly within:* Bow, wow.]

Hark, hark! I hear
The strain of strutting chanticleer
Cry, Cock-a-doodle-doo.

Ferdinand. Where should this music be? i' the air or
th' earth?
It sounds no more: and sure it waits upon
Some god o' th' island. Sitting on a bank
Weeping again the king my father's wreck,
This music crept by me upon the waters,
Allaying both their fury and my passion
With its sweet air; thence I have follow'd it,
Or it hath drawn me rather:—but 'tis gone.—
No, it begins again.

ARIEL *sings:*

Full fathom five thy father lies,
Of his bones are coral made:
Those are pearls that were his eyes,
Nothing of him that doth fade,
But doth suffer a sea change
Into something rich and strange.
Sea-nymphs hourly ring his knell—

[*Burden within:* Ding, dong.]

Hark! now I hear them, Ding-dong, bell.

Ferdinand. The ditty does remember my drown d father.
This is no mortal business, nor no sound
That the earth owes: I hear it now above me."—[1]

The courtship between Ferdinand and Miranda is one of
the chief beauties of this play. It is the very purity of
love. The pretended interference of Prospero with it
heightens its interest, and is in character with the magician, whose sense of preternatural power makes him
arbitrary, tetchy, and impatient of opposition.

[[1] **Act** i., sc. 2.]

The 'Tempest' is a finer play than the 'Midsummer
Night's Dream,' which has sometimes been compared with
it; but it is not so fine a poem.   There are a greater
number of beautiful passages in the latter.   Two of the
most striking in the 'Tempest' are spoken by Prospero.
The one is that admirable one when the vision which he has
conjured up disappears, beginning "The cloud-capp'd
towers, the gorgeous palaces," &c., which has been so often
quoted, that every school-boy knows it by heart; the other
is that which Prospero makes in abjuring his art:

> "Ye elves of hills, brooks, standing lakes, and groves,
> And ye that on the sands with printless foot
> Do chase the ebbing Neptune, and do fly him
> When he comes back; you demi-puppets that
> By moonshine do the green sour ringlets make,
> Whereof the ewe not bites; and you whose pastime
> Is to make midnight mushrooms, that rejoice
> To hear the solemn curfew, by whose aid—
> Weak masters though ye be—I have be-dimm'd
> The noon-tide sun, call'd forth the mutinous winds,
> And 'twixt the green sea and the azur'd vault
> Set roaring war; to the dread rattling thunder
> Have I given fire, and rifted Jove's stout oak
> With his own bolt; the strong-bas'd promontory
> Have I made shake, and by the spurs pluck'd up
> The pine and cedar: graves at my command
> Have wak'd their sleepers, oped, and let them forth
> By my so potent art.   But this rough magic
> I here abjure; and when I have requir'd
> Some heavenly music—which even now I do—
> To work mine end upon their senses that
> This airy charm is for, I'll break my staff,
> Bury it certain fadoms in the earth,
> And deeper than did ever plummet sound,
> I'll drown my book." [1]

We must not forget to mention among other things in
this play, that Shakespear has anticipated nearly all the
arguments on the Utopian schemes of modern philosophy

[1 Act V, sc. 1.]

" *Gonzalo.* Had I plantation of this isle, my lord—
Antonio. He'd sow't with nettle-seed.
Sebastian.   Or docks, or mallows
Gonzalo. And were the king on't, what would I do?
Sebastian. 'Scape being drunk, for want of wine.
Gonzalo. I' the commonwealth I would by contraries
Execute all things : for no kind of traffic
Would I admit ; no name of magistrate ;
Letters should not be known ; riches, poverty,
And use of service, none ; contract, succession,
Bourn, bound of land, tilth, vineyard, none ;
No use of metal, corn, or wine, or oil ;
No occupation, all men idle, all,
And women too—but innocent and pure :
No sovereignty.
Sebastian.   Yet he would be king on't.
Antonio. The latter end of his commonwealth forgets the
    beginning.
Gonzalo. All things in common nature should produce
Without sweat or endeavour ; treason, felony,
Sword, pike, knife, gun, or need of any engine
Would I not have ; but nature should bring forth,
Of its own kind, all foison, all abundance
To feed my innocent people !
Sebastian. No marrying 'mong his subjects?
Antonio. None, man ; all idle :—whores and knaves.
Gonzalo. I would with such perfection govern, sir,
T' excel the golden age.
Sebastian.   Save his majesty !" [1]

A MIDSUMMER NIGHT'S DREAM.

BOTTOM the Weaver is a character that has not had justice
done him. He is the most romantic of mechanics. And
what a list of companions he has—Quince the Carpenter,
Snug the Joiner, Flute the Bellows-mender, Snout the
Tinker, Starveling the Tailor ; and then again, what a
group of fairy attendants, Puck, Peaseblossom, Cobweb,
Moth, and Mustard-seed ! It has been observed that

[1] Act ii., sc. 1.]

Shakespear's characters are constructed upon deep physiological principles; and there is something in this play which looks very like it. Bottom the Weaver, who takes the lead of

> " A crew of patches, rude mechanicals,
> That work for bread upon Athenian stalls," [1]

follows a sedentary trade, and he is accordingly represented as conceited, serious, and fantastical. He is ready to undertake anything and everything, as if it was as much a matter of course as the motion of his loom and shuttle. He is for playing the truant, the lover, the lady, the lion. " I will roar that it shall do any man's heart good to hear me ;" [2] and this being objected to as improper, he still has a resource in his good opinion of himself, and " I will roar you an 'twere any nightingale." [3] Snug the Joiner is the moral man of the piece, who proceeds by measurement and discretion in all things. You see him with his rule and compasses in his hand :

> "*Snug.* Have you the lion's part written? Pray you, if it be, give it me, for I am slow of study.
> *Quince.* You may do it extempore, for it is nothing but roaring." [4]

Starveling the Tailor keeps the peace, and objects to the lion and the drawn sword. " I believe we must leave the killing out when all is done." [5] Starveling, however, does not start the objections himself, but seconds them when made by others, as if he had not spirit to express his fears without encouragement. It is too much to suppose all this intentional : but it very luckily falls out so. Nature includes all that is implied in the most subtle analytical distinctions; and the same distinctions will be found in Shakespear. Bottom, who is not only chief actor, but stage-manager for the occasion, has a device to obviate the danger of frightening the ladies :

[1 Act iii., sc. 1.]   [2 Act i., sc. 2.]   [3 *Ibid.*]
    [4 *Ibid.*]   [5 Act iii., sc. 1.]

" Write me a prologue, and let the prologue seem to say, we will do no harm with our swords, and that Pyramus is not killed indeed; and for the more better assurance, tell them that I Pyramus am not Pyramus, but Bottom the Weaver: this will put them out of fear." [1]

Bottom seems to have understood the subject of dramatic illusion at least as well as any modern essayist. If our holiday mechanic rules the roast amongst his fellows, he is no less at home in his new character of an ass, " with amiable cheeks, and fair large ears." He instinctively acquires a most learned taste, and grows fastidious in the choice of dried peas and bottled hay. He is quite familiar with his new attendants, and assigns them their parts with all due gravity :

" Monsieur Cobweb, good monsieur, get your weapons in your hand, and kill me a red-hipped humble bee on the top of a thistle, and, good monsieur, bring me the honey-bag." [2]

What an exact knowledge is here shown of natural history !

Puck, or Robin Goodfellow, is the leader of the fairy band. He is the Ariel of the 'Midsummer Night's Dream;' and yet as unlike as can be to the Ariel in the ' Tempest. No other poet could have made two such different characters out of the same fanciful materials and situations. Ariel is a minister of retribution, who is touched with the sense of pity at the woes he inflicts. Puck is a madcap sprite, full of wantonness and mischief, who laughs at those whom he misleads—" Lord, what fools these mortals be !" Ariel cleaves the air, and executes his mission with the zeal of a winged messenger ; Puck is borne along on his fairy errand like the light and glittering gossamer before the breeze. He is, indeed, a most Epicurean little gentleman, dealing in quaint devices, and faring in dainty delights. Prospero and his world of spirits are a set of moralists : but with Oberon and his fairies we are launched at once into the empire of the butterflies. How beautifully is this race of beings contrasted with the men

[¹ Act iii., sc. 1.]   [² Act iv., sc. 1]

and women actors in the scene, by a single epithet which Titania gives to the latter, "the human mortals!" It is astonishing that Shakespear should be considered, not only by foreigners, but by many of our own critics, as a gloomy and heavy writer, who painted nothing but "gorgons and hydras, and chimeras dire." His subtlety exceeds that of all other dramatic writers, insomuch that a celebrated person of the present day said that he regarded him rather as a metaphysician than a poet. His delicacy and sportive gaiety are infinite. In the 'Midsummer Night's Dream' alone, we should imagine, there is more sweetness and beauty of description than in the whole range of French poetry put together. What we mean is this, that we will produce out of that single play ten passages, to which we do not think any ten passages in the works of the French poets can be opposed, displaying equal fancy and imagery. Shall we mention the remonstrance of Helena to Hermia, or Titania's description of her fairy train, or her disputes with Oberon about the Indian boy, or Puck's account of himself and his employments, or the Fairy Queen's exhortation to the elves to pay due attendance upon her favourite, Bottom ; or Hippolita's description of a chase, or Theseus's answer ? The two last are as heroical and spirited as the others are full of luscious tenderness. The reading of this play is like wandering in a grove by moonlight ; the descriptions breathe a sweetness like odours thrown from beds of flowers.

Titania's exhortation to the fairies to wait upon Bottom, which is remarkable for a certain cloying sweetness in the repetition of the rhymes, is as follows :—

> " Be kind and courteous to this gentleman.
> Hop in his walks, and gambol in his eyes,
> Feed him with apricocks and dewberries,
> With purple grapes, green figs and mulberries
> The honey-bags steal from the humble bees,
> And for night tapers crop their waxen thighs,
> And light them at the fiery glow-worm's eyes.

To have my love to bed and to arise:
And pluck the wings from painted butterflies,
To fan the moonbeams from his sleeping eyes;
Nod to him, elves, and do him courtesies." [1]

The sounds of the lute and of the trumpet are not more distinct than the poetry of the foregoing passage, and of the conversation between Theseus and Hippolita.

" *Theseus.* Go, one of you, find out the forester,
For now our observation is perform'd;
And since we have the vaward of the day,
My love shall hear the music of my hounds.
Uncouple in the western valley, go,—
Despatch, I say, and find the forester. [*Exit an Attend.*]
We will, fair Queen, up to the mountain's top,
And mark the musical confusion
Of hounds and echo in conjunction.
 Hippolita. I was with Hercules and Cadmus once,
When in a wood of Crete they bay'd the boar
With hounds of Sparta; never did I hear
Such gallant chiding; for besides the groves,
The skies, the fountains, every region near
Seem'd all one mutual cry;—I never heard
So musical a discord, such sweet thunder.
 Theseus. My hounds are bred out of the Spartan kind,
So flew'd, so sanded, and their heads are hung
With ears that sweep away the morning dew;
Crook-knee'd and dew-lapp'd, like Thessalian bulls,
Slow in pursuit, but matched in mouth like bells.
Each under each. A cry more tuneable
Was never holla'd to, nor cheer'd with horn,
In Crete, in Sparta, nor in Thessaly:
Judge when you hear." [2]

Even Titian never made a hunting-piece of a *gusto* so fresh and lusty, and so near the first ages of the world as this.—

It had been suggested to us, that the 'Midsummer Night's Dream' would do admirably to get up as a Christmas after-piece; and our prompter proposed that Mr. Kean should play the part of Bottom, as worthy of his

[1 Act iii., sc. 1.] [2 Act iv., sc. 1.]

great talents. He might, in the discharge of his duty offer to play the lady like any of our actresses that he pleased, the lover or the tyrant like any of our actors that he pleased, and the lion like "the most fearful wild-fowl" living. The carpenter, the tailor, and joiner, it was thought, would hit the galleries. The young ladies in love would interest the side-boxes; and Robin Goodfellow and his companions excite a lively fellow-feeling in the children from school. There would be two courts, an empire within an empire, the Athenian and the Fairy King and Queen, with their attendants, and with all their finery. What an opportunity for processions, for the sound of trumpets and glittering of spears! What a fluttering of urchins' painted wings; what a delightful profusion of gauze clouds and airy spirits floating on them

Alas! the experiment has been tried, and has failed;[1] not through the fault of Mr. Kean, who did not play the part of Bottom, nor of Mr. Liston, who did, and who played it well, but from the nature of things. The 'Midsummer Night's Dream,' when acted, is converted from a delightful fiction into a dull pantomime. All that is finest in the play is lost in the representation. The spectacle was grand; but the spirit was evaporated, the genius was fled. Poetry and the stage do not agree well together. The attempt to reconcile them in this instance fails not only of effect, but of decorum. The *ideal* can have no place upon the stage, which is a picture without perspective ; everything there is in the fore-ground. That which was merely an airy shape, a dream, a passing thought, immediately becomes an unmanageable reality. Where all is left to the imagination (as is the case in reading), every circumstance, near or remote, has

---

[1] 'The Midsummer Night's Dream,' altered by Reynolds into a three-act drama, was brought out at Covent-garden, January 17 1816. See Geneste's Acc. of the English Stage, viii., 545-9.—ED.

an equal chance of being kept in mind, and tells accordingly to the mixed impression of all that has been suggested. But the imagination cannot sufficiently qualify the actual impressions of the senses. Any offence given to the eye is not to be got rid of by explanation. Thus Bottom's head in the play is a fantastic illusion, produced by magic spells : on the stage it is an ass's head, and nothing more ; certainly a very strange costume for a gentleman to appear in. Fancy cannot be embodied any more than a simile can be painted ; and it is as idle to attempt it as to personate *Wall* or *Moonshine.* Fairies are not incredible, but fairies six feet high are so. Monsters are not shocking, if they are seen at a proper distance. When ghosts appear at mid-day, when apparitions stalk along Cheapside, then may the 'Midsummer Night's Dream' be represented without injury at Covent-garden or at Drury-lane. The boards of a theatre and the regions of fancy are not the same thing.

----◆----

ROMEO AND JULIET.[1]

' ROMEO AND JULIET' is the only tragedy which Shakespear has written entirely on a love-story. It is supposed to have been his first play,[2] and it deserves to stand in that proud rank. There is the buoyant spirit of youth in every line, in the rapturous intoxication of hope, and in the bitterness of despair. It has been said of ' Romeo and Juliet' by a great critic, that " whatever is most intoxi-

[1] It now seems to be generally admitted that this drama was not written, or at least finished, quite at so early a date as was formerly believed. It is supposed to have been composed in 1596, and was first printed (very imperfectly) in 1597—a circumstance which, as the edition of 1597 is nowhere described as a pirated one, appears to me to militate rather against the hypothesis that the author was at work on the play as long prior to its production as 1591.—ED.

[2] This is now to be regarded as extremely doubtful. —ED.

cating in the odour of a southern spring, languishing in the song of the nightingale, or voluptuous in the first opening of the rose, is to be found in this poem." The description is true; and yet it does not answer to our idea of the play. For if it has the sweetness of the rose, it has its freshness too ; if it has the languor of the nightingale's song, it has also its giddy transport ; if it has the softness of a southern spring, it is as glowing and as bright. There is nothing of a sickly and sentimental cast. Romeo and Juliet are in love, but they are not love-sick. Everything speaks the very soul of pleasure, the high and healthy pulse of the passions : the heart beats, the blood circulates and mantles throughout. Their courtship is not an insipid interchange of sentiments lip-deep, learnt at second-hand from poems and plays,—made up of beauties of the most shadowy kind, of " fancies wan that hang the pensive head," of evanescent smiles, and sighs that breathe not, of delicacy that shrinks from the touch, and feebleness that scarce supports itself, an elaborate vacuity of thought, and an artificial dearth of sense, spirit, truth, and nature ! It is the reverse of all this. It is Shakespear all over, and Shakespear when he was young.

We have heard it objected to 'Romeo and Juliet,' that it is founded on an idle passion between a boy and a girl, who have scarcely seen and can have but little sympathy or rational esteem for one another,[1] who have had no experience of the good or ills of life, and whose raptures or despair must be therefore equally groundless and fantastical. Whoever objects to the youth of the parties in this play as "too unripe and crude" to pluck the sweets of love, and wishes to see a first-love carried on into a good

[1] Shakespear was portraying the manners of a more southern people than ourselves, where women arrive at womanhood early, and where, especially in high families, it would scarcely have been etiquette for the lover and his mistress to see much of each other prior to the nuptials. Where there were meetings, they were usually clandestine, and connived at by the nurse or governess.—ED.

old age, and the passions taken at the rebound, when their
force is spent, may find all this done in the 'Stranger' and
in other German plays, where they do things by contraries,
and transpose nature to inspire sentiment and create philosophy. Shakespear proceeded in a more straightforward,
and, we think, effectual way. He did not endeavour to
extract beauty from wrinkles, or the wild throb of passion
from the last expiring sigh of indifference. He did not
" gather grapes of thorns nor figs of thistles." It was not
his way. But he has given a picture of human life, such
as it is in the order of nature. He has founded the passion of the two lovers not on the pleasures they had experienced, but on all the pleasures they had *not* experienced.
All that was to come of life was theirs. At that untried
source of promised happiness they slaked their thirst, and
the first eager draught made them drunk with love and
joy. They were in full possession of their senses and
their affections. Their hopes were of air, their desires of
fire. Youth is the season of love, because the heart is then
first melted in tenderness from the touch of novelty, and
kindled to rapture, for it knows no end of its enjoyments
or its wishes. Desire has no limit but itself. Passion,
the love and expectation of pleasure, is infinite, extravagant, inexhaustible, till experience comes to check and
kill it. Juliet exclaims on her first interview with
Romeo—

> " My bounty is as boundless as the sea,
> My love as deep."

And why should it not? What was to hinder the thrilling
tide of pleasure, which had just gushed from her heart,
from flowing on without stint or measure, but experience
which she was yet without? What was to abate the transport of the first sweet sense of pleasure, which her heart
and her senses had just tasted, but indifference which she
was yet a stranger to? What was there to check the
ardour of hope, of faith, of constancy, just rising in her

breast, but disappointment which she had not yet felt? As are the desires and the hopes of youthful passion, such is the keenness of its disappointments, and their baleful effect. Such is the transition in this play from the highest bliss to the lowest despair, from the nuptial couch to an untimely grave. The only evil that even in apprehension befalls the two lovers is the loss of the greatest possible felicity; yet this loss is fatal to both, for they had rather part with life than bear the thought of surviving all that had made life dear to them. In all this, Shakespear has but followed nature, which existed in his time, as well as now. The modern philosophy, which reduces the whole theory of the mind to habitual impressions, and leaves the natural impulses of passion and imagination out of the account, had not then been discovered; or if it had, would have been little calculated for the uses of poetry.

It is the inadequacy of the same false system of philosophy to account for the strength of our earliest attachments, which has led Mr. Wordsworth to indulge in the mystical visions of Platonism in his Ode on the Progress of Life. He has very admirably described the vividness of our impressions in youth and childhood, and how " they fade by degrees into the light of common day," and he ascribes the change to the supposition of a pre-existent state, as if our early thoughts were nearer heaven, reflections of former trials of glory, shadows of our past being. This is idle. It is not from the knowledge of the past that the first impressions of things derive their gloss and splendour, but from our ignorance of the future, which fills the void to come with the warmth of our desires, with our gayest hopes, and brightest fancies. It is the obscurity spread before it that colours the prospect of life with hope, as it is the cloud which reflects the rainbow. There is no occasion to resort to any mystical union and transmission of feeling through different states of being to account for the romantic enthusiasm of youth; nor to plant the root of hope in the grave, nor to derive it from the skies. Its root is in the heart of man: it lifts its head above the stars. Desire and imagination are inmates of the human breast. The heaven "that lies about us in our infancy" is only a new world, of which we know nothing but what we wish it to be, and believe all that we wish. In youth and boyhood, the world we live in is the world of desire, and of fancy : it is experience that brings us down to the world of reality. What is it that in youth sheds a dewy light round the evening star ? That makes the daisy look so bright ? That perfumes the hyacinth ? That embalms the first kiss of love? It is the delight of novelty, and the seeing no end to the pleasure that we fondly believe is still in store for us. The heart revels in the luxury of its own thoughts, and is unable to sustain the weight of hope and love that presses upon it.—The effects of the passion of love alone might have dissipated Mr. Wordsworth's theory, if he means anything more by it than an ingenious and poetical allegory. *That* at least is not a link in the chain let down from other worlds ; " the purple light of love " is not a dim reflection of the smiles of celestial bliss. It does not appear till the middle of life, and then seems like " another morn risen on mid-day." In this respect the soul comes into the world " in utter nakedness." Love waits for the ripening of the youthful blood. The sense of pleasure precedes the love of pleasure, but with the sense of pleasure, as soon as it is felt, come thronging infinite desires and hopes of pleasure, and love is mature as soon as born. It withers and it dies almost as soon !

This play presents a beautiful *coup-d'œil* of the progress of human life. In thought it occupies years, and embraces the circle of the affections from childhood to old age. Juliet has become a great girl, a young woman since we first remember her a little thing in the idle prattle of the Nurse. Lady Capulet was about her age when she became a mother, and old Capulet somewhat impatiently tells his younger visitors,

> ————————" I have seen the day,
> That I have worn a visor, and could tell
> A whispering tale in a fair lady's ear,
> Such as would please:—'tis gone, 'tis gone, 'tis gone." [1]

Thus one period of life makes way for the following, and one generation pushes another off the stage. One of the most striking passages to show the intense feeling of youth in this play is Capulet's invitation to Paris to visit his entertainment :

> " At my poor house look to behold this night
> Earth-treading stars that make dark heaven light :
> Such comfort as do lusty young men feel
> When well-apparell'd April on the heel
> Of limping Winter treads, even such delight
> Among fresh female buds shall you this night
> Inherit at my house." [2]

The feelings of youth and of the spring are here blended together like the breath of opening flowers. Images of vernal beauty appear to have floated before the author's mind, in writing this poem, in profusion. Here is another of exquisite beauty, brought in more by accident than by necessity. Montague declares of his son smit with a hopeless passion, which he will not reveal :

> "But he, his own affection's counsellor,
> Is to himself—I will not say how true—
> But to himself so secret and so close,
> So far from sounding and discovery,
> As is the bud bit with an envicus worm,
> Ere he can spread his sweet leaves to the air,
> Or dedicate his beauty to the sun." [3]

This casual description is as full of passionate beauty as when Romeo dwells in frantic fondness on " the white wonder of his Juliet's hand." The reader may, if he pleases, contrast the exquisite pastoral simplicity of the above lines with the gorgeous description of Juliet, when

[1 Act i., sc. 5.]   [2 Act i., sc. 2.]   [3 Act i., sc. 1.]

Romeo first sees her at her father's house, surrounded by company and artificial splendour :

> "What lady's that which doth enrich the hand
> Of yonder knight? . . . . .
> O she doth teach the torches to burn bright ;
> Her beauty hangs upon the cheek of night,
> Like a rich jewel in an Æthiop's ear." [1]

It would be hard to say which of the two garden scenes is the finest, that where he first converses with his love, or takes leave of her the morning after their marriage. Both are like a heaven upon earth ; the blissful bowers of Paradise let down upon this lower world. We will give only one passage of these well-known scenes to show the perfect refinement and delicacy of Shakespear's conception of the female character. It is wonderful how Collins, who was a critic and a poet of great sensibility, should have encouraged the common error on this subject by saying— " But stronger Shakespear felt for man alone."

The passage we mean is Juliet's apology for her maiden boldness.

> "Thou know'st the mask of night is on my face ;
> Else would a maiden blush bepaint my cheek
> For that which thou hast heard me speak to-night.
> Fain would I dwell on form, fain, fain deny
> What I have spoke : but farewell compliment :
> Dost thou love me ? I know thou wilt say, Ay,
> And I will take thee at thy word : yet if thou swear'st,
> Thou may'st prove false ; at lovers' perjuries,
> They say, Jove laughs. O gentle Romeo,
> If thou dost love, pronounce it faithfully ;
> Or if thou think I am too quickly won,
> I'll frown and be perverse, and say thee nay,
> So thou wilt woo : but else, not for the world.
> In truth, fair Montague, I am too fond ;
> And therefore thou may'st think my 'haviour light ;
> But trust me, gentleman, I'll prove more true
> Than those that have more cunning to be strange.
> I should have been more strange, I must confess,

---

[1] Act i, sc, 5.]

> But that thou overheard'st, ere I was ware,
> My true love's passion ; therefore pardon me,
> And not impute this yielding to light love,
> Which the dark night hath so discovered." [1]

In this and all the rest, her heart, fluttering between pleasure, hope, and fear, seems to have dictated to her tongue, and " calls true love spoken simple modesty." Of the same sort, but bolder in virgin innocence, is her soliloquy after her marriage with Romeo.

> " Gallop apace, you fiery-footed steeds,
> Towards Phœbus' lodging ; such a wagoner
> As Phaëton would whip you to the west,
> And bring in cloudy night immediately.
> Spread thy close curtain, love-performing night;
> That rude day's eyes may wink ; and Romeo
> Leap to these arms, untalk'd of and unseen !—
> Lovers can see to do their amorous rites
> By their own beauties : or, if love be blind,
> It best agrees with night.—Come, civil night,
> Thou sober-suited matron, all in black,
> And learn me how to lose a winning match,
> Play'd for a pair of stainless maidenhoods:
> Hold my unmann'd blood, bating in my cheeks,
> With thy black mantle ; till strange love, grown bold,
> Thinks true love acted simple modesty.
> Come, night !—come, Romeo !—come, thou day in night—
> For thou wilt lie upon the wings of night
> Whiter than new snow upon a raven's back.—
> Come, gentle night—come, loving, black-brow'd night,
> Give me my Romeo : and when he shall die,
> Take him and cut him out in little stars,
> And he will make the face of heaven so fine,
> That all the world will be in love with night,
> And pay no worship to the garish sun.—
> O, I have bought the mansion of a love,
> But not possess'd it ; and though I am sold,
> Not yet enjoy'd : so tedious is this day,
> As is the night before some festival
> To an impatient child, that hath new robes,
> And may not wear them." [2]

[1 Act ii., sc. 2.]   [2 Act iii., sc. 2.]

We the rather insert this passage here, inasmuch as we have no doubt it has been expunged from the Family Shakespear. Such critics do not perceive that the feelings of the heart sanctify, without disguising, the impulses of nature. Without refinement themselves, they confound modesty with hypocrisy. Not so the German critic, Schlegel. Speaking of 'Romeo and Juliet,' he says, "It was reserved for Shakespear to unite purity of heart and the glow of imagination, sweetness and dignity of manners and passionate violence, in one ideal picture." The character is indeed one of perfect truth and sweetness. It has nothing forward, nothing coy, nothing affected or coquettish about it; it is a pure effusion of nature. It is as frank as it is modest, for it has no thought that it wishes to conceal. It reposes in conscious innocence on the strength of its affections. Its delicacy does not consist in coldness and reserve, but in combining warmth of imagination and tenderness of heart with the most voluptuous sensibility. Love is a gentle flame that rarefies and expands her whole being. What an idea of trembling haste and airy grace, borne upon the thoughts of love, does the Friar's exclamation give of her, as she approaches his cell to be married!

> " Here comes the lady :—O, so light of foot
> Will ne'er wear out the everlasting flint :
> A lover may bestride the gossamer,
> That idles in the wanton summer air,
> And yet not fall; so light is vanity." [1]

The tragic part of this character is of a piece with the rest. It is the heroic founded on tenderness and delicacy. Of this kind are her resolution to follow the Friar's advice, and the conflict in her bosom between apprehension and love when she comes to take the sleeping potion. Shakespear is blamed for the mixture of low characters. If this is a deformity, it is the source of a thousand

[1] Act ii., sc. 6.]

beauties. One instance is the contrast between the guile-less simplicity of Juliet's attachment to her first love, and the convenient policy of the Nurse in advising her to marry Paris, which excites such indignation in her mistress "Ancient damnation! O most wicked fiend," &c.

Romeo is Hamlet in love. There is the same rich exuberance of passion and sentiment in the one, that there is of thought and sentiment in the other. Both are absent and self-involved, both live out of themselves in a world of imagination. Hamlet is abstracted from everything; Romeo is abstracted from everything but his love, and lost in it. His "frail thoughts dally with faint surmise," and are fashioned out of the suggestions of hope, "the flattery of sleep." He is himself only in his Juliet; she is his only reality, his heart's true home and idol. The rest of the world is to him a passing dream. How finely is this character portrayed where he recollects himself on seeing Paris slain at the tomb of Juliet!—

> "What said my man when my betossèd soul
> Did not attend him as we rode? I think
> He told me Paris should have married Juliet." [1]

And again, just before he hears the sudden tidings of her death—

> "If I may trust the flattering eye of sleep,
> My dreams presage some joyful news at hand
> My bosom's lord sits lightly on his throne,
> And all this day an unaccustom'd spirit
> Lifts me above the ground with cheerful thoughts.
> I dreamt my lady came and found me dead,—
> Strange dream, that gives a dead man leave to think!—
> And breath'd such life with kisses on my lips,
> That I reviv'd and was an emperor.
> Ah me! how sweet is love itself possess'd,
> When but love's shadows are so rich in joy!" [2]

Romeo's passion for Juliet is not a first love: it succeeds and drives out his passion for another mistress, Rosaline

[1 Act v, sc. 3.]   [2 Act v, sc. 1.]

as the sun hides the stars. This is perhaps an artifice (not absolutely necessary) to give us a higher opinion of the lady, while the first absolute surrender of her heart to him enhances the richness of the prize. The commencement, progress, and ending of his second passion are however complete in themselves, not injured if they are not bettered by the first. The outline of the play is taken from an Italian novel; but the dramatic arrangement of the different scenes between the lovers, the more than dramatic interest in the progress of the story, the development of the characters with time and circumstances, just according to the degree and kind of interest excited, are not inferior to the expression of passion and nature. It has been ingeniously remarked among other proofs of skill in the contrivance of the fable, that the improbability of the main incident in the piece, the administering of the sleeping-potion, is softened and obviated from the beginning by the introduction of the Friar on his first appearance culling simples and descanting on their virtues. Of the passionate scenes in this tragedy, that between the Friar and Romeo when he is told of his sentence of banishment, that between Juliet and the Nurse when she hears of it, and of the death of her cousin Tybalt (which bear no proportion in her mind, when passion after the first shock of surprise throws its weight into the scale of her affections), and the last scene at the tomb, are among the most natural and overpowering. In all of these it is not merely the force of any one passion that is given, but the slightest and most unlooked-for transitions from one to another, the mingling currents of every different feeling rising up and prevailing in turn, swayed by the mastermind of the poet, as the waves undulate beneath the gliding storm. Thus when Juliet has by her complaints encouraged the Nurse to say, " Shame come to Romeo," she instantly repels the wish, which she had herself occasioned, by answering :

> ——————" Blister'd be thy tongue
> For such a wish ! He was not born to shame.
> Upon his brow shame is asham'd to sit,
> For tis a throne where honour may be crown'd
> Sole monarch of the universal earth !
> O, what a beast was I to chide at him ?
>   *Nurse.* Will you speak well of him that kill'd your
>   cousin ?
>   *Juliet.* Shall I speak ill of him that is my husband ?
> Ah, poor my lord, what tongue shall smooth thy name,
> When I, thy three-hours' wife, have mangled it ?" [1]

And then follows on the neck of her remorse and returning
fondness, that wish treading almost on the brink of im-
piety, but still held back by the strength of her devotion
to her lord, that " father, mother, nay, or both were dead,"
rather than Romeo banished. If she requires any other
excuse, it is in the manner in which Romeo echoes her
frantic grief and disappointment in the next scene at being
banished from her. Perhaps one of the finest pieces of
acting that ever was witnessed on the stage, is Mr. Kean's
manner of doing this scene and his repetition of the word,
Banished. He treads close indeed upon the genius of his
author.

A passage which this celebrated actor and able com-
mentator on Shakespear (actors are the best commentators
on the poets) did not give with equal truth or force of
feeling was the one which Romeo makes at the tomb of
Juliet, before he drinks the poison :

> ——————" Let me peruse this face—
> Mercutio's kinsman ! noble County Paris !
> What said my man, when my betossèd soul
> Did not attend him as we rode ! I think,
> He told me Paris should have married Juliet
> Said he not so ? or did I dream it so ?
> Or am I mad, hearing him talk of Juliet,
> To think it was so ?—O, give me thy hand,
> One writ with me in sour misfortune's book !
> I'll bury thee in a triumphant grave ;—

---

[1] Act iii., sc. 2.]

A grave? O, no, a lantern, slaughter'd youth,
For here lies Juliet.
*   *   *   *   *   *   *   *
——————O my love! my wife!
Death, that hath suck'd the honey of thy breath,
Hath had no power yet upon thy beauty:
Thou art not conquer'd; beauty's ensign yet
Is crimson in thy lips and in thy cheeks,
And Death's pale flag is not advanced there.—
Tybalt, liest thou there in thy bloody sheet?
O, what more favour can I do to thee,
Than with that hand that cut thy youth in twain,
To sunder his that was thine enemy?
Forgive me, cousin!—Ah, dear Juliet,
Why art thou yet so fair! Shall I believe
That unsubstantial death is amorous;
And that the lean abhorred monster keeps
Thee here in dark to be his paramour!
For fear of that, I still will stay with thee;
And never from this palace of dim night
Depart again: here, here will I remain
With worms that are thy chamber-maids; O, here
Will I set up my everlasting rest;
And shake the yoke of inauspicious stars
From this world-wearied flesh.—Eyes, look your last!
Arms, take your last embrace! and lips, O you,
The doors of breath, seal with a righteous kiss
A dateless bargain to engrossing death!—
Come, bitter conduct: come, unsavoury guide!
Thou desperate pilot, now at once run on
The dashing rock my sea-sick weary bark!
Here's to my love!—[*Drinks.*] O true apothecary!
Thy drugs are quick.—Thus with a kiss I die.' [1]

The lines in this speech, describing the loveliness of
Juliet, who is supposed to be dead, have been compared
to those in which it is said of Cleopatra after her death,
that she looked "as she would take another Antony in her
strong toil of grace;" and a question has been started
which is the finest, that we do not pretend to decide. We
can more easily decide between Shakespear and any other
author, than between him and himself. Shall we quote

[1] Act v., sc. 3.]

any more passages to show his genius or the beauty of 'Romeo and Juliet?' At that rate, we might quote the whole. The late Mr. Sheridan, on being shown a volume of the Beauties of Shakespear, very properly asked : "But where are the other eleven ?" The character of Mercutio in this play is one of the most mercurial and spirited of the productions of Shakespear's comic muse.

——◆◆◆——

LEAR.[1]

WE wish that we could pass this play over, and say nothing about it. All that we can say must fall far short of the subject; or even of what we ourselves conceive of it. To attempt to give a description of the play itself or of its effect upon the mind, is mere impertinence : yet we must say something. It is then the best of all Shakespear's plays, for it is the one in which he was the most in earnest. He was here fairly caught in the web of his own imagination. The passion which he has taken as his subject is that which strikes its root deepest into the human heart; of which the bond is the hardest to be unloosed; and the cancelling and tearing to pieces of which gives the greatest revulsion to the frame. This depth of nature, this force of passion, this tug and war of the elements of our being, this firm faith in filial piety, and the giddy anarchy and whirling tumult of the thoughts at finding this prop failing it, the contrast between the fixed, immoveable basis of natural affection, and the rapid, irregular starts of imagina-

[1] This drama having been performed before King James the First, at Christmas, 1606, it is to be taken for granted that it had been written some time before that date. Steevens seems to have shown satisfactorily that it followed the publication of Harsnet's ' Discoveries of Egregious Popish Impostures,' 1603. But whether it was anterior in execution to the old play of 'King Leir and his Three Daughters,' printed in 1605, appears questionable.— ED.

tion, **suddenly** wrenched from all its accustomed holds **and resting-places** in the soul, this is what Shakespear has given, and what nobody else but he could give. So we believe. The mind of Lear, staggering between the weight of attachment and the hurried movements of passion, is like a tall ship driven about by the winds, buffetted by the furious waves, but that still rides above the storm, having its anchor fixed in the bottom of the sea ; or it is like the sharp rock circled by the eddying whirlpool that foams and beats against it, or like the solid promontory pushed from its basis by the force of an earthquake.

The character of Lear itself is very finely conceived for the purpose. It is the only ground on which such a story could be built with the greatest truth and effect. It is his rash haste, his violent impetuosity, his blindness to everything but the dictates of his passions or affections, that produces all his misfortunes, that aggravates his impatience of them, that enforces our pity for him. The part which Cordelia bears in the scene is extremely beautiful : the story is almost told in the first words she utters. We see at once the precipice on which the poor old king stands from his own extravagant and credulous importunity, the indiscreet simplicity of her love (which, to be sure, has a little of her father's obstinacy in it), and the hollowness of her sisters' pretensions. Almost the first burst of that noble tide of passion, which runs through the play, is in the remonstrance of Kent to his royal master on the injustice of his sentence against his youngest daughter : " Be Kent unmannerly, when Lear is mad !" This manly plainness, which draws down on him the displeasure of the unadvised king, is worthy of the fidelity with which he adheres to his fallen fortunes. The true character of the two eldest daughters, Regan and Goneril (they are so thoroughly hateful that we do not even like to repeat their names), breaks out in their answer to Cordelia, who desires them to treat their father well : " Prescribe not us our

duties"—their hatred of advice being in proportion to
their determination to do wrong, and to their hypocritical
pretensions to do right. Their deliberate hypocrisy adds
the last finishing to the odiousness of their characters. It
is the absence of this detestable quality that is the only
relief in the character of Edmund the Bastard, and that at
times reconciles us to him. We are not tempted to ex-
aggerate the guilt of his conduct, when he himself gives it
up as a bad business, and writes himself down "plain
villain." Nothing more can be said about it. His religious honesty in this respect is admirable. One speech of
his is worth a million. His father, Gloster, whom he has
just deluded with a forged story of his brother Edgar's
designs against his life, accounts for his unnatural behaviour and the strange depravity of the times from the late
eclipses in the sun and moon. Edmund, who is in the
secret, says when he is gone :

"This is the excellent foppery of the world, that when we are
sick in fortune—often the surfeit of our own behaviour—we make
guilty of our disasters the sun, the moon, and stars : as if we were
villains on necessity ; fools by heavenly compulsion ; knaves, thieves,
and treachers by spherical predominance ; drunkards, liars, and
adulterers by an enforced obedience of planetary influence ; and all
that we are evil in, by a divine thrusting on : an admirable evasion
of whore-master man, to lay his goatish disposition to the charge of
a star ! My father compounded with my mother under the dragon's
tail, and my nativity was under Ursa Major : so that it follows, I am
rough and lecherous. Tut ! I should have been what I am, had the
maidenliest star in the firmament twinkled on my bastardising."

The whole character, its careless, light-hearted villainy,
contrasted with the sullen, rancorous malignity of Regan
and Goneril, its connection with the conduct of the under-
plot, in which Gloster's persecution of one of his sons and
the ingratitude of another, form a counterpart to the mistakes and misfortunes of Lear : his double amour with the
two sisters, and the share which he has in bringing about
the fatal catastrophe, are all managed with an uncommon
degree of skill and power.

It has been said, and we think justly, that the third act of 'Othello' and the three first acts of 'Lear,' are Shakespear's great masterpieces in the logic of passion : that they contain the highest examples not only of the force of individual passion, but of its dramatic vicissitudes and striking effects arising from the different circumstances and characters of the persons speaking. We see the ebb and flow of the feeling, its pauses and feverish starts, its impatience of opposition, its accumulating force when it has time to recollect itself, the manner in which it avails itself of every passing word or gesture, its haste to repel insinuation, the alternate contraction and dilatation of the soul, and all " the dazzling fence of controversy " in this mortal combat with poisoned weapons, aimed at the heart, where each wound is fatal. We have seen in 'Othello,' how the unsuspecting frankness and impetuous passions of the Moor are played upon and exasperated by the artful dexterity of Iago. In the present play, that which aggravates the sense of sympathy in the reader, and of uncontrollable anguish in the swoln heart of Lear, is the petrifying indifference, the cold, calculating, obdurate selfishness of his daughters. His keen passions seem whetted on their stony hearts. The contrast would be too painful, the shock too great, but for the intervention of the Fool, whose well-timed levity comes in to break the continuity of feeling when it can no longer be borne, and to bring into play again the fibres of the heart just as they are growing rigid from over-strained excitement. The imagination is glad to take refuge in the half-comic, half-serious comments of the Fool, just as the mind under the extreme anguish of a surgical operation vents itself in sallies of wit. The character was also a grotesque ornament of the barbarous times, in which alone the tragic ground-work of the story could be laid. In another point of view it is indispensable, inasmuch as while it is a diversion to the too great intensity of our disgust, it carries the pathos to the highest

pitch of which it is capable, by showing the pitiable weak
ness of the old king's conduct and its irretrievable consequences in the most familiar point of view. Lear may
well " beat at the gate which let his folly in," after, as the
Fool says, " he has made his daughters his mothers." The
character is dropped in the third act to make room for the
entrance of Edgar as Mad Tom, which well accords with
the increasing bustle and wildness of the incidents ; and
nothing can be more complete than the distinction between
Lear's real and Edgar's assumed madness, while the resemblance in the cause of their distresses, from the severing
of the nearest ties of natural affection, keeps up a unity of
interest.   Shakespear's mastery over his subject, if it was
not art, was owing to a knowledge of the connecting links
of the passions, and their effect upon the mind, still more
wonderful than any systematic adherence to rules, and
that anticipated and outdid all the efforts of the most
refined art, not inspired and rendered instinctive by
genius.

One of the most perfect displays of dramatic power is
the first interview between Lear and his daughter, after
the designed affronts upon him, which till one of his
knights reminds him of them, his sanguine temperament
had led him to overlook.   He returns with his train from
hunting, and his usual impatience breaks out in his first
words, " Let me not stay a jot for dinner; go, get it
ready."   He then encounters the faithful Kent in disguise,
and retains him in his service; and the first trial of his
honest duty is to trip up the heels of the officious Steward
who makes so prominent and despicable a figure through
the piece.   On the entrance of Goneril the following
dialogue takes place :—

" *Lear.* How now, daughter? what makes that frontlet on?
Methinks you are too much of late i' the frown.

Fool. Thou wast a pretty fellow, when thou hadst no need to
care for her frowning; now thou art an O without a figure : I am

better than thou art now; I am a fool, thou art nothing. [*To Gon.*]
Yes, forsooth, I will hold my tongue; so your face bids me, though
you say nothing. Mum, mum.

> He that keeps nor crust nor crumb,
> Weary of all, shall want some.—

That's a sheal'd peascod !   [*Pointing to Lear.*

  Goneril. Not only, sir, this your all-licens'd fool,
But other of your insolent retinue
Do hourly carp and quarrel ; breaking forth
In rank and not-to-be-endured riots.

                                  Sir,
I had thought, by making this well known unto you,
T' have found a safe redress ; but now grow fearful,
By what yourself too late have spoke and done,
That you protect this course, and put it on
By your allowance ; which if you should, the fault
Would not 'scape censure, nor the redresses sleep,
Which, in the tender of a wholesome weal,
Might in their working do you that offence,
Which else were shame, that then necessity
Will call discreet proceeding.

  Fool. For, you trow, nuncle,

> The hedge-sparrow fed the cuckoo so long,
> That it had its head bit off by its young.

So out went the candle, and we were left darkling.

  Lear. Are you our daughter ?

  Goneril. Come, sir,
I would you would make use of that good wisdom
Whereof I know you're fraught ; and put away
These dispositions, which of late transform you
From what you rightly are.

  Fool. May not an ass know when the cart draws the horse ?—
Whoop, Jug ! I love thee.

  Lear. Does any here know me ?—Why, this is not Lear :
Doth Lear walk thus ? speak thus ? Where are his eyes ?
Either his notion weakens, or his discernings
Are lethargied——Ha ! waking ?—'Tis not so.——
Who is it that can tell me who I am ?

  Fool. Lear's shadow.

  Lear. I would learn that : for by the marks of sovereignty
Knowledge, and reason, I should be false-persuaded
I had daughters.——

  Fool. Which they will make an obedient father.

  Lear. Your name, fair gentlewoman ?

Goneril. This admiration, sir, is much o' the savour
Of other your new pranks. I do beseech you
To understand my purposes aright:
As you are old and reverend, should be wise :
Here do you keep a hundred knights and squires ;
Men so disorder'd, so debauch'd, and bold,
That this our court, infected with their manners,
Shows like a riotous inn : epicurism and lust
Make it more like a tavern, or a brothel,
Than a grac'd palace. The shame itself doth speak
For instant remedy : be then desir'd
By her, that else will take the thing she begs,
A little to disquantity your train ;
And the remainder, that shall still depend,
To be such men as may besort your age,
Which know themselves and you.

    Lear.   Darkness and devils !-.
Saddle my horses ; call my train together.—
Degenerate bastard ! I'll not trouble thee ;
Yet have I left a daughter.

    Goneril. You strike my people ; and your disorder'd rabble
Make servants of their betters.

Enter ALBANY.

    Lear. Woe, that too late repents—[*To Albany.*] O, sir, are
      you come ?
Is it your will? speak, sir.—Prepare my horses.—
Ingratitude ! thou marble-hearted fiend,
More hideous, when thou show'st thee in a child,
Than the sea-monster !

    Albany,   Pray, sir, be patient.

    Lear. Detested kite ! thou liest.   [*To Goneril.*
My train are men of choice and rarest parts,
That all particulars of duty know ;
And in the most exact regard support
The worships of their name.—O most small fault,
How ugly didst thou in Cordelia show !
Which, like an engine, wrench'd my frame of nature
From the fixt place ; drew from my heart all love,
And added to the gall. O Lear, Lear, Lear !
Beat at this gate, that let thy folly in,   [*Striking his head.*
And thy dear judgment out!—Go, go, my people !

    Albany. My lord, I'm guiltless, as I'm ignorant
Of what hath mov'd you.

Lear. It may be so, my lord——
Hear, nature, hear! dear goddess, hear!
Suspend thy purpose, if thou didst intend
To make this creature fruitful!
Into her womb convey sterility!
Dry up in her the organs of increase;
And from her derogate body never spring
A babe to honour her! If she must teem,
Create her child of spleen: that it may live,
And be a thwart disnatur'd torment to her!
Let it stamp wrinkles in her brow of youth;
With cadent tears fret channels in her cheeks;
Turn all her mother's pains and benefits
To laughter and contempt; that she may feel
How sharper than a serpent's tooth it is
To have a thankless child!——Away, away!   [*Exit*
   Albany. Now, gods, that we adore, whereof comes this?
   Goneril. Never afflict yourself to know the cause;
But let his disposition have that scope
That dotage gives it.
             Re-enter LEAR.

   Lear. What, fifty of my followers at a clap!
Within a fortnight!
   Albany.   What's the matter, sir?
   Lear. I'll tell thee;—[*To Gon.*] life and death! I am asham'd
That thou hast power to shake my manhood thus:
That these hot tears, which break from me perforce,
Should make thee worth them.——Blasts and fogs upon thee!
Th' untented woundings of a father's curse
Pierce every sense about thee!——Old fond eyes
Beweep this cause again, I'll pluck you out;
And cast you, with the waters that you lose,
To temper clay.——Ha! is it come to this?
Let it be so:——I have another daughter,
Who, I am sure, is kind and comfortable;
When she shall hear this of thee, with her nails
She'll flay thy wolfish visage. Thou shalt find
That I'll resume the shape, which thou dost think
I have cast off for ever.
        [*Exeunt Lear, Kent, and Attendants.*" [1]

This is certainly fine: no wonder that Lear says after
it, " O let me not be mad, not mad, sweet heavens," feeling

[[1] Act i., sc. 4.]

its effects by anticipation; but fine as is this burst of rage
and indignation at the first blow aimed at his hopes and
expectations, it is nothing near so fine as what follows
from his double disappointment, and his lingering efforts
to see which of them he shall lean upon for support and
find comfort in, when both his daughters turn against his
age and weakness. It is with some difficulty that Lear
gets to speak with his daughter Regan, and her husband,
at Gloster's castle. In concert with Goneril they have
left their own home on purpose to avoid him. His apprehensions are first alarmed by this circumstance, and when
Gloster, whose guests they are, urges the fiery temper of
the Duke of Cornwall as an excuse for not importuning
him a second time, Lear breaks out—

> " Vengeance! Plague! Death! Confusion!——
> Fiery? What quality? Why, Gloster, Gloster,
> I'd speak with the Duke of Cornwall, and his wife." [1]

Afterwards, feeling perhaps not well himself, he is
inclined to admit their excuse from illness, but then recollecting that they have set his messenger (Kent) in the
stocks, all his suspicions are roused again, and he insists
on seeing them.

> " *Enter* CORNWALL, REGAN, GLOSTER, *and Servants.*
>
> *Lear.* Good-morrow to you both.
> *Cornwall.* Hail to your grace !   [*Kent is set at liberty.*
> *Regan.* I am glad to see your highness.
> *Lear.* Regan, I think you are; I know what reason
> I have to think so: if thou should'st not be glad,
> I would divorce me from thy mother's tomb,
> Sepulchring an adultress.——[*To Kent.*] O, are you free ?
> Some other time for that.——Beloved Regan,
> Thy sister's naught: O Regan, she hath tied
> Sharp-tooth'd unkindness, like a vulture, here——
>   [*Points to his heart*
> I can scarce speak to thee; thou'lt not believe,
> Of how deprav'd a quality——O Regan !

---

[1] Act ii., sc. 4.]

Regan. I pray you, sir, take patience ; I have hope
You less know how to value her desert,
Than she to scant her duty.

    Lear.   Say, how is that ?

    Regan. I cannot think my sister in the least
Would fail her obligation ; if, sir, perchance,
She have restrain'd the riots of your follow···
'Tis on such ground, and to such wholesome ···,
As clears her from all blame.

    Lear.   My curses on her

    Regan. O, sir, you are old ;
Nature in you stands on the very verge
Of her confine : you should be rul'd and le·
By some discretion, that discerns your state
Better than yourself. Therefore, I pr· y you,
That to our sister you do make return ;
Say you have wrong'd her, sir.

    Lear.   Ask her forgiveness ?
Do you but mark how this becomes the house ?
Dear daughter, I confess that I am old ;
Age is unnecessary ; on my knees I beg,
That you'll vouchsafe me raiment, bed, and food.

    Regan. Good sir, no more ; these are unsightly tricks :
Return you to my sister.

    Lear. [*Rising.*] Never, Regan :
She hath abated me of half my train ;
Look'd blank upon me ; struck me with her tongue,
Most serpent-like, upon the very heart :—
All the stor'd vengeances of heaven fall
On her ungrateful top ! Strike her young bones,
You taking airs, with lameness !

    Cornwall.   Fie, sir, fie !

    Lear. You nimble lightnings, dart your blinding flames
Into her scornful eyes ! Infect her beauty,
You fen-suck'd fogs, drawn by the powerful sun,
To fall and blast her pride !

    Regan. O the blest gods ! So will you wish on me,
When the rash mood is on.

    Lear. No, Regan, thou shalt never have my curse :
Thy tender-hefted nature shall not give
Thee o'er to harshness ; her eyes are fierce ; but thine
Do comfort, and not burn. 'Tis not in thee
To grudge my pleasures, to cut off my train,
To bandy hasty words, to scant my sizes,

And, in conclusion, to oppose the bolt
Against my coming in : thou better know'st
The offices of nature, bond of childhood,
Effects of courtesy, dues of gratitude ;
Thy half o' the kingdom thou hast not forgot,
Wherein I thee endow'd.

 Regan.   Good sir, to the purpose.
 Lear. Who put my man i' the stocks ? [*Trumpets within*
 Cornwall. What trumpet's that ?
 Regan. I know't, my sister's : this approves her letter,
That she would soon be here.

      Enter OSWALD.

     Is your lady come ?
 Lear. This is a slave, whose easy-borrow'd pride
Dwells in the fickle grace of her he follows :——
Out, varlet, from my sight !
 Cornwall.   What means your grace ?
 Lear. Who stock'd my servant ? Regan, I have good hope
Thou did'st not know on't.——Who comes here ? O heavens,

      Enter GONERIL.

If you do love old men, if your sweet sway
Allow obedience, if yourselves are old,
Make it your cause ; send down, and take my part !—
[*To Gon.*] Art not asham'd to look upon this beard ?—
O, Regan, wilt thou take her by the hand ?
 Goneril. Why not by the hand, sir ? How have I offended ?
All's not offence, that indiscretion finds,
And dotage terms so.
 Lear.   O, sides, you are too tough !
Will you yet hold ?—How came my man i' the stocks ?
 Cornwall. I set him there, sir : but his own disorders
Deserv'd much less advancement.
 Lear.   You ! did you ?
 Regan. I pray you, father, being weak, seem so.
If, till the expiration of your month,
You will return and sojourn with my sister,
Dismissing half your train, come then to me ;
I'm now from home, and out of that provision
Which shall be needful for your entertainment.
 Lear. Return to her, and fifty men dismiss'd ?
No, rather I abjure all roofs, and choose
To be a comrade with the wolf and owl——
To wage against the enmity o' th' air,

Necessity's sharp pinch !——Return with her !
Why, the hot-blooded France, that dowerless took
Our youngest born, I could as well be brought
To knee his throne, and, squire-like, pension beg
To keep base life afoot.——Return with her !
Persuade me rather to be slave and sumpter
To this detested groom.   [*Pointing at Oswald*

    Goneril.   At your choice, sir.

    Lear. I prithee, daughters, do not make me mad;
I will not trouble thee, my child ; farewell :
We'll no more meet, no more see one another :——
But yet thou art my flesh, my blood, my daughter ;
Or rather a disease that's in my flesh,
Which I must needs call mine : thou art a bile,
A plague-sore, an embossed carbuncle,
In my corrupted blood.   But I'll not chide thee;
Let shame come when it will, I do not call it :
I did not bid the thunder-bearer shoot,
Nor tell tales of thee to high-judging Jove :
Mend when thou canst; be better at thy leisure.
I can be patient ; I can stay with Regan,
I and my hundred knights.

    Regan.   Not altogether so ;
I look'd not for you yet, nor am provided
For your fit welcome.   Give ear, sir, to my sister ;
For those that mingle reason with your passion
Must be content to think you old, and so——
But she knows what she does.

    Lear.   Is this well spoken ?

    Regan. I dare avouch it, sir: What, fifty followers?
Is it not well ? What should you need of more ?
Yea, or so many? sith that both charge and danger
Speak 'gainst so great a number?   How, in one house,
Should many people, under two commands,
Hold amity ?   'Tis hard—almost impossible.

    Goneril. Why might not you, my lord, receive attendance
From those that she calls servants, or from mine ?

    Regan. Why not, my lord?   If then they chanc'd to slack you,
We would control them : If you will come to me—
For now I spy a danger—I entreat you
To bring but five-and-twenty; to no more
Will I give place, or notice.

    Lear. I gave you all——

    Regan.   And in good time you gave it.

Lear. Made you my guardians, my depositaries:
But kept a reservation to be follow'd
With such a number: what, must I come to you
With five-and-twenty, Regan! said you so?
  Regan. And speak 't again, my lord: no more with me.
  Lear. Those wicked creatures yet do look well-favour'd,
When others are more wicked; not being the worst,
Stands in some rank of praise:——I'll go with thee;
                                                  [*To Gonerill.*

Thy fifty yet doth double five-and-twenty,
And thou art twice her love.
  Gonerill.   Hear me, my lord;
What need you five-and-twenty, ten, or five,
To follow in a house, where twice so many
Have a command to tend you?
  Regan.   What need one?
  Lear. O, reason not the need: our basest beggars
Are in the poorest thing superfluous:
Allow not nature more than nature needs,
Man's life is cheap as beast's: thou art a lady;
If only to go warm were gorgeous,
Why, nature needs not what thou gorgeous wear'st;
Which scarcely keeps thee warm.—But for true need—
You heavens, give me that patience which I need!
You see me here, you gods, a poor old man,
As full of grief as age; wretched in both!
If it be you that stir these daughters' hearts
Against their father, fool me not so much
To bear it tamely; touch me with noble anger!
O, let no women's weapons, water-drops,
Stain my man's cheeks!—No, you unnatural hags,
I will have such revenges on you both,
That all the world shall—I will do such things—
What they are, yet I know not; but they shall be
The terrors of the earth.   You think I'll weep:
No, I'll not weep·—
I have full cause of weeping; but this heart
Shall break into a hundred thousand flaws,
Or e'er I'll weep:—O, fool, I shall go mad!—
                          [*Exeunt Lear, Gloster, Kent, and Fool.*"

If there is anything in any author like this yearning of
the heart, these throes of tenderness, this profound expression of all that can be thought and felt in the most

heartrending situations, we are glad of it; but it is in
some author that we have not read.

The scene in the storm, where he is exposed to all the
fury of the elements, though grand and terrible, is not so
fine, but the moralising scenes with Mad Tom, Kent,
and Gloster, are upon a par with the former. His exclamation in the supposed trial-scene of his daughters, " The
little dogs and all, Tray, Blanch, and Sweetheart, see,
they bark at me,"[1] his issuing his orders, " Then let them
anatomize Regan, see what breeds about her heart,"[2] and
his reflection when he sees the misery of Edgar, " Nothing
could have subdued nature to such a lowness but his
unkind daughters,"[3] are in a style of pathos, where the
extremest resources of the imagination are called in to
lay open the deepest movements of the heart, which was
peculiar to Shakespear. In the same style and spirit is
his interrupting the Fool, who asks, " whether a madman
be a gentleman or a yeoman," by answering " A king,
a king."[4]—

The indirect part that Gloster takes in these scenes
where his generosity leads him to relieve Lear and resent
the cruelty of his daughters, at the very time that he is
himself instigated to seek the life of his son, and suffering
under the sting of his supposed ingratitude, is a striking
accompaniment to the situation of Lear. Indeed, the
manner in which the threads of the story are woven
together is almost as wonderful in the way of art as the
carrying on the tide of passion, still varying and unim-
paired, is on the score of nature. Among the remarkable
instances of this kind are Edgar's meeting with his old
blind father ; the deception he practises upon him when
he pretends to lead him to the top of Dover-cliff—" Come
on, sir, here's the place,"[5] to prevent his ending his life
and miseries together ; his encounter with the perfidious

[1] Act iii., sc. 6.]   [2] *Ibid.*]   [3] Act iii., sc. 4.]
     [4] Act iii., sc. 6.]   [5] Act iv., sc. 6.]

Steward whom he kills, and his finding the letter from Goneril to his brother upon him which leads to the final catastrophe, and brings the wheel of Justice "full circle" home to the guilty parties. The bustle and rapid succession of events in the last scenes is surprising. But the meeting between Lear and Cordelia is by far the most affecting part of them. It has all the wildness of poetry, and all the heartfelt truth of nature. The previous account of her reception of the news of his unkind treatment, her involuntary reproaches to her sisters, "Shame of ladies, sisters," Lear's backwardness to see his daughter, the picture of the desolate state to which he is reduced, "Alack, 'tis he; why he was met even now, as mad as the vex'd sea, singing aloud," [1] only prepare the way for and heighten our expectation of what follows, and assuredly this expectation is not disappointed when through the tender care of Cordelia he revives and recollects her.

> "*Cordelia.* How does my royal lord? How fares your majesty!
> *Lear.* You do me wrong to take me out o' the grave:
> Thou art a soul in bliss; but I am bound
> Upon a wheel of fire, that mine own tears
> Do scald like molten lead.
> *Cordelia.*   Sir, do you know me?
> *Lear.* You are a spirit, I know: when did you die?
> *Cordelia.* Still, still, far wide!
> *Doct.* He's scarce awake; let him alone awhile.
> *Lear.* Where have I been? Where am I?—Fair day-light?——
> I'm mightily abus'd.—I should e'en die with pity,
> To see another thus.—I know not what to say.——
> I will not swear these are my hands:—let's see;
> I feel this pin prick. 'Would I were assured
> Of my condition.
> *Cordelia.* O, look upon me, sir,
> And hold your hands in benediction o'er me:——
> No, sir, you must not kneel.

[1 Act iv., sc. 4.]

Lear.   Pray, do not mock me:
I am a very foolish fond old man,
Fourscore and upward; not an hour more nor less;
And, to deal plainly,
I fear, I am not in my perfect mind.
Methinks, I should know you, and know this man;
Yet I am doubtful; for I'm mainly ignorant
What place this is; and all the skill I have
Remembers not these garments; nor I know not
Where I did lodge last night. Do not laugh at me;
For, as I am a man, I think this lady
To be my child Cordelia.
    Cordelia.   And so I am, I am!"[1]

Almost equal to this in awful beauty is their consolation
of each other when, after the triumph of their enemies,
they are led to prison:

   " *Cordelia.*   We are not the first
Who, with best meaning, have incurr'd the worst.
For thee, oppressed king, am I cast down;
Myself could else outfrown false fortune's frown.—
Shall we not see these daughters and these sisters?
   Lear. No, no, no, no! Come, let's away to prison:
We two alone will sing like birds i' the cage:
When thou dost ask me blessing, I'll kneel down
And ask of thee forgiveness: so we'll live,
And pray, and sing, and tell old tales, and laugh
At gilded butterflies, and hear poor rogues
Talk of court news; and we'll talk with them too—
Who loses, and who wins; who's in, who's out;—
And take upon 's the mystery of things,
As if we were God's spies: and we'll wear out,
In a wall'd prison, packs and sects of great ones,
That ebb and flow by the moon.
   Edmund.   Take them away.
   Lear. Upon such sacrifices, my Cordelia,
The gods themselves throw incense."[2]

The concluding events are sad, painfully sad; but their
pathos is extreme. The oppression of the feelings is
relieved by the very interest we take in the misfortunes of
others, and by the reflections to which they give birth.

    [1 Act iv., sc. 7.]   [2 Act v., sc. 3.

Cordelia is hanged in prison by the orders of the bastard Edmund, which are known too late to be countermanded, and Lear dies broken-hearted, lamenting over her.

> " *Lear.* And my poor fool is hang'd ! No, no, no, life :
> Why should a dog, a horse, a rat, have life,
> And thou no breath at all ? Thou wilt come no more,
> Never, never, never, never, never !——
> Pray you, undo this button: thank you, sir."[1]

He dies, and indeed we feel the truth of what Kent says on the occasion—

> " Vex not his ghost: O let him pass ! he hates him,
> That would upon the rack of this tough world
> Stretch him out longer." [2]

Yet a happy ending has been contrived for this play, which is approved of by Dr. Johnson and condemned by Schlegel. A better authority than either, on any subject in which poetry and feeling are concerned, has given it in favour of Shakespear, in some remarks on the acting of Lear, with which we shall conclude this account.

" The ' Lear ' of Shakespear cannot be acted. The contemptible machinery with which they mimic the storm which he goes out in, is not more inadequate to represent the horrors of the real elements than any actor can be to represent Lear. The greatness of Lear is not in corporal dimension, but in intellectual; the explosions of his passions are terrible as a volcano: they are storms turning up and disclosing to the bottom that rich sea, his mind, with all its vast riches. It is his mind which is laid bare. This case of flesh and blood seems too insignificant to be thought on ; even as he himself neglects it. On the stage we see nothing but corporal infirmities and weakness, the impotence of rage ; while we read it, we see not Lear, but we are Lear ;—we are in his mind : we are sustained by a grandeur which baffles the malice of daughters and storms; in the aberrations of his reason, we discover a mighty

[1 Act v., sc. 3.]   [2 *Ibid.*]

irregular power of reasoning, immethodised from the ordinary purposes of life, but exerting its powers, as the wind blows where it listeth, at will on the corruptions and abuses of mankind. What have looks or tones to do with that sublime identification of his age with that of *the heavens themselves*, when in his reproaches to them for conniving at the injustice of his children, he reminds them that ' they themselves are old ?' What gesture shall we appropriate to this? What has the voice or the eye to do with such things? But the play is beyond all art, as the tamperings with it show: it is too hard and stony: it must have love-scenes, and a happy ending. It is not enough that Cordelia is a daughter, she must shine as a lover too. Tate has put his hook in the nostrils of this Leviathan, for Garrick and his followers, the showmen of the scene, to draw it about more easily. A happy ending!—as if the living martyrdom that Lear had gone through,—the flaying of his feelings alive, did not make a fair dismissal from the stage of life the only decorous thing for him. If he is to live and be happy after, if he could sustain this world's burden after, why all this puddel and preparation—why torment us with all this unnecessary sympathy? As if the childish pleasure of getting his gilt robes and sceptre again could tempt him to act over again his misused station,—as if at his years and with his ex·perience, anything was left but to die." [1]

Four things have struck us in reading ' Lear :'

1. That poetry is an interesting study, for this reason, that it relates to whatever is most interesting in human life. Whoever therefore has a contempt for poetry, has a contempt for himself and humanity.

2. That the language of poetry is superior to the language of painting; because the strongest of our recollections relate to feelings, not to faces.

[1] See an article, called ' Theatralia,' in the second volume of the Reflector,' by Charles Lamb [or in his ' Works,' 1818. 2 vols., 12mo.].

3. That the greatest strength of genius is shown in describing the strongest passions : for the power of the imagination, in works of invention, must be in proportion to the force of the natural impressions, which are the subject of them.

4. That the circumstance which balances the pleasure against the pain in tragedy is, that in proportion to the greatness of the evil, is our sense and desire of the opposite good excited ; and that our sympathy with actual suffering is lost in the strong impulse given to our natural affections, and carried away with the swelling tide of passion, that gushes from and relieves the heart.

RICHARD II.[2]

' RICHARD II.' is a play little known compared with ' Richard III.,' which last is a play that every unfledged candidate for theatrical fame chooses to strut and fret his hour upon the stage in ; yet we confess that we prefer the nature and feeling of the one to the noise and bustle of the other ; at least, as we are so often forced to see it acted. In ' Richard II.' the weakness of the king leaves us leisure to take a greater interest in the misfortunes of the man. After the first act, in which the arbitrariness of his behaviour only proves his want of resolution, we see him staggering under the unlooked-for blows of fortune, bewailing his loss of kingly power, not preventing it, sinking under the aspiring genius of Bolingbroke, his authority trampled on, his hopes failing him, and his

---

[1] The date of its composition seems to be uncertain. It was first printed in 1597. In 1608 were first incorporated ' New Additions of the Parliament Scene, and the Deposing of King Richard.' There were two other early dramas on this subject ; but to what extent, if any, Shakespear was indebted to them cannot at present be ascertained.—ED.

pride crushed and broken down under insults and injuries, which his own misconduct had provoked, but which he has not courage or manliness to resent. The change of tone and behaviour in the two competitors for the throne according to their change of fortune, from the capricious sentence of banishment passed by Richard upon Boling-broke, the suppliant offers and modest pretensions of the latter on his return to the high and haughty tone with which he accepts Richard's resignation of the crown after the loss of all his power, the use which he makes of the deposed king to grace his triumphal progress through the streets of London, and the final intimation of his wish for his death, which immediately finds a servile executioner, is marked throughout with complete effect and without the slightest appearance of effort. The steps by which Boling-broke mounts the throne are those by which Richard sinks into the grave. We feel neither respect nor love for the deposed monarch; for he is as wanting in energy as in principle: but we pity him, for he pities himself. His heart is by no means hardened against himself, but bleeds afresh at every new stroke of mischance, and his sensibility, absorbed in his own person, and unused to misfortune, is not only tenderly alive to its own sufferings, but without the fortitude to bear them. He is, however, human in his distresses; for to feel pain, and sorrow, weakness, disappointment, remorse, and anguish, is the lot of humanity, and we sympathise with him accordingly. The sufferings of the man make us forget that he ever was a king.

The right assumed by sovereign power to trifle at its will with the happiness of others as a matter of course, or to remit its exercise as a matter of favour, is strikingly shown in the sentence of banishment so unjustly pro-nounced on Bolingbroke and Mowbray, and in what Bolingbroke says when four years of his banishment are taken off, with as little reason :

> " How long a time lies in one little word !
> Four lagging winters and four wanton springs
> End in a word: such is the breath of kings." [1]

A more affecting image of the loneliness of a state of exile can hardly be given than by what Bolingbroke afterwards observes of his having " sighed my English breath in foreign clouds ;" [2] or than that conveyed in Mowbray's complaint at being banished for life :

> " The language I have learned these forty years,
> My native English, now I must forego ;
> And now my tongue's use is to me no more
> Than an unstringed viol or a harp,
> Or like a cunning instrument cas'd up,
> Or being open, put into his hands
> That knows no touch to tune the harmony. . .
> I am too old to fawn upon a nurse,
> Too far in years to be a pupil now."—[3]

How very beautiful is all this, and at the same time how very *English* too !

' Richard II.' may be considered as the first of that series of English historical plays, in which " is hung armour of the invincible knights of old," in which their hearts seem to strike against their coats of mail, where their blood tingles for the fight, and words are but the harbingers of blows. Of this state of accomplished barbarism the appeal of Bolingbroke and Mowbray is an admirable specimen. Another of these " keen encounters of their wits," which serve to whet the talkers' swords, is where Aumerle answers in the presence of Bolingbroke to the charge which Bagot brings against him of being an accessory in Gloster's death :

> " *Fitzwater.* If that thy valour stand on sympathy,
> There is my gage, Aumerle, in gage to thine ;
> By that fair sun that shows me where thou stand'st,
> I heard thee say, and vauntingly thou spak'st it,

[1 Act i., sc 3.]   [2 Act iii., sc. 1.]   [3 Act i., sc. 3.]

That thou wert cause of noble Gloster's death.
If thou deny'st it twenty times thou liest,
And I will turn thy falsehood to thy heart
Where it was forged, with my rapier's point.
    Aumerle. Thou dar'st not, coward, live to see the day.
    Fitzwater. Now, by my soul, I would it were this hour.
    Aumerle. Fitzwater, thou art damn'd to hell for this.
    Percy. Aumerle, thou liest; his honour is as true,
In this appeal, as thou art all unjust ;
And that thou art so, there I throw my gage
To prove it on thee, to the extremest point
Of mortal breathing.   Seize it, if thou dar'st.
    Aumerle. And if I do not, may my hands rot off,
And never brandish more revengeful steel
Over the glittering helmet of my foe. . . . .
Who sets me else ? By heav'n, I'll throw at all.
I have a thousand spirits in my breast,
To answer twenty thousand such as you.
    Surrey. My lord Fitzwater, I do remember well
The very time Aumerle and you did talk.
    Fitzwater. My lord, 'tis true: you were in presence then
And you can witness with me, this is true.
    Surrey. As false, by heav'n, as heav'n itself is true.
    Fitzwater. Surrey, thou liest.
    Surrey.   Dishonourable boy,
That lie shall lie so heavy on my sword,
That it shall render vengeance and revenge,
Till thou the lie-giver, and that lie do lie
In earth as quiet as thy father's skull.
In proof whereof, there is my honour's pawn :
Engage it to the trial, if thou dar'st.
    Fitzwater. How fondly dost thou spur a forward horse :
If I dare eat or drink, or breathe, or live,
I dare meet Surrey in a wilderness,
And spit upon him, whilst I say he lies,
And lies, and lies : there is my bond of faith,
To tie thee to my strong correction.
As I do hope to thrive in this new world,
Aumerle is guilty of my true appeal—" [1]

The truth is, that there is neither truth nor honour in
all these noble persons : they answer words with words,
as they do blows with blows, in mere self-defence : nor

[1 Act iv., sc. 1.]

have they any principle whatever but that of courage in maintaining any wrong they dare commit, or any false-hood which they find it useful to assert. How different were these noble knights and "barons bold" from their more refined descendants in the present day, who, instead of deciding questions of right by brute force, refer every-thing to convenience, fashion, and good breeding! In point of any abstract love of truth or justice, they are just the same now that they were then.

The characters of old John of Gaunt and of his brother York, uncles to the King, the one stern and foreboding, the other honest, good-natured, doing all for the best, and therefore doing nothing, are well kept up. The speech of the former, in praise of England, is one of the most elo-quent that ever was penned. We should perhaps hardly be disposed to feed the pampered egotism of our country-men by quoting this description, were it not that the con-clusion of it (which looks prophetic) may qualify any improper degree of exultation:

> " This royal throne of kings, this scepter'd isle,
> This earth of Majesty, this seat of Mars,
> This other Eden, demi-Paradise,
> This fortress built by Nature for herself
> Against infection and the hand of war ;
> This happy breed of men, this little world,
> This precious stone set in the silver sea,
> Which serves it in the office of a wall,
> Or as a moat defensive to a house
> Against the envy of less happier lands:
> This blessed plot, this earth, this realm, this England,
> This nurse, this teeming womb of royal kings,
> Fear'd by their breed and famous by their birth,
> Renowned for their deeds as far from home
> (For Christian service and true chivalry),
> As is the sepulchre, in stubborn Jewry,
> Of the world's ransom, blessed Mary's Son ;
> This land of such dear souls, this dear dear land,
> Dear for her reputation through the world,
> Is now leas'd out—I die pronouncing it—

Like to a tenement or pelting farm :
England bound in with the triumphant sea,
Whose rocky shore beats back the envious surge
Of watery Neptune, 's now bound in with shame,
With inky-blots and rotten parchment bonds.
That England that was wont to conquer others,
Hath made a shameful conquest of itself." [1]

The character of Bolingbroke, afterwards Henry IV., is drawn with a masterly hand :—patient for occasion, and then steadily availing himself of it, seeing his advantage afar off, but only seizing on it when he has it within his reach, humble, crafty, bold, and aspiring, encroaching by regular but slow degrees, building power on opinion, and cementing opinion by power. His disposition is first unfolded by Richard himself, who however is too self-willed and secure to make a proper use of his knowledge :

" Ourself and Bushy, Bagot here and Green,
Observed his courtship to the common people :
How he did seem to dive into their hearts,
With humble and familiar courtesy,
What reverence he did throw away on slaves ;
Wooing poor craftsmen with the craft of smiles
And patient under-bearing of his fortune,
As 'twere to banish their affections with him.
Off goes his bonnet to an oyster-wench ;
A brace of draymen bid God speed him well,
And had the tribute of his supple knee,
With, Thanks my countrymen, my loving friends ;
As were our England in reversion his,
And he our subjects' next degree in hope." [2]

Afterwards, he gives his own character to Percy, in these words :

" I thank thee, gentle Percy, and be sure
I count myself in nothing else so happy,
As in a soul rememb'ring my good friends ;
And as my fortune ripens with thy love,
It shall be still thy true love's recompense." [3]

We know how he afterwards kept his promise. His bold assertion of his own rights, his pretended submission to

[1] Act ii., sc. 1.]   [2] Act i., sc. 4.]   [3] Act ii., sc. 3.]

the king, and the ascendency which he tacitly assumes over him without openly claiming it, as soon as he has him in his power, are characteristic traits of this ambitious and politic usurper. But the part of Richard himself gives the chief interest to the play. His folly, his vices, his misfortunes, his reluctance to part with the crown, his fear to keep it, his weak and womanish regrets, his starting tears, his fits of hectic passion, his smothered majesty, pass in succession before us, and make a picture as natural as it is affecting. Among the most striking touches of pathos are his wish :

> " O, that I were a mockery king of snow,
> Standing before the sun of Bolingbroke,
> To melt myself away in water-drops !" [1]

and the incident of the poor groom who comes to visit him in prison, and tells him :

> "O, how it yearn'd my heart, when I beheld,
> In London streets, that coronation-day,
> When Bolingbroke rode on roan Barbary—" [2]

We shall have occasion to return hereafter to the character of Richard II. in speaking of Henry VI. There is only one passage more, the description of his entrance into London with Bolingbroke, which we should like to quote here, if it had not been so used and worn out, so thumbed and got by rote, so praised and painted; but its beauty surmounts all these considerations :

> " *Duchess.* My lord, you told me you would tell the rest,
> When weeping made you break the story off
> Of our two cousins coming into London.
>   *York.* Where did I leave ?
>   *Duchess.*   At that sad stop, my lord,
> Where rude misgovern'd hands from window tops
> Threw dust and rubbish on King Richard's head.
>   *York.* Then, as I said, the duke, great Bolingbroke,
> Mounted upon a hot and fiery steed,

[1 Act iv., sc. 1.]   [2 Act v., sc. 5.]

Which his aspiring rider seem'd to know,
With slow but stately pace kept on his course,
While all tongues cried—God save thee, Bolingbroke!
You would have thought the very windows spake,
So many greedy looks of young and old
Through casements darted their desiring eyes
Upon his visage; and that all the walls
With painted imagery had said at once—
Jesu preserve thee! welcome, Bolingbroke!
Whilst he, from one side to the other turning,
Bare-headed, lower than his proud steed's neck,
Bespake them thus, I thank you, countrymen:
And thus still doing, thus he pass'd along.
    Duchess. Alas, poor Richard! where rides he the while?
    York. As in a theatre, the eyes of men,
After a well-grac'd actor leaves the stage,
Are idly bent on him that enters next,
Thinking his prattle to be tedious:
Even so, or with much more contempt, men's eyes
Did scowl on Richard; no man cried, God save him!
No joyful tongue gave him his welcome home:
But dust was thrown upon his sacred head!
Which with such gentle sorrow he shook off—
His face still combating with tears and smiles,
The badges of his grief and patience—
That had not God, for some strong purpose, steel'd
The hearts of men, they must perforce have melted,
And barbarism itself have pitied him." [1]

———◦◇◦———

HENRY IV.

IN TWO PARTS. [2]

IF Shakespear's fondness for the ludicrous sometimes led
to faults in his tragedies (which was not often the case) he
has made us amends by the character of Falstaff. This is
perhaps the most substantial comic character that ever was

[1] Act v., sc. 2.]
[2] The *First Part* was printed in 1598, the *Second* in 1600. See
for further particulars, Dyce's 2nd edit., iv., 204-5.—ED.

invented. Sir John carries a most portly presence in the mind's eye; and in him, not to speak it profanely, " we behold the fulness of the spirit of wit and humour bodily." We are as well acquainted with his person as his mind, and his jokes come upon us with double force and relish from the quantity of flesh through which they make their way, as he shakes his fat sides with laughter, or " lards the lean earth as he walks along." Other comic characters seem, if we approach and handle them, to resolve themselves into air, " into thin air;" but this is embodied and palpable to the grossest apprehension : it lies " three fingers deep upon the ribs," it plays about the lungs and diaphragm with all the force of animal enjoyment. His body is like a good estate to his mind, from which he receives rents and revenues of profit and pleasure in kind, according to its extent and the richness of the soil. Wit is often a meagre substitute for pleasurable sensation; an effusion of spleen and petty spite at the comforts of others, from feeling none in itself. Falstaff's wit is an emanation of a fine constitution ; an exuberance of good-humour and good-nature ; an overflowing of his love of laughter and good-fellowship ; a giving vent to his heart's ease, and over-contentment with himself and others. He would not be in character, if he were not so fat as he is ; for there is the greatest keeping in the boundless luxury of his imagination and the pampered self-indulgence of his physical appetites. He manures and nourishes his mind with jests, as he does his body with sack and sugar. He carves out his jokes, as he would a capon or a haunch of venison, where there is *cut and come again ;* and pours out upon them the oil of gladness. His tongue drops fatness, and in the chambers of his brain " it snows of meat and drink." He keeps up perpetual holiday and open house, and we live with him in a round of invitations to a rump and dozen. Yet we are not to suppose that he was a mere sensualist All this is as much in imagination as in reality.

His sensuality does not engross and stupify his other faculties, but "ascends me into the brain, dries me there all the foolish and dull and crudy vapours which environ it, makes it apprehensive, quick, forgetive, full of nimble, fiery, and delectable shapes."[1] His imagination keeps up the ball after his senses have done with it. He seems to have even a greater enjoyment of the freedom from restraint, of good cheer, of his ease, of his vanity, in the ideal exaggerated description which he gives of them, than in fact. He never fails to enrich his discourse with allusions to eating and drinking, but we never see him at table. He carries his own larder about with him, and he is himself "a tun of man." His pulling out the bottle in the field of battle is a joke to show his contempt for glory accompanied with danger, his systematic adherence to his Epicurean philosophy in the most trying circumstances. Again, such is his deliberate exaggeration of his own vices, that it does not seem quite certain whether the account of his hostess's bill, found in his pocket, with such an out-of-the-way charge for capons and sack with only one half-penny-worth of bread, was not put there by himself as a trick to humour the jest upon his favourite propensities, and as a conscious caricature of himself. He is represented as a liar, a braggart, a coward, a glutton, &c., and yet we are not offended but delighted with him; for he is all these as much to amuse others as to gratify himself. He openly assumes all these characters to show the humorous part of them. The unrestrained indulgence of his own ease, appetites, and convenience, has neither malice nor hypocrisy in it. In a word, he is an actor in himself almost as much as upon the stage, and we no more object to the character of Falstaff in a moral point of view than we should think of bringing an excellent comedian, who should represent him to the life, before one of the police offices. We only consider the number of pleasant

[Part II., act iv., sc. 3.]

lights in which he puts certain foibles (the more pleasant as they are opposed to the received rules and necessary restraints of society), and do not trouble ourselves about the consequences resulting from them, for no mischievous consequences do result. Sir John is old as well as fat, which gives a melancholy retrospective tinge to the character; and by the disparity between his inclinations and his capacity for enjoyment, makes it still more ludicrous and fantastical.

The secret of Falstaff's wit is for the most part a masterly presence of mind, an absolute self-possession, which nothing can disturb. His repartees are involuntary suggestions of his self-love; instinctive evasions of everything that threatens to interrupt the career of his triumphant jollity and self-complacency. His very size floats him out of all his difficulties in a sea of rich conceits; and he turns round on the pivot of his convenience, with every occasion and at a moment's warning. His natural repugnance to every unpleasant thought or circumstance, of itself makes light of objections, and provokes the most extravagant and licentious answers in his own justification. His indifference to truth puts no check upon his invention, and the more improbable and unexpected his contrivances are, the more happily does he seem to be delivered of them, the anticipation of their effect acting as a stimulus to the gaiety of his fancy. The success of one adventurous sally gives him spirits to undertake another: he deals always in round numbers, and his exaggerations and excuses are " open, palpable, monstrous as the father that begets them." His dissolute carelessness of what he says discovers itself in the first dialogue with the Prince:

" *Falstaff.* By the Lord, thou sayest true, lad. And is not my hostess of the tavern a most sweet wench ?

P. Henry. As the honey of Hibla, my old lad of the castle. And is not a buff-jerkin a most sweet robe of durance ?

Falstaff. How now, how now, mad wag ? what, in thy quips and thy quiddities ? what a plague have I to do with a buff-jerkin ?

P. Henry. Why, what a pox have I to do with my hostess of the tavern?" [1]

In the same scene he afterwards affects melancholy, from pure satisfaction of heart, and professes reform, because it is the farthest thing in the world from his thoughts. He has no qualms of conscience, and therefore would as soon talk of them as of anything else when the humour takes him:

"*Falstaff.* But Hal, I prithee, trouble me no more with vanity. I would to God thou and I knew where a commodity of good names were to be bought. An old lord of the council rated me the other day in the street about you, sir; but I marked him not, and yet he talked very wisely, but I regarded him not; and yet he talked wisely, and in the street too.

P. Henry. Thou didst well, for wisdom cries out in the streets, and no man regards it.

Falstaff. O, thou hast damnable iteration, and art indeed able to corrupt a saint. Thou hast done much harm upon me, Hal—God forgive thee for it! Before I knew thee, Hal, I knew nothing, and now I am, if a man should speak truly, little better than one of the wicked. I must give over this life, and I will give it over; by the Lord, an I do not, I am a villain. I'll be damn'd for never a king's son in Christendom.

P. Henry. Where shall we take a purse to-morrow, Jack?

Falstaff. Zounds! where thou wilt, lad, I'll make one; an I do not, call me villain, and baffle me.

P. Henry. I see a good amendment of life in thee, from praying to purse-taking.

Falstaff. Why, Hal, 'tis my vocation, Hal. 'Tis no sin for a man to labour in his vocation." [2]

Of the other prominent passages, his account of his pretended resistance to the robbers, " who grew from four men in buckram into eleven" as the imagination of his own valour increased with his relating it, his getting off when the truth is discovered by pretending he knew the Prince, the scene in which in the person of the old King he lectures the Prince and gives himself a good character, the soliloquy on honour, and description of his new-raised recruits, his meeting with the chief-justice, his abuse of the Prince and Poins, who over-

[1 Act i., sc. 2.]   [2 *Ibid.*]

hear him, to Doll Tearsheet, his reconciliation with Mrs. Quickly, who has arrested him for an old debt, and whom he persuades to pawn her plate to lend him ten pounds more, and the scenes with Shallow and Silence, are all inimitable. Of all of them, the scene in which Falstaff plays the part, first, of the King, and then of Prince Henry, is the one that has been the most often quoted. We must quote it once more in illustration of our remarks :—

"*Falstaff.* Harry, I do not only marvel where thou spendest thy time, but also how thou art accompanied : for though the camomile, the more it is trodden on, the faster it grows, yet youth, the more it is wasted, the sooner it wears. That thou art my son, I have partly thy mother's word, partly my own opinion ; but chiefly, a villainous trick of thine eye, and a foolish hanging of thy nether lip, that doth warrant me. If then thou be son to me, here lies the point ;—Why, being son to me, art thou so pointed at ? Shall the blessed sun of heaven prove a micher, and eat blackberries ? A question not to be asked. Shall the son of England prove a thief, and take purses ? a question to be asked. There is a thing, Harry, which thou hast often heard of, and it is known to many in our land by the name of pitch : this pitch, as ancient writers do report, doth defile ; so doth the company thou keepest : for, Harry, now I do not speak to thee in drink, but in tears; not in pleasure, but in passion; not in words only, but in woes also :—and yet there is a virtuous man, whom I have often noted in thy company, but I know not his name.

P. Henry. What manner of man, an it like your majesty ?

Falstaff. A goodly portly man, i'faith, and a corpulent ; of a cheerful look, a pleasing eye, and a most noble carriage ; and, as I think, his age some fifty, or, by'r-lady, inclining to threescore ; and now I remember me, his name is Falstaff : if that man should be lewdly given, he deceiveth me ; for, Harry, I see virtue in his looks. If then the tree may be known by the fruit, as the fruit by the tree, then peremptorily I speak it, there is virtue in that Falstaff : him keep with, the rest banish. And tell me now, thou naughty varlet, tell me, where hast thou been this month ?

P. Henry. Dost thou speak like a king ? Do thou stand for me, and I'll play my father.

Falstaff. Depose me ? if thou dost it half so gravely, so majestically, both in word and matter, hang me up by the heels for a rabbit-sucker, or a poulter's hare.

P. Henry. Will, here I am set.

Falstaff. And here I stand :—judge, my masters.

P. Henry. Now, Harry, whence come you?

Falstaff. My noble lord, from Eastcheap.

P. Henry. The complaints I hear of thee are grievous.

Falstaff. S'blood, my lord, they are false :—nay, I'll tickle ye for a young prince, i'faith.

P. Henry. Swearest thou, ungracious boy? henceforth ne'er look on me. Thou art violently carried away from grace: there is a devil haunts thee, in the likeness of an old fat man; a tun of man is thy companion. Why dost thou converse with that trunk of humours, that bolting-hutch of beastliness. that swollen parcel of dropsies, that huge bombard of sack, that stuffed cloak-bag of guts, that roasted Manningtree ox with the pudding in his belly, that reverend vice, that grey iniquity, that father ruffian, that vanity in years? Wherein is he good, but to taste sack and drink it? wherein neat and cleanly, but to carve a capon and eat it? wherein cunning, but in craft? wherein crafty, but in villainy? wherein villainous, but in all things? wherein worthy, but in nothing?

Falstaff. I would, your grace would take me with you : whom means your grace?

P. Henry. That villainous, abominable mislcader of youth, Falstaff, that old white-bearded Satan.

Falstaff. My lord, the man I know.

P. Henry. I know thou dost.

Falstaff. But to say, I know more harm in him than in myself, were to say more than I know. That he is old (the more the pity) his white hairs do witness it: but that he is (saving your reverence) a whore-master, that I utterly deny. If sack and sugar be a fault, God help the wicked! if to be old and merry be a sin, then many an old host that I know is damned : if to be fat be to be hated, then Pharaoh's lean kine are to be loved. No, my good lord ; banish Peto, banish Bardolph, banish Poins : but for sweet Jack Falstaff, kind Jack Falstaff, true Jack Falstaff, valiant Jack Falstaff, and therefore more valiant, being as he is, old Jack Falstaff, banish not him thy Harry's company ; banish plump Jack, and banish all the world.

P. Henry. I do, I will.

[*A knocking heard : Exeunt Hostess, Francis, and Bardolph.*

Re-enter BARDOLPH, *running.*

Bardolph. O, my lord, my lord; the sheriff, with a most monstrous watch, is at the door.

Falstaff. Out, ye rogue! Play out the play: I have much to say in the behalf of that Falstaff." [1]

[1 Act ii. sc. 4]

One of the most characteristic descriptions of Sir John is that which Mrs. Quickly gives of him when he asks her " What is the gross sum that I owe thee ?"

" *Hostess.* Marry, if thou wert an honest man, thyself and the money too. Thou didst swear to me upon a parcel-gilt goblet, sitting in my Dolphin-chamber, at the round table, by a sea-coal fire on Wednesday in Wheeson-week, when the prince broke thy head for likening his father to a singing man of Windsor—thou didst swear to me then, as I was washing thy wound, to marry me, and make me my lady thy wife. Canst thou deny it ? Did not goodwife Keech, the butcher's wife, come in then, and call me gossip Quickly ? coming in to borrow a mess of vinegar; telling us, she had a good dish of prawns; whereby thou didst desire to eat some ; whereby I told thee they were ill for a green wound ? And didst thou not, when she was gone down stairs, desire me to be no more so familiarity with such poor people; saying, that ere long they should call me madam ? And didst thou not kiss me, and bid me fetch thee thirty shillings ? I put thee now to thy book-oath : deny it, if thou canst." [1]

This scene is to us the most convincing proof of Falstaff's power of gaining over the good-will of those he was familiar with, except indeed Bardolph's somewhat profane exclamation on hearing the account of his death, " Would I were with him, wheresome'er he is, whether in heaven or in hell." [2]

One of the topics of exulting superiority over others most common in Sir John's mouth is his corpulence and the exterior marks of good living which he carries about him, thus " turning his vices into commodity." He accounts for the friendship between the Prince and Poins, from " their legs being both of a bigness ;" and compares Justice Shallow to " a man made after supper of a cheese-paring." There cannot be a more striking gradation of character than that between Falstaff and Shallow, and Shallow and Silence. It seems difficult at first to fall lower than the squire ; but this fool, great as he is, finds an admirer and humble foil in his cousin Silence. Vain

[1 Part II., act ii., sc. 1.]   [2 'Henry V.,' act ii., sc. 3.]

of his acquaintance with Sir John, who makes a butt of him, he exclaims, " Would, cousin Silence, that thou hadst seen that which this knight and I have seen!"—"Ay, Master Shallow, we have heard the chimes at midnight," says Sir John. To Falstaff's observation, "I did not think Master Silence had been a man of this mettle," Silence answers, "Who, I? I have been merry twice and once ere now." What an idea is here conveyed of a prodigality of living! What good husbandry and economical self-denial in his pleasures! What a stock of lively recollections! It is curious that Shakespear has ridiculed in Justice Shallow, who was "in some authority under the king," that disposition to unmeaning tautology which is the regal infirmity of later times, and which, it may be supposed, he acquired from talking to his cousin Silence, and receiving no answers :

" *Falstaff.* 'Fore God, you have here a goodly dwelling and a rich.
Shallow. Barren, barren, barren ; beggars all, beggars all, Sir John : marry, good air. Spread, Davy, spread, Davy. Well said, Davy.
Falstaff. This Davy serves you for good uses.
Shallow. A good varlet, a good varlet, a very good varlet, Sir John. By the mass, I have drank too much sack at supper—a good varlet. Now sit down, now sit down. Come, cousin." [1]

The true spirit of humanity, the thorough knowledge of the stuff we are made of, the practical wisdom with the seeming fooleries in the whole of the garden-scene at Shallow's country-seat, and just before in the exquisite dialogue between him and Silence on the death of old Double, have no parallel anywhere else. In one point of view, they are laughable in the extreme ; in another they are equally affecting, if it is affecting to show *what a little thing is human life*, what a poor forked creature man is!

The heroic and serious part of these two plays founded on the story of Henry IV. is not inferior to the comic and

[1 Part II., act v., sc. 3.]

farcical. The characters of Hotspur and Prince Henry are two of the most beautiful and dramatic, both in themselves and from contrast, that ever were drawn. They are the essence of chivalry. We like Hotspur the best upon the whole, perhaps because he was unfortunate. The characters of their fathers, Henry IV. and old Northumberland, are kept up equally well. Henry naturally succeeds by his prudence and caution in keeping what he has got; Northumberland fails in his enterprise from an excess of the same quality, and is caught in the web of his own cold, dilatory policy. Owen Glendower is a masterly character. It is as bold and original as it is intelligible and thoroughly natural. The disputes between him and Hotspur are managed with infinite address and insight into nature. We cannot help pointing out here some very beautiful lines, where Hotspur describes the fight between Glendower and Mortimer:

> ————" When on the gentle Severn's sedgy bank,
> In single opposition, hand to hand,
> He did confound the best part of an hour
> In changing hardiment with great Glendower :
> Three times they breath'd, and three times did they drink,
> Upon agreement, of swift Severn's flood ;
> Who then, affrighted with their bloody looks,
> Ran fearfully among the trembling reeds,
> And hid his crisp head in the hollow bank,
> Blood-stained with these valiant combatants." [1]

The peculiarity and the excellence of Shakespear's poetry is, that it seems as if he made his imagination the handmaid of nature, and nature the plaything of his imagination. He appears to have been all the characters, and in all the situations he describes. It is as if either he had had all their feelings, or had lent them all his genius to express themselves. There cannot be stronger instances of this than Hotspur's rage when Henry IV. forbids him to speak of Mortimer, his insensibility to all that his

[1] Part I., act i., sc. 3.]

father and uncle urge to calm him, and his fine abstracted
apostrophe to honour, " By heaven methinks it were an
easy leap to pluck bright honour from the moon," &c.
After all, notwithstanding the gallantry, generosity, good
temper, and idle freaks of the madcap Prince of Wales,
we should not have been sorry, if Northumberland's force
had come up in time to decide the fate of the battle at
Shrewsbury ; at least, we always heartily sympathise with
Lady Percy's grief, when she exclaims,

" Had my sweet Harry had but half their numbers,
To-day might I, hanging on Hotspur's neck,
Have talked of Monmouth's grave." [1]

The truth is, that we never could forgive the Prince's
treatment of Falstaff; though perhaps Shakespear knew
what was best, according to the history, the nature of the
times, and of the man. We speak only as dramatic
critics. Whatever terror the French in those days might
have of Henry V., yet, to the readers of poetry at present,
Falstaff is the better man of the two. We think of him
and quote him oftener.

HENRY V.[2]

HENRY V. is a very favourite monarch with the English
nation, and he appears to have been also a favourite with
Shakespear, who labours hard to apologise for the actions
of the king, by showing us the character of the man, as " the
king of good fellows." He scarcely deserves this honour.
He was fond of war and low company ;—we know little

[1] Part II., act ii., sc. 3.]
[2] This drama is supposed to have been written in 1599; it was
printed (very incorrectly) in 1600. There was an older play on
the same subject, entitled ' The Famous Victories of Henry the
Fifth ;' this was first published in 1598, but had been written and
performed more than ten years before.—ED.

else of him. He was careless, dissolute, and ambitious;—
idle, or doing mischief. In private, he seemed to have no
idea of the common decencies of life, which he subjected
to a kind of regal licence; in public affairs, he seemed to
have no idea of any rule of right or wrong, but brute
force, glossed over with a little religious hypocrisy and
archiepiscopal advice. His principles did not change
with his situation and professions. His adventure on
Gadshill was a prelude to the affair of Agincourt, only a
bloodless one; Falstaff was a puny prompter of violence
and outrage, compared with the pious and politic Archbishop of Canterbury, who gave the king *carte blanche*, in
a genealogical tree of his family, to rob and murder in
circles of latitude and longitude abroad—to save the
possessions of the church at home. This appears in the
speeches in Shakespear, where the hidden motives that
actuate princes and their advisers in war and policy are
better laid open than in speeches from the throne or
woolsack. Henry, because he did not know how to
govern his own kingdom, determined to make war upon
his neighbours. Because his own title to the crown was
doubtful, he laid claim to that of France. Because he
did not know how to exercise the enormous power which
had just dropped into his hands, to any one good purpose,
he immediately undertook (a cheap and obvious resource
of sovereignty) to do all the mischief he could. Even if
absolute monarchs had the wit to find out objects of laud-
able ambition, they could only " plume up their wills " in
adhering to the more sacred formula of the royal prerogative, "the right divine of kings to govern wrong,"
because will is only then triumphant when it is opposed
to the will of others, because the pride of power is only
then shown, not when it consults the rights and interests
of others, but when it insults and tramples on all justice
and all humanity. Henry declares his resolution, " France
being ours, we'll bend it to our awe, or break it all to

pieces "[1]—a resolution worthy of a conqueror, to destroy
all that he cannot enslave; and what adds to the joke, he
lays all the blame of the consequences of his ambition on
those who will not submit tamely to his tyranny. Such
is the history of kingly power, from the beginning to the
end of the world;—with this difference, that the object of
war formerly, when the people adhered to their allegiance,
was to depose kings; the object latterly, since the people
swerved from their allegiance, has been to restore kings,
and to make common cause against mankind. The
object of our late invasion and conquest of France was to
restore the legitimate monarch, the descendant of Hugh
Capet, to the throne: Henry V. in his time made war on
and deposed the descendant of this very Hugh Capet, on
the plea that he was a usurper and illegitimate. What
would the great modern catspaw of legitimacy and re-
storer of divine right have said to the claim of Henry and
the title of the descendants of Hugh Capet? Henry V.,
it is true, was a hero, a King of England, and the conqueror of the king of France. Yet we feel little love or
admiration for him. He was a hero, that is, he was
ready to sacrifice his own life for the pleasure of destroying thousands of other lives: he was a king of England,
but not a constitutional one, and we only like kings according to the law; lastly, he was a conqueror of the
French king, and for this we dislike him less than if he
had conquered the French people. How then do we like
him? We like him in the play. There he is a very
amiable monster, a very splendid pageant. As we like to
gaze at a panther or a young lion in their cages in the
Tower, and catch a pleasing horror from their glistening
eyes, their velvet paws, and dreadless roar, so we take a
very romantic, heroic, patriotic, and poetical delight in
the boasts and feats of our younger Harry, as they appear
on the stage and are confined to lines of ten syllables;

[1] Act i., sc. 2.]

where no blood follows the stroke that wounds our ears, where no harvest bends beneath horses' hoofs, no city flames, no little child is butchered, no dead men's bodies are found piled on heaps and festering the next morning —in the orchestra !

So much for the politics of this play ; now for the poetry. Perhaps one of the most striking images in all Shakespear is that given of war in the first lines of the Chorus :

> " O for a muse of fire, that would ascend
>   The brightest heaven of invention,
>   A kingdom for a stage, princes to act,
>   And monarchs to behold the swelling scene !
>   Then should the warlike Harry, like himself,
>   Assume the port of Mars, and *at his heels*
>   *Leash'd in like hounds, should famine, sword, and fire*
>   *Crouch for employment.*"

Rubens, if he had painted it, would not have improved upon this simile.

The conversation between the Archbishop of Canterbury and the Bishop of Ely, relating to the sudden change in the manners of Henry V., is among the well-known *Beauties* of Shakespear. It is indeed admirable both for strength and grace. It has sometimes occurred to us that Shakespear, in describing "the reformation" of the Prince, might have had an eye to himself—

> " Which is a wonder how his grace should glean it,
>   Since his addiction was to courses vain,
>   His companies unletter'd, rude and shallow,
>   His hours fill'd up with riots, banquets, sports;
>   And never noted in him any study,
>   Any retirement, any sequestration
>   From open haunts and popularity.
>   *Ely.* The strawberry grows underneath the nettle,
>   And wholesome berries thrive and ripen best
>   Neighbour'd by fruit of baser quality :
>   And so the prince obscur'd his contemplation
>   Under the veil of wildness, which no doubt

> Grew, like the summer-grass, fastest by night,
> Unseen, yet crescive in his faculty."[1]

This at least is as probable an account of the progress of the poet's mind as we have met with in any of the Essays on the Learning of Shakespear.

Nothing can be better managed than the caution which the king gives the meddling Archbishop, not to advise him rashly to engage in the war with France, his scrupulous dread of the consequences of that advice, and his eager desire to hear and follow it :

> " And God forbid, my dear and faithful lord,
> That you should fashion, wrest, or bow your reading,
> Or nicely charge your understanding soul
> With opening titles miscreate, whose right
> Suits not in native colours with the truth.
> For God doth know how many now in health
> Shall drop their blood in approbation
> Of what your reverence shall incite us to.
> Therefore take heed how you impawn your person,
> How you awake the sleeping sword of war ;
> We charge you in the name of God, take heed.
> For never two such kingdoms did contend
> Without much fall of blood, whose guiltless drops
> Are every one a woe, a sore complaint
> 'Gainst him, whose wrong gives edge unto the sword,
> That makes such waste in brief mortality.
> Under this conjuration, speak, my lord ;
> For we will hear, note, and believe in heart,
> That what you speak, is in your conscience wash'd,
> As pure as sin with baptism." [2]

Another characteristic instance of the blindness of human nature to everything but its own interests, is the complaint made by the king of " the ill neighbourhood " of the Scot in attacking England when she was attacking France.

> " For once the eagle England being in prey,
> To her unguarded nest the weasel Scot
> Comes sneaking, and so sucks her princely eggs." [3]

[1 Act i., sc. 1.]　　　[2 Act i., sc. 2.]　　　[3 *Ibid.*]

It is worth observing that in all these plays, which give an admirable picture of the spirit of the *good old times*, the moral inference does not at all depend upon the nature of the actions, but on the dignity or meanness of the persons committing them. "The eagle England" has a right "to be in prey," but "the weasel Scot" has none "to come sneaking to her nest," which she has left to pounce upon others. Might was right, without equivocation or disguise, in that heroic and chivalrous age. The substitution of right for might, even in theory, is among the refinements and abuses of modern philosophy.

A more beautiful rhetorical delineation of the effects of subordination in a commonwealth can hardly be conceived than the following :—

> "For government, though high, and low, and lower,
>   Put into parts, doth keep in one concent,
>   Congreeing in a full and natural close,
>   Like music.
>   ————— Therefore doth heaven divide
> The state of man in divers functions,
> Setting endeavour in continual motion;
> To which is fixed, as an aim or butt,
> Obedience: for so work the honey-bees,
> Creatures that, by a rule in nature, teach
> The art of order to a peopled kingdom.
> They have a king, and officers of sorts :
> Where some, like magistrates, correct at home;
> Others, like merchants, venture trade abroad;
> Others, like soldiers, armed in their stings,
> Make boot upon the summer's velvet buds;
> Which pillage they with merry march bring home
> To the tent-royal of their emperor;
> Who, busied in his majesty, surveys
> The singing mason building roofs of gold;
> The civil citizens kneading up the honey;
> The poor mechanic porters crowding in
> Their heavy burthens at his narrow gate;
> The sad-eyed justice, with his surly hum,
> Delivering o'er to executors pale
> The lazy yawning drone. I this infer,—

That many things, having full reference
To one concent, may work contrariously:
As many arrows, loosed several ways,
Fly to one mark;
As many several streets meet in one town;
As many fresh streams run in one salt sea;
As many lines close in the dial's centre;
So may a thousand actions, once a-foot,
End in one purpose, and be all well borne
Without defeat." [1]

'Henry V.' is but one of Shakespear's second-rate plays. Yet by quoting passages, like this, from his second-rate plays alone, we might make a volume "rich with his praise :"

" As is the oozy bottom of the sea
With sunken wreck and sumless treasuries."

Of this sort are the king's remonstrance to Scroop, Grey, and Cambridge, on the detection of their treason, his address to the soldiers at the siege of Harfleur, and the still finer one before the battle of Agincourt, the description of the night before the battle, and the reflections on ceremony put into the mouth of the king :

—————" O hard condition,
Twin-born with greatness, subject to the breath
Of every fool, whose sense no more can feel
But his own wringing!
What infinite heart's ease must kings neglect,
That private men enjoy!
And what have kings, that privates have not too,
Save ceremony—save general ceremony?
And what art thou, thou idol ceremony?
What kind of god art thou, that suffer'st more
Of mortal griefs, than do thy worshippers?
What are thy rents? what are thy comings-in?
O ceremony, show me but thy worth!
What is thy soul, O adoration?
Art thou aught else but place, degree, and form,
Creating awe and fear in other men?
Wherein thou art less happy, being feared,

[- Act i., sc. 2.]

Than they in fearing.
What drink'st thou oft, instead of homage sweet,
But poison'd flattery? O, be sick, great greatness,
And bid thy ceremony give thee cure!
Think'st thou, the fiery fever will go out
With titles blown from adulation?
Will it give place to flexure and low bending?
Canst thou, when thou command'st the beggar's knee,
Command the health of it? No, thou proud dream,
That play'st so subtly with a king's repose,
I am a king that find thee: and I know
'Tis not the balm, the sceptre, and the ball,
The sword, the mace, the crown imperial,
The inter-tissu'd robe of gold and pearl,
The farsed title running 'fore the king,
The throne he sits on, nor the tide of pomp
That beats upon the high shore of this world—
No, not all these, thrice-gorgeous ceremony,
Not all these, laid in bed majestical,
Can sleep so soundly as the wretched slave
Who, with a body fill'd and vacant mind,
Gets him to rest, cramm'd with distressful bread,
Never sees horrid night, the child of hell:
But, like a lacquey, from the rise to set,
Sweats in the eye of Phœbus, and all night
Sleeps in Elysium; next day, after dawn,
Doth rise, and help Hyperion to his horse;
And follows so the ever-running year
With profitable labour, to his grave:
And, but for ceremony, such a wretch,
Winding up days with toil and nights with sleep,
Has the fore-hand and vantage of a king.
The slave, a member of the country's peace,
Enjoys it; but in gross brain little wots,
What watch the king keeps to maintain the peace,
Whose hours the peasant best advantages."

Most of these passages are well known: there is one,
which we do not remember to have seen noticed, and yet
it is no whit inferior to the rest in heroic beauty. It is
the account of the deaths of York and Suffolk:

" *Exeter.* The duke of York commends him to your majesty,
   K. Henry. Lives he, good uncle? thrice within this hour

I saw him down; thrice up again, and fighting;
From helmet to the spur all blood he was.
Exeter. In which array (brave soldier) doth he lie,
Larding the plain: and by his bloody side
(Yoke-fellow to his honour-owing wounds)
The noble earl of Suffolk also lies.
Suffolk first died: and York, all haggled o'er,
Comes to him, where in gore he lay insteep'd,
And takes him by the beard: kisses the gashes,
That bloodily did yawn upon his face;
And cries aloud—*Tarry, dear cousin Suffolk!*
My soul shall thine keep company to heaven:
Tarry, sweet soul, for mine, then fly abreast;
As, in this glorious and well-foughten field,
We kept together in our chivalry!
Upon these words I came, and cheer'd him up:
He smil'd me in the face, raught me his hand,
And, with a feeble gripe, says—*Dear my lord,*
Commend my service to my sovereign.
So did he turn, and over Suffolk's neck
He threw his wounded arm, and kiss'd his lips;
And so, espous'd to death, with blood he seal'd
A testament of noble-ending love." [1]

But we must have done with splendid quotations. The
behaviour of the king, in the difficult and doubtful circumstances in which he is placed, is as patient and
modest as it is spirited and lofty in his prosperous
fortune. The character of the French nobles is also
very admirably depicted; and the Dauphin's praise of
his horse shows the vanity of that class of persons in
a very striking point of view. Shakespear always accompanies a foolish prince with a satirical courtier, as
we see in this instance. The comic parts of 'Henry V.'
are very inferior to those of 'Henry IV.' Falstaff is
dead, and without him, Pistol, Nym, and Bardolph are
satellites without a sun. Fluellen the Welchman is the
most entertaining character in the piece. He is good-
natured, brave, choleric, and pedantic. His parallel
between Alexander and Harry of Monmouth, and his

[1 Act iv., sc. 6.]

desire to have "some disputations" with Captain Mac-
morris on the discipline of the Roman wars, in the
heat of the battle, are never to be forgotten. His treatment of Pistol is as good as Pistol's treatment of his
French prisoner. There are two other remarkable prose
passages in this play : the conversation of Henry in disguise with the three sentinels on the duties of a
soldier, and his courtship of Katherine in broken
French. We like them both exceedingly, though the
first savours perhaps too much of the king, and the
last too little of the lover.

HENRY VI.

IN THREE PARTS.[1]

DURING the time of the civil wars of York and Lancaster,
England was a perfect bear-garden, and Shakespear has
given us a very lively picture of the scene. The three
parts of 'Henry VI.' convey a picture of very little else ;
and are inferior to the other historical plays. They have
brilliant passages ; but the general ground-work is comparatively poor and meagre, the style "flat and unraised."
There are few lines like the following :—

> "Glory is like a circle in the water ;
> Which never ceaseth to enlarge itself,
> Till, by broad spreading, it disperse to naught."[2]

The first part relates to the wars in France after the
death of Henry V. and the story of the Maid of Orleans.
She is here almost as scurvily treated as in Voltaire's
Pucelle. Talbot is a very magnificent sketch : there is

---

[1] First printed in the folio of 1623. It seems to be extremely
difficult to arrive at any conclusion as to Shakespear's amount of
participation in the authorship of this tripartite drama, founded on
older plays, which are likewise unidentified with the writers.—ED.

[2 Part I., act i., sc. 2.]

something as formidable in this portrait cf him, as there would be in a monumental figure of him or in the sight of the armour which he wore. The scene in which he visits the Countess of Auvergne, who seeks to entrap him, is a very spirited one, and his description of his own treatment while a prisoner to the French not less remarkable :

" *Salisbury.* Yet tell'st thou not how thou wert entertain'd.
 Talbot. With scoffs and scorns, and contumelious taunts.
In open market-place produced they me,
To be a public spectacle to all.
Here, said they, is the terror of the French,
The scarecrow that affrights our children so.
Then broke I from the officers that led me,
And with my nails digg'd stones out of the ground,
To hurl at the beholders of my shame.
My grisly countenance made others fly,
None durst come near for fear of sudden death.
In iron walls they deem'd me not secure :
So great fear of my name 'mongst them was spread,
That they suppos'd I could rend bars of steel,
And spurn in pieces posts of adamant.
Wherefore a guard of chosen shot I had :
They walk'd about me every minute-while ;
And if I did but stir out of my bed,
Ready they were to shoot me to the heart." [1]

The second part relates chiefly to the contests between the nobles during the minority of Henry, and the death of Gloucester, the good Duke Humphrey. The character of Cardinal Beaufort is the most prominent in the group : the account of his death is one of our author's masterpieces. So is the speech of Gloucester to the nobles on the loss of the provinces of France by the King's marriage with Margaret of Anjou. The pretensions and growing ambition of the Duke of York, the father of Richard III., are also very ably developed. Among the episodes, the tragi-comedy of Jack Cade, and the detection of the impostor Simcox are truly edifying.

The third part describes Henry's loss of his crown : his

[1] Part I., act i., sc. 4.

death takes place in the last act, which is usually thrust
into the common acting play of 'Richard III.' The
character of Gloucester, afterwards King Richard, is here
very powerfully commenced, and his dangerous designs
and long-reaching ambition are fully described in his
soliloquy in the third act, beginning, " Ay, Edward will
use women honourably." Henry VI. is drawn as distinctly as his high-spirited Queen, and notwithstanding
the very mean figure which Henry makes as a King, we
still feel more respect for him than for his wife.

We have already observed that Shakespear was scarcely
more remarkable for the force and marked contrasts of
his characters than for the truth and subtlety with which
he has distinguished those which approached the nearest
to each other.   For instance, the soul of Othello is hardly
more distinct from that of Iago than that of Desdemona is
shown to be from Æmilia's ; the ambition of Macbeth is as
distinct from the ambition of Richard III. as it is from
the meekness as Duncan ; the real madness of Lear is as
different from the feigned madness of Edgar [1] as from the
babbling of the fool ; the contrast between wit and folly
in Falstaff and Shallow is not more characteristic though
more obvious than the gradations of folly, loquacious or
reserved, in Shallow and Silence ; and again, the gallantry
of Prince Henry is as little confounded with that of
Hotspur as with the cowardice of Falstaff, or as the
sensual and philosophic cowardice of the Knight is with
the pitiful and cringing cowardice of Parolles.   All these
several personages were as different in Shakespear as they
would have been in themselves : his imagination borrowed
from the life, and every circumstance, object, motive,
passion, operated there as it would in reality, and produced a world of men and women as distinct, as true and

[1] There is another instance of the same distinction in Hamlet
and Ophelia.   Hamlet's pretended madness would make a very
good real madness in any other author.

as various as those that exist in nature. The peculiar property of Shakespear's imagination was this truth, accompanied with the unconsciousness of nature : indeed, imagination to be perfect must be unconscious, at least in production; for nature is so. We shall attempt one example more in the characters of Richard II. and Henry VI.

The characters and situations of both these persons were so nearly alike, that they would have been completely confounded by a common-place poet. Yet they are kept quite distinct in Shakespear. Both were kings, and both unfortunate. Both lost their crowns owing to their mismanagement and imbecility; the one from a thoughtless wilful abuse of power, the other from an indifference to it. The manner in which they bear their misfortunes corresponds exactly to the causes which led to them. The one is always lamenting the loss of his power which he has not the spirit to regain ; the other seems only to regret that he had ever been king, and is glad to be rid of the power, with the trouble; the effeminacy of the one is that of a voluptuary, proud, revengeful, impatient of contradiction, and inconsolable in his misfortunes; the effeminacy of the other is that of an indolent, good-natured mind, naturally averse to the turmoils of ambition and the cares of greatness, and who wishes to pass his time in monkish indolence and contemplation. Richard bewails the loss of the kingly power only as it was the means of gratifying his pride and luxury ; Henry regards it only as a means of doing right, and is less desirous of the advantages to be derived from possessing it than afraid of exercising it wrong. In knighting a young soldier, he gives him ghostly advice —

> " Edward Plantagenet, arise a knight,
> And learn this lesson—draw thy sword in right."[1]

Richard II. in the first speeches of the play betrays his

[1 Part III., act ii., sc. 2.]

real character.   In the first alarm of his pride, on hearing
of Bolingbroke's rebellion, before his presumption has met
with any check, he exclaims—

> " Mock not my senseless conjuration. lords :
> This earth shall have a feeling, and these stones
> Prove armed soldiers, ere her native king
> Shall falter under proud rebellion's arms.
>   *   *   *   *   *
> Not all the water in the rough rude sea
> Can wash the balm from an anointed king ;
> The breath of worldly men cannot depose
> The deputy elected by the Lord.
> For every man that Bolingbroke hath press'd,
> To lift shrewd steel against our golden crown,
> Heaven for his Richard hath in heavenly pay
> A glorious angel ; then, if angels fight,
> Weak men must fall ; for heaven still guards the right." [1]

Yet, notwithstanding this royal confession of faith, on
the very first news of actual disaster, all his conceit of
himself as the peculiar favourite of Providence vanishes
into air :

> " But now the blood of twenty thousand men
>   Did triumph in my face, and they are fled. . . .
> All souls that will be safe fly from my side ;
>   For time hath set a blot upon my pride." [2]

Immediately after, however, recollecting that " cheap
defence " of the divinity of kings which is to be found in
opinion, he is for arming his name against his enemies :

> " Awake, thou sluggard majesty, thou sleep'st ;
> Is not the King's name forty thousand names ?
> Arm, arm, my name : a puny subject strikes
> At thy great glory—" [3]

King Henry does not make any such vapouring resistance to the loss of his crown, but lets it slip from off his
head as a weight which he is neither able nor willing to
bear ; stands quietly by to see the issue of the contest for
his kingdom, as if it were a game at push-pin, and is
pleased when the odds prove against him.

[1 ' Richard II.,' act iii., sc. 2.   [2 *Ibid.*]   [3 *Ibid.*]

When Richard first hears of the death of his favourites, Bushy, Bagot, and the rest, he indignantly rejects all idea of any further efforts, and only indulges in the extravagant impatience of his grief and his despair, in that fine speech which has been so often quoted :—

> " *Aumerle.* Where is the duke my father with his power ?
>   *K. Richard.* No matter where : of comfort no man speak:
> Let's talk of graves, of worms, and epitaphs,
> Make dust our paper, and with rainy eyes
> Write sorrow on the bosom of the earth !
> Let's choose executors, and talk of wills :
> And yet not so—for what can we bequeath,
> Save our deposed bodies to the ground ?
> Our lands, our lives, and all are Bolingbroke's,
> And nothing can we call our own but death,
> And that small model of the barren earth,
> Which serves as paste and cover to our bones.
> For God's sake, let us sit upon the ground,
> And tell sad stories of the death of kings :
> How some have been depos'd, some slain in war ;
> Some haunted by the ghosts they have depos'd ;
> Some poison'd by their wives, some sleeping kill'd ;
> All murder'd :—for within the hollow crown,
> That rounds the mortal temples of a king,
> Keeps Death his court : and there the antic sits,
> Scoffing his state, and grinning at his pomp ;
> Allowing him a breath, a little scene
> To monarchize, be fear'd, and kill with looks ;
> Infusing him with self and vain conceit—
> As if this flesh, which walls about our life,
> Were brass impregnable ; and humour'd thus,
> Comes at the last, and with a little pin
> Bores through his castle wall, and—farewell king !
> Cover your heads, and mock not flesh and blood
> With solemn reverence ; throw away respect,
> Tradition, form, and ceremonious duty,
> For you have but mistook me all this while :
> I live on bread like you, feel want, taste grief,
> Need friends, like you ;—subjected thus,
> How can you say to me—I am a king ?"[1]

There is as little sincerity afterwards in his affected

[1 'Richard II.,' act ii., sc. 2.]

resignation to his fate, as there is fortitude in this exaggerated picture of his misfortunes before they have happened.

When Northumberland comes back with the message from Bolingbroke, he exclaims, anticipating the result:

> " What must the king do now?   Must he submit?
> The king shall do it: must he be depos'd?
> The king shall be contented: must he lose
> The name of king?   O' God's name let it go.
> I'll give my jewels for a set of beads;
> My gorgeous palace for a hermitage;
> My gay apparel for an alms-man's gown;
> My figur'd goblets for a dish of wood;
> My sceptre for a palmer's walking staff;
> My subjects for a pair of carved saints;
> And my large kingdom for a little grave—
> A little little grave, an obscure grave." [1]

How differently is all this expressed in King Henry's soliloquy, during the battle with Edward's party:—

> " This battle fares like to the morning's war,
> When dying clouds contend with growing light,
> What time the shepherd, blowing of his nails,
> Can neither call it perfect day nor night. . . . .
> Here on this mole-hill will I sit me down;
> To whom God will, there be the victory!
> For Margaret my Queen and Clifford too
> Have chid me from the battle, swearing both
> They prosper best of all, when I am thence.
> Would I were dead, if God's good will were so
> For what is in this world but grief and woe?
> O God! methinks it were a happy life
> To be no better than a homely swain,
> To sit upon a hill as I do now,
> To carve out dials quaintly, point by point,
> Thereby to see the minutes how they run:
> How many make the hour full complete,
> How many hours bring about the day,
> How many days will finish up the year,
> How many years a mortal man may live.

[1 ' Richard II.,' act iii., sc. 3.]

When this is known, then to divide the times:
So many hours must I tend my flock,
So many hours must I take my rest,
So many hours must I contemplate,
So many hours must I sport myself ;
So many days my ewes have been with young,
So many weeks ere the poor fools will yean,
So many months ere I shall shear the fleece :
So many minutes, hours, weeks, months, and years
Pass'd over to the end they were created,
Would bring white hairs unto a quiet grave.
Ah ! what a life were this ! how sweet, how lovely !
Gives not the hawthorn bush a sweeter shade
To shepherds looking on their silly sheep,
Than doth a rich-embroider'd canopy
To kings that fear their subjects' treachery ?
O yes, it doth, a thousandfold it doth.
And to conclude, the shepherds' homely curds,
His cold thin drink out of his leather bottle,
His wonted sleep under a fresh tree's shade,
All which secure and sweetly he enjoys,
Is far beyond a prince's delicates,
His viands sparkling in a golden cup,
His body couched in a curious bed,
When care, mistrust, and treasons wait on him."[1]

This is a true and beautiful description of a naturally quiet and contented disposition, and not, like the former, the splenetic effusion of disappointed ambition.

In the last scene of ' Richard II.' his despair lends him courage : he beats the keeper, slays two of his assassins, and dies with imprecations in his mouth against Sir Pierce Exton, who "had staggered his royal person." Henry, when he is seized by the deer-stealers, only reads them a moral lecture on the duty of allegiance and the sanctity of an oath ; and when stabbed by Gloucester in the Tower, reproaches him with his crimes, but pardons him his own death.

[[1] ' Henry VI.,' Part III., act ii., sc. 5.]

RICHARD III.[1]

' RICHARD III.' may be considered as properly a stage-play:
it belongs to the theatre, rather than to the closet. We
shall therefore criticise it chiefly with a reference to the
manner in which we have seen it performed. It is the
character in which Garrick came out: it was the second
character in which Mr. Kean appeared, and in which he
acquired his fame. Shakespear we have always with us:
actors we have only for a few seasons; and therefore some
account of them may be acceptable, if not to our cotem-
poraries, to those who come after us, if " that rich and idle
personage, Posterity," should deign to look into our
writings.

It is possible to form a higher conception of the character of Richard than that given by Mr. Kean: but we
cannot imagine any character represented with greater
distinctness and precision, more perfectly *articulated* in
every part. Perhaps indeed there is too much of what is
technically called execution. When we first saw this
celebrated actor in the part,[2] we thought he sometimes
failed from an exuberance of manner, and dissipated the
impression of the general character by the variety of his
resources. To be complete, his delineation of it should
have more solidity, depth, sustained and impassioned feeling, with somewhat less brilliancy, with fewer glancing
lights, pointed transitions, and pantomimic evolutions.[3]

[1] First printed in 1597, about which date it seems to have been
composed. In the folio of 1623 it is republished with a very varying
text.—ED.

[2] February 15, 1814.—ED.

[3] See, for fuller particulars on this part of the subject, ' View of
the English Stage,' 1821, pp. 5–13.—ED.

The Richard of Shakespear is towering and lofty; equally impetuous and commanding; haughty, violent, and subtle; bold and treacherous; confident in his strength as well as in his cunning; raised high by his birth, and higher by his talents and his crimes; a royal usurper, a princely hypocrite, a tyrant, and a murderer of the house of Plantagenet:

> ————"But I was born so high:
> Our aery buildeth in the cedar's top,
> And dallies with the wind, and scorns the sun." [1]

The idea conveyed in these lines (which are indeed omitted in the miserable medley acted for 'Richard III.') is never lost sight of by Shakespear, and should not be out of the actor's mind for a moment. The restless and sanguinary Richard is not a man striving to be great, but to be greater than he is; conscious of his strength of will, his power of intellect, his daring courage, his elevated station; and making use of these advantages to commit unheard-of crimes, and to shield himself from remorse and infamy.

If Mr. Kean does not entirely succeed in concentrating all the lines of the character, as drawn by Shakespear, he gives an animation, vigour, and relief to the part which we have not seen equalled. He is more refined than Cooke; more bold, varied, and original than Kemble in the same character. In some parts he is deficient in dignity, and particularly in the scenes of state business, he has by no means an air of artificial authority. There is at times an aspiring elevation, an enthusiastic rapture in his expectations of attaining the crown, and at others a gloating expression of sullen delight, as if he already clenched the bauble, and held it in his grasp. The court-ship scene with Lady Anne is an admirable exhibition of smooth and smiling villainy. The progress of wily adulation, of encroaching humility, is finely marked by his

[1 Act i., sc. 3.]

action, voice, and eye. He seems, like the first Tempter, to approach his prey, secure of the event, and as if success had smoothed his way before him. The late Mr. Cooke's manner of representing this scene was more vehement, hurried, and full of anxious uncertainty.[1] This, though more natural in general, was less in character in this particular instance. Richard should woo less as a lover than as an actor—to show his mental superiority, and power of making others the playthings of his purposes. Mr. Kean's attitude in leaning against the side of the stage before he comes forward to address Lady Anne, is one of the most graceful and striking ever witnessed on the stage. It would do for Titian to paint. The frequent and rapid transition of his voice from the expression of the fiercest passion to the most familiar tones of conversation was that which gave a peculiar grace of novelty to his acting on his first appearance. This has been since imitated and caricatured by others, and he himself uses the artifice more sparingly than he did. His byplay is excellent. His manner of bidding his friends " Good-night," after pausing with the point of his sword, drawn slowly backward and forward on the ground, as if considering the plan of the battle next day, is a particularly happy and natural thought. He gives to the two last acts of the play the greatest animation and effect. He fills every part of the stage ; and makes up for the deficiency of his person by what has been sometimes objected to as an excess of action. The concluding scene, in which he is killed by Richmond, is the most brilliant of the whole. He fights at last like one drunk with wounds; and the

---

[1] The writer may have seen George Frederick Cooke perform in ' Richard III.,' Sept. 20, 1809, at Covent Garden. He also filled the parts of *Falstaff* and *Sir John Restless* in ' A New Way to pay Old Debts.' See Geneste, viii., 178, *et seqq.* Cooke died, I believe, at New York, in 1821, in extreme distress. See a singular letter respecting him in ' Memoirs of William Hazlitt,' 1867, ii., 1.--ED.

attitude in which he stands with his hands stretched out, after his sword is wrested from him, has a preternatural and terrific grandeur, as if his will could not be disarmed, and the very phantoms of his despair had power to kill. Mr. Kean has since in a great measure effaced the impression of his Richard III. by the superior efforts of his genius in Othello (his master-piece), in the murder-scene in Macbeth, in Richard II., in Sir Giles Overreach, and lastly in Oroonoko; but we still like to look back to his first performance of this part, both because it first assured his admirers of his future success, and because we bore our feeble but, at that time, not useless testimony to the merits of this very original actor, on which the town was considerably divided for no other reason than because they *were* original.

The manner in which Shakespear's plays have been generally altered or rather mangled by modern mechanists is a disgrace to the English stage. The patch-work 'Richard III.,' which is acted under the sanction of his name, and which was manufactured by Cibber, is a striking example of this remark.

The play itself is undoubtedly a very powerful effusion of Shakespear's genius. The ground-work of the character of Richard—that mixture of intellectual vigour with moral depravity, in which Shakespear delighted to show his strength—gave full scope as well as temptation to the exercise of his imagination. The character of his hero is almost everywhere predominant, and marks his lurid track throughout. The original play is however too long for representation, and there are some few scenes which might be better spared than preserved, and by omitting which it would remain a complete whole. The only rule, indeed, for altering Shakespear is to retrench certain passages which may be considered either as superfluous or obsolete, but not to add or transpose anything. The arrangement and development of the story, and the mutual contrast and combination of the *dramatis personæ*, are in general as finely managed as the development of the characters or the expression of the passions.

This rule has not been adhered to in the present instance. Some of the most important and striking passages in the principal character have been omitted, to make room for idle and misplaced extracts from other plays; the only intention of which seems to have been to make the character of Richard as odious and disgusting as possible. It is apparently for no other purpose than to make Gloucester stab King Henry on the stage, that the fine abrupt introduction of the character in the opening of the play is lost in the tedious whining morality of the uxorious king (taken from another play);—we say *tedious*, because it interrupts the business of the scene, and loses its beauty and effect by having no intelligible connection with the previous character of the mild, well-meaning monarch. The passages which the unfortunate Henry has to recite are beautiful and pathetic in themselves, but they have nothing to do with the world that Richard has to " bustle in." In the same spirit of vulgar caricature is the scene between Richard and Lady Anne (when his wife) interpolated without any authority, merely to gratify this favourite propensity to disgust and loathing. With the same perverse consistency, Richard, after his last fatal struggle, is raised up by some galvanic process, to utter the imprecation, without any motive but pure malignity, which Shakespear has so properly put into the mouth of Northumberland on hearing of Percy's death. To make room for these worse than needless additions, many of the most striking passages in the real play have been omitted by the foppery and ignorance of the prompt-book critics. We do not mean to insist merely on passages which are fine as poetry and to the reader, such as Clarence's dream, &c., but on those which are important to the understanding of the character, and peculiarly sdapted for stage effect. We will give the following as instances among several others. The first is the scene where Richard enters abruptly to the Queen and her friends to defend himself:—

> " *Gloucester.* They do me wrong, and I will not endure it.
> Who are they that complain unto the king,
> That I forsooth am stern, and love them not?
> By holy Paul, they love his grace but lightly,
> That fill his ears with such dissentious rumours:
> Because I cannot flatter and speak fair,
> Smile in men's faces, smooth, deceive, and cog,
> Duck with French nods and apish courtesy,
> I must be held a rancorous enemy.
> Cannot a plain man live, and think no harm,
> But thus his simple truth must be abus'd
> By silken, sly, insinuating Jacks?
>   *Gray.* To whom in all this presence speaks your grace?
>   *Gloucester.* To thee, that hast nor honesty nor grace;
> When have I injur'd thee? when done thee wrong?
> Or thee? or thee? or any of your faction?
> A plague upon you all!" [1]

Nothing can be more characteristic than the turbulent pretensions to meekness and simplicity in this address. Again, the versatility and adroitness of Richard is admirably described in the following ironical conversation with Brakenbury :—

> " *Brakenbury.* Beseech your graces both to pardon me.
> His majesty hath straitly given in charge,
> That no man shall have private conference,
> Of what degree soever, with your brother.
>   *Gloucester.* Even so, and please your worship, Brakenbury,
> You may partake of anything we say:
> We speak no treason, man—we say the king
> Is wise and virtuous, and his noble queen
> Well struck in years, fair, and not jealous.
> We say that Shore's wife hath a pretty foot,
> A cherry lip, a bonny eye, a passing pleasing tongue;
> And that the queen's kindred are made gentlefolks.
> How say you, sir? Can you deny all this?

---

[1] Act I., sc. 3.

> *Brakenbury.* With this, my lord, myself have nought to do.
> *Gloucester.* Naught to do with Mistress Shore? I tell thee,
>   fellow;
> He that doth naught with her, excepting one,
> Were best to do it secretly alone.
> *Brakenbury.* What one, my lord?
> *Gloucester.* Her husband, knave—would'st thou betray me?"[1]

The feigned reconciliation of Gloucester with the
Queen's kinsmen is also a master-piece. One of the finest
strokes in the play, and which serves to show as much as
anything the deep, plausible manners of Richard, is the
unsuspecting security of Hastings, at the very time when
the former is plotting his death, and when that very
appearance of cordiality and good-humour on which
Hastings builds his confidence arises from Richard's
consciousness of having betrayed him to his ruin. This,
with the whole character of Hastings, is omitted.

Perhaps the two most beautiful passages in the original
play are the farewell apostrophe of the Queen to the
Tower, where the children are shut up from her, and
Tyrrel's description of their death. We will finish our
quotations with them:

> " *Queen.* Stay, yet look back with me unto the Tower;
> Pity, you ancient stones, those tender babes,
> Whom envy hath immured within your walls;
> Rough cradle for such little pretty ones,
> Rude, rugged nurse, old sullen playfellow,
> For tender princes—"[2]

The other passage is the account of their death by
Tyrrel:—

> " Dighton and Forrest, whom I did suborn
> To do this ruthless piece of butchery,
> Albeit they were flesh'd villains, bloody dogs,—
> Melting with tenderness and mild compassion,
> Wept like two children in their death's sad story:
> O, thus! quoth Dighton, lay the gentle babes,
> Thus, thus, quoth Forrest, girdling one another

[1 Act i., sc. 1.]   [2 Act iv., sc. 1.]

Within their innocent alabaster arms;
Their lips were four red roses on a stalk,
And in their summer beauty kiss'd each other;
A book of prayers on their pillow lay,
Which once, quoth Forrest, almost changed my mind;
But O the devil!—there the villain stopped;
When Dighton thus told on—we smothered
The most replenished sweet work of nature,
That from the prime creation e'er she fram'd."

These are some of those wonderful bursts of feeling, done to the life, to the very height of fancy and nature, which our Shakespear alone could give. We do not insist on the repetition of these last passages as proper for the stage: we should indeed be loth to trust them in the mouth of almost any actor; but we should wish them to be retained in preference at least to the fantoccini exhibition of the young princes, Edward and York, bandying childish wit with their uncle.

HENRY VIII.[1]

THIS play contains little action or violence of passion, yet it has considerable interest of a more mild and thoughtful cast, and some of the most striking passages in the author's works. The character of Queen Katherine is the most perfect delineation of matronly dignity, sweetness, and resignation that can be conceived. Her appeals to the protection of the king, her remonstrances to the cardinals, her conversations with her women, show a noble and

[1] First printed in the folio of 1623. It is supposed to have been written after the death of Queen Elizabeth; but the precise date is not known. An historical play on the reign of Henry VIII., by Samuel Rowley, was published in 1605. The latter is, beyond reasonable doubt, the play entered at Stationers' Hall, Feb. 12, 1604–5, and not Shakespear's piece, as Mr. Collier appears to think.—ED.

generous spirit accompanied with the utmost gentleness
of nature. What can be more affecting than her answer
to Campeius and Wolsey, who come to visit her as pre-
\tended friends.

> ————————" Nay, forsooth, my friends,
> They that must weigh out my afflictions,
> They that my trust must grow to, live not here;
> They are, as all my comforts are, far hence,
> In mine own country, lords." [1]

Dr. Johnson observes of this play, that " the meek sorrows and virtuous distress of Katherine have furnished
some scenes, which may be justly numbered among the
greatest efforts of tragedy. But the genius of Shakespear
comes in and goes out with Katherine. Every other part
may be easily conceived and easily written." This is
easily said; but with all due deference to so great a
reputed authority as that of Johnson, it is not true. For
instance, the scene of Buckingham led to execution is one
of the most affecting and natural in Shakespear, and one
to which there is hardly an approach in any other author.
Again, the character of Wolsey,[2] the description of his
pride and of his fall, are inimitable, and have, besides
their gorgeousness of effect, a pathos, which only the
genius of Shakespear could lend to the distresses of a
proud, bad man, like Wolsey. There is a sort of child-
like simplicity in the very helplessness of his situation,
arising from the recollection of his past overbearing ambition. After the cutting sarcasms of his enemies on his
disgrace, against which he bears up with a spirit conscious
of his own superiority, he breaks out into that fine apostrophe—

[1 Act iii., sc. 1.]

2 Possibly Shakespear may have seen an earlier drama in two
parts, performed in 1601–2, but apparently (in some shape or other)
in existence even before that date, in which Wolsey was the foremost character. See Halliwell's ' Dict. of Old Plays,' 18⁶⁹, in v.—
ED.

" Farewell, a long farewell, to all my greatness !
This is the state of man : to-day he puts forth
The tender leaves of hope, to-morrow blossoms,
And bears his blushing honours thick upon him;
The third day comes a frost, a killing frost;
And—when he thinks, good easy man, full surely
His greatness is a-ripening—nips his root,
And then he falls, as I do. I have ventur'd,
Like little wanton boys that swim on bladders,
These many summers in a sea of glory;
But far beyond my depth : my high-blown pride
At length broke under me; and now has left me,
Weary and old with service, to the mercy
Of a rude stream, that must for ever hide me.
Vain pomp and glory of the world, I hate ye:
I feel my heart new open'd.   O how wretched
Is that poor man, that hangs on princes' favours !
There is betwixt that smile we would aspire to,
That sweet aspect of princes, and their ruin,
More pangs and fears than wars or women have ;
And when he falls, he falls like Lucifer,
Never to hope again !"—[1]

There is in this passage, as well as in the well-known
dialogue with Cromwell which follows, something which
stretches beyond commonplace; nor is the account which
Griffith gives of Wolsey's death less Shakespearian ; and
the candour with which Queen Katherine listens to the
praise of " him whom I most hated living "[2] adds the last
graceful finishing to her character.

Among other images of great individual beauty might
be mentioned the description of the effect of Ann Boleyn's
presenting herself to the crowd at her coronation :

————" While her grace sat down
To rest awhile, some half an hour or so,
In a rich chair of state, opposing freely
The beauty of her person to the people.
Believe me, sir, she is the goodliest woman
That ever lay by man: which when the people
Had the full view of, *such a noise arose*

[1 Act iii., sc. 2.]   [2 Act iv., sc. 2.]

As the shrouds make at sea in a stiff tempest,
As loud and to as many tunes —" [1]

The character of Henry VIII. is drawn with great truth
and spirit. It is like a very disagreeable portrait, sketched
by the hand of a master. His gross appearance, his blustering demeanour, his vulgarity, his arrogance, his sensuality, his cruelty, his hypocrisy, his want of common
decency and common humanity, are marked in strong
lines. His traditional peculiarities of expression complete
the reality of the picture. The authoritative expletive,
" Ha!" with which he intimates his indignation or surprise, has an effect like the first startling sound that breaks
from a thunder-cloud. He is of all the monarchs in our
history the most disgusting : for he unites in himself all
the vices of barbarism and refinement, without their virtues. Other kings before him (such as Richard III.) were
tyrants and murderers out of ambition or necessity : they
gained or established unjust power by violent means :
they destroyed their enemies, or those who barred their
access to the throne, or made its tenure insecure. But
Henry VIII.'s power is most fatal to those whom he loves :
he is cruel and remorseless to pamper his luxurious appetites : bloody and voluptuous; an amorous murderer; an
uxorious debauchee. His hardened insensibility to the
feelings of others is strengthened by the most profligate
self-indulgence. The religious hypocrisy under which he
masks his cruelty and his lust, is admirably displayed in
the speech in which he describes the first misgivings of
his conscience and its increasing throes and terrors, which
have induced him to divorce his queen. The only thing
in his favour in this play is his treatment of Cranmer :
there is also another circumstance in his favour, which is
his patronage of Hans Holbein.—It has been said of
Shakespear—" No maid could live near such a man." It
might with as good reason be said—" No king could live

[1 Act iv., sc. 1.]

near such a man." His eye would have penetrated through the pomp of circumstance and the veil of opinion. As it is, he has represented such persons to the life—his plays are in this respect the glass of history—he has done them the same justice as if he had been a privy councillor all his life, and in each successive reign. Kings ought never to be seen upon the stage. In the abstract, they are very disagreeable characters; it is only while living that they are "the best of kings." It is their power, their splendour, it is the apprehension of the personal consequences of their favour or their hatred that dazzles the imagination and suspends the judgment of their favourites or their vassals; but death cancels the bond of allegiance and of interest; and seen *as they were*, their power and their pretensions look monstrous and ridiculous. The charge brought against modern philosophy as inimical to loyalty is unjust, because it might as well be brought against other things. No reader of history can be a lover of kings. We have often wondered that Henry VIII. as he is drawn by Shakespear, and as we have seen him represented in all the bloated deformity of mind and person, is not hooted from the English stage.

———◦◦◦———

KING JOHN.[1]

'King John' is the last of the historical plays we shall have to speak of; and we are not sorry that it is. If we are to indulge our imaginations, we had rather do it upon an imaginary theme; if we are to find subjects for the exercise of our pity and terror, we prefer seeking them in fictitious danger and fictitious distress. It gives a *soreness*

[1] First printed in the folio of 1623. It is founded on an anonymous drama entitled 'The Troublesome Reign of John, King of England,' first published in 1591. Shakespear's play is mentioned by Meres in his 'Palladis Tamia,' 1598.—Ed.

to our feelings of indignation or sympathy, when we know that in tracing the progress of sufferings and crimes, we are treading upon real ground, and recollect that the poet's dream *"denoted a foregone conclusion"*—irrevocable ills, not conjured up by fancy, but placed beyond the reach of poetical justice. That the treachery of King John, the death of Arthur, the grief of Constance, had a real truth in history, sharpens the sense of pain, while it hangs a leaden weight on the heart and the imagination. Something whispers us that we have no right to make a mock of calamities like these, or to turn the truth of things into the puppet and plaything of our fancies. "To consider thus" may be " to consider too curiously;" but still we think that the actual truth of the particular events, in proportion as we are conscious of it, is a drawback on the pleasure as well as the dignity of tragedy.

'King John' has all the beauties of language and all the richness of the imagination to relieve the painfulness of the subject. The character of King John himself is kept pretty much in the background; it is only marked in by comparatively slight indications. The crimes he is tempted to commit are such as are thrust upon him rather by circumstances and opportunity than of his own seeking: he is here represented as more cowardly than cruel, and as more contemptible than odious. The play embraces only a part of his history. There are, however, few characters on the stage that excite more disgust and loathing. He has no intellectual grandeur or strength of character to shield him from the indignation which his immediate conduct provokes: he stands naked and defenceless, in that respect, to the worst we can think of him: and besides, we are impelled to put the very worst construction on his meanness and cruelty by the tender picture of the beauty and helplessness of the object of it, as well as by the frantic and heartrending pleadings of maternal despair. We do not forgive him the death of Arthur, because he had too late revoked his doom and tried to prevent it; and perhaps because he has himself repented of his black design, our *moral sense* gains courage to hate him the more for it. We take him at his word, and think his purposes must be odious indeed, when he himself shrinks back from them. The scene in which King John suggests to Hubert the design of murdering his nephew is a master-piece of dramatic skill, but it is still inferior— very inferior—to the scene between Hubert and Arthur, when the latter learns the orders to put out his eyes. If anything ever was penned, heart-piercing, mixing the extremes of terror and pity, of that which shocks and that which soothes the mind, it is this scene. We will give it entire, though perhaps it is tasking the reader's sympathy too much : —

"*Enter* HUBERT *and two Attendants.*

Hubert. Heat me these irons hot, and look you stand
Within the arras; when I strike my foot
Upon the bosom of the ground, rush forth
And bind the boy, which you shall find with me,
Fast to the chair : be heedful : hence, and watch.
  First Attend. I hope your warrant will bear out the deed.
  Hubert. Uncleanly scruples! fear not you; look to't.—
                          [*Exeunt Attendants.*
Young lad, come forth; I have to say with you.

Enter ARTHUR.

Arthur. Good morrow, Hubert.
Hubert. Good morrow, little Prince.
Arthur. As little prince, having so great a title
To be more prince, as may be. You are sad.
Hubert. Indeed I have been merrier.
Arthur.   Mercy on me'
Methinks nobody should be sad but I :
Yet I remember when I was in France,
Young gentlemen would be as sad as night,
Only for wantonness. By my christendom,
So I were out of prison, and kept sheep,
I should be merry as the day is long.
And so I would be here, but that I doubt
My uncle practises more harm to me.

He is afraid of me, and I of him.
Is it my fault that I was Geffrey's son?
Indeed it is not, and I would to heav'n
I were your son, so you would love me, Hubert.

Hubert. [*Aside.*] If I talk to him, with his innocent prate
He will awake my mercy, which lies dead;
Therefore I will be sudden, and dispatch.

Arthur. Are you sick, Hubert? you look pale to-day?
In sooth, I would you were a little sick,
That I might sit all night and watch with you.
Alas, I love you more than you do me.

Hubert. [*Aside.*] His words do take possession of my bosom.
Read here, young Arthur. [*Showing a paper.*—How now, foolish
rheum!
Turning dis-piteous torture out of door!
I must be brief, lest resolution drop
Out at mine eyes in tender womanish tears.—
Can you not read it? is it not fair writ?

Arthur. Too fairly, Hubert, for so foul effect:
Must you with irons burn out both mine eyes?

Hubert. Young boy, I must.

Arthur.   And will you?

Hubert.   And I will.

Arthur. Have you the heart? When your head did but ache,
I knit my handkerchief about your brows
(The best I had, a princess wrought it me),
And I did never ask it you again;
And with my hand at midnight held your head;
And like the watchful minutes to the hour,
Still and anon cheer'd up the heavy time,
Saying, What lack you? and, Where lies your grief?
Or, What good love may I perform for you?
Many a poor man's son would have lien still,
And ne'er have spoke a loving word to you;
But you at your sick service had a prince.
Nay, you may think my love was crafty love,
And call it cunning:—do, and if you will:
If heaven be pleased that you must use me ill,
Why then you must——Will you put out mine eyes?
These eyes that never did, nor never shall,
So much as frown on you?

Hubert.   I've sworn to do it;
And with hot irons must I burn them out.

Arthur. Ah, none but in this iron age would do it!

The iron of itself, though heat[ed] red-hot,
Approaching near these eyes, would drink my tears,
And quench his fiery indignation
Even in the water of mine innocence ;
Nay, after that consume away in rust,
But for containing fire to harm mine eyes.
Are you more stubborn-hard than hammer'd iron?
An if an angel should have come to me,
And told me Hubert should put out mine eyes,
I would not have believ'd him,—no tongue but Hubert's.

 Hubert. Come forth.   [*Stamps*

   Re-enter Attendants with cord, irons, &c.

Do as I bid you.

 Arthur. O save me, Hubert, save me ! my eyes are out
Even with the fierce looks of these bloody men.

 Hubert. Give me the iron, I say, and bind him here.

 Arthur. Alas, what need you be so boisterous-rough?
I will not struggle, I will stand stone-still.
For heaven-sake, Hubert, let me not be bound !
Nay, hear me, Hubert ! drive these men away,
And I will sit as quiet as a lamb ;
I will not stir, nor wince, nor speak a word,
Nor look upon the iron angerly ;
Thrust but these men away, and I'll forgive you,
Whatever torment you do put me to.

 Hubert. Go, stand within ; let me alone with him.

 First Attend. I am best pleas'd to be from such a deed.

            [*Exeunt*

 Arthur. Alas, I then have chid away my friend.
He hath a stern look, but a gentle heart;
Let him come back, that his compassion may
Give life to yours.

 Hubert.   Come, boy, prepare yourself.

 Arthur. Is there no remedy?

 Hubert.   None, but to lose your eyes.

 Arthur. O heaven ! that there were but a mote in yours,
A grain, a dust, a gnat, a wandering hair,
Any annoyance in that precious sense !
Then, feeling what small things are boisterous there,
Your vile intent must needs seem horrible.

 Hubert. Is this your promise? go to, hold your tongue.

 Arthur. Hubert, the utterance of a brace of tongues
Must needs want pleading for a pair of eyes :
Let me not hold my tongue;—let me not Hubert;

Or, Hubert, if you will, cut out my tongue,
So I may keep mine eyes: O, spare mine eyes!
Though to no use but still to look on you.
Lo, by my troth, the instrument is cold,
And would not harm me.
    Hubert.   I can heat it, boy.
    Arthur. No, in good sooth, the fire is dead with grief,
Being create for comfort, to be us'd
In undeserv'd extremes; see else yourself;
There is no malice in this burning coal;
The breath of heaven hath blown his spirit out,
And strew'd repentant ashes on his head.
    Hubert. But with my breath I can revive it, boy.
    Arthur. And if you do, you will but make it blush,
And glow with shame of your proceedings, Hubert:
Nay, it perchance will sparkle in your eyes,
And, like a dog that is compell'd to fight,
Snatch at his master that doth tarre him on.
All things that you should use to do me wrong,
Deny their office; only you do lack
That mercy which fierce fire and iron extend,
Creatures of note for mercy-lacking uses.
    Hubert. Well, see to live; I will not touch thine eyes
For all the treasure that thine uncle owes:
Yet I am sworn, and I did purpose, boy,
With this same very iron to burn them out.
    Arthur. O, now you look like Hubert. All this while
You were disguised.
    Hubert.   Peace; no more. Adieu,
Your uncle must not know but you are dead.
I'll fill these dogged spies with false reports:
And, pretty child, sleep doubtless and secure,
That Hubert, for the wealth of all the world,
Will not offend thee.
    Arthur.   O heaven! I thank you, Hubert.
    Hubert. Silence, no more; go closely in with me;
Much danger do I undergo for thee.   *[Exeunt.*"

His death afterwards, when he throws himself from his
prison walls, excites the utmost pity for his innocence
and friendless situation, and well justifies the exaggerated
denunciations of Falconbridge to Hubert, whom he suspects wrongfully of the deed:

[¹ Act iv., sc. 1.]

> " There is not yet so ugly a fiend of hell
> As thou shalt be, if thou didst kill this child.
> —If thou didst but consent
> To this most cruel act, do but despair :
> And if thou want'st a cord, the smallest thread
> That ever spider twisted from her womb
> Will serve to strangle thee ; a rush will be a beam
> To hang thee on ; or would'st thou drown thyself,
> Put but a little water in a spoon,
> And it shall be as all the ocean,
> Enough to stifle such a villain up."[1]

The excess of maternal tenderness, rendered desperate by the fickleness of friends and the injustice of fortune, and made stronger in will, in proportion to the want of all other power, was never more finely expressed than in Constance. The dignity of her answer to King Philip, when she refuses to accompany his messenger, " To me and to the state of my great grief, let kings assemble," her indignant reproach to Austria for deserting her cause, her invocation to death, " that love of misery," however fine and spirited, all yield to the beauty of the passage, where, her passion subsiding into tenderness, she addresses the Cardinal in these words :—

> " And, father Cardinal, I have heard you say
> That we shall see and know our friends in heaven :
> If that be true, I shall see my boy again,
> For since the birth of Cain, the first male child,
> To him that did but yesterday suspire,
> There was not such a gracious creature born.
> But now will canker-sorrow eat my bud,
> And chase the native beauty from his cheek,
> And he will look as hollow as a ghost,
> As dim and meagre as an ague-fit,
> And so he'll die ; and rising so again,
> When I shall meet him in the court of heaven,
> I shall not know him ; therefore never, never
> Must I behold my pretty Arthur more. . . . .
> *K. Philip.* You are as fond of grief as of your child.
> *Constance.* Grief fills the room up of my absent child."

[1 Act iv., sc. 3.]

> Lies in his bed, walks up and down with me ;
> Puts on his pretty looks, repeats his words.
> Remembers me of all his gracious parts ;
> Stuffs out his vacant garments with his form.
> Then have I reason to be fond of grief." [1]

The contrast between the mild resignation of Queen
Katherine to her own wrongs, and the wild, uncontrollable
affliction of Constance for the wrongs which she sustains
as a mother, is no less naturally conceived than it is ably
sustained throughout these two wonderful characters.

The accompaniment of the comic character of the
Bastard was well chosen to relieve the poignant agony of
suffering, and the cold cowardly policy of behaviour in
the principal characters of this play.   Its spirit, invention,
volubility of tongue and forwardness in action, are unbounded.   *Aliquando sufflaminandus erat,* says Ben Jonson
of Shakespear.   But we should be sorry if Ben Jonson
had been his licenser.   We prefer the heedless magnanimity of his wit infinitely to all Jonson's laborious
caution.   The character of the Bastard's comic humour is
the same in essence as that of other comic characters in
Shakespear ; they always run on with good things and are
never exhausted ; they are always daring and successful.
They have words at will, and a flow of wit like a flow of
animal spirits.   The difference between Falconbridge and
the others is that he is a soldier, and brings his wit to
bear upon action, is courageous with his sword as well as
tongue, and stimulates his gallantry by his jokes, his
enemies feeling the sharpness of his blows and the sting
of his sarcasms at the same time.   Among his happiest
sallies are his descanting on the composition of his own
person, his invective against "commodity, tickling commodity," and his expression of contempt for the Archduke
of Austria, who had killed his father, which begins in jest
but ends in serious earnest.   His conduct at the siege of

[1 Act iii., sc. 4.]

Angiors shows that his resources were not confined to verbal retorts. The same exposure of the policy of courts and camps, of kings, nobles, priests, and cardinals, takes place here as in the other plays we have gone through, and we shall not go into a disgusting repetition.

This, like the other plays taken from English history, is written in a remarkably smooth and flowing style, very different from some of the tragedies, ' Macbeth,' for instance. The passages consist of a series of single lines, not running into one another. This peculiarity in the versification, which is most common in the three parts of 'Henry VI.,' has been assigned as a reason why those plays were not written by Shakespear. But the same structure of verse occurs in his other undoubted plays, as in ' Richard II.' and in ' King John.' The following are instances :—

> " That daughter there of Spain, the lady Blanch,
> Is niece to England; look upon the years
> Of Lewis the dauphin and that lovely maid.
> If lusty love should go in quest of beauty,
> Where should he find it fairer than in Blanch ?
> If zealous love should go in search of virtue,
> Where should he find it purer than in Blanch ?
> If love ambitious sought a match of birth,
> Whose veins bound richer blood than lady Blanch ?
> Such as she is, in beauty, virtue, birth,
> Is the young dauphin every way complete :
> If not complete, O say he is not she ;
> And she again wants nothing, to name want,
> If want it be not, that she is not he.
> He is the half part of a blessed man,
> Left to be finished by such as she ;
> And she a fair divided excellence,
> Whose fulness of perfection lies in him.
> O, two such silver currents, when they join,
> Do glorify the banks that bound them in :
> And two such shores to two such streams made one,
> Two such controlling bounds shall you be, kings,
> To these two princes if you marry them."[1]

[Act ii., sc. 1.]

Another instance, which is certainly very happy as an example of the simple enumeration of a number of particulars, is Salisbury's remonstrance against the second crowning of the king.

> " Therefore to be possessed with double pomp,
> To guard a title that was rich before ;
> To gild refined gold, to paint the lily,
> To throw a perfume on the violet,
> To smooth the ice, to add another hue
> Unto the rainbow, or with taper-light
> To seek the beauteous eye of heaven to garnish ;
> Is wasteful and ridiculous excess."[1]

TWELFTH NIGHT; OR, WHAT YOU WILL.[2]

THIS is justly considered as one of the most delightful of Shakespear's comedies. It is full of sweetness and pleasantry. It is perhaps too good-natured for comedy. It has little satire, and no spleen. It aims at the ludicrous rather than the ridiculous. It makes us laugh at the follies of mankind, not despise them, and still less bear any ill-will towards them. Shakespear's comic genius resembles the bee rather in its power of extracting sweets from weeds or poisons, than in leaving a sting behind it. He gives the most amusing exaggeration of the prevailing foibles of his characters, but in a way that they themselves, instead of being offended at, would almost join in to humour ; he rather contrives opportunities for them to show themselves off in the happiest lights, than renders them contemptible in the perverse construc-

[1] Act iv., sc. 2.]
[2] First printed in 1623. From Manningham's Diary, lately edited by Mr. Bruce for the Camden Society, it appears that the drama was performed at the Middle Temple, Feb. 2, 1601-2. How much earlier it was written, cannot be ascertained at present, but Meres does not mention it in 1598.—ED.

tion of the wit or malice of others.   There is a certain
stage of society in which people become conscious of their
peculiarities and absurdities, affect to disguise what they
are, and set up pretensions to what they are not.   This
gives rise to a corresponding style of comedy, the object
of which is to detect the disguises of self-love, and to
make reprisals on these preposterous assumptions of vanity,
by marking the contrast between the real and the affected
character as severely as possible, and denying to those
who would impose on us for what they are not even the
merit which they have.   This is the comedy of artificial
life, of wit and satire, such as we see it in Congreve,
Wycherley, Vanbrugh, &c.   To this succeeds a state of
society from which the same sort of affectation and pretence are banished by a greater knowledge of the world
or by their successful exposure on the stage; and which by
neutralising the materials of comic character, both natural
and artificial, leaves no comedy at all—but *the sentimental.*
Such is our modern comedy.   There is a period in the
progress of manners anterior to both these, in which the
foibles and follies of individuals are of nature's planting,
not the growth of art or study; in which they are therefore unconscious of them themselves, or care not who
knows them, if they can but have their whim out; and
in which, as there is no attempt at imposition, the spectators rather receive pleasure from humouring the inclinations of the persons they laugh at, than wish to give
them pain by exposing their absurdity.   This may be
called the comedy of nature, and it is the comedy which
we generally find in Shakespear.   Whether the analysis
here given be just or not, the spirit of his comedies is
evidently quite distinct from that of the authors above
mentioned, as it is in its essence the same with that of
Cervantes, and also very frequently of Molière, though
he was more systematic in his extravagance than Shakespear.   Shakespear's comedy is of a pastoral and poetical

cast. Folly is indigenous to the soil, and shoots out
with native, happy, unchecked luxuriance. Absurdity has
every encouragement afforded it; and nonsense has room
to flourish in. Nothing is stunted by the churlish, icy
hand of indifference or severity. The poet runs riot in a
conceit, and idolises a quibble. His whole object is to
turn the meanest or rudest objects to a pleasurable account. The relish which he has of a pun, or of the quaint
humour of a low character, does not interfere with the
delight with which he describes a beautiful image, or the
most refined love. The clown's forced jests do not spoil
the sweetness of the character of Viola; the same house
is big enough to hold Malvolio, the Countess, Maria, Sir
Toby, and Sir Andrew Aguecheek. For instance, nothing
can fall much lower than this last character in intellect
or morals : yet how are his weaknesses nursed and dandled
by Sir Toby into something "high fantastical," when on
Sir Andrew's commendation of himself for dancing and
fencing, Sir Toby answers—"Wherefore are these things
hid ? Wherefore have these gifts a curtain before them?
Are they like to take dust like Mistress Moll's picture ?
Why dost thou not go to church in a galliard, and come
home in a coranto? My very walk should be a jig! I
would not so much as make water but in a cinque-pace.
What dost thou mean ? Is this a world to hide virtues
in ? I did think by the excellent constitution of thy leg,
it was framed under the star of a galliard !" How Sir
Toby, Sir Andrew, and the Clown afterwards *chirp over
their cups,* how they "rouse the night-owl in a catch, that
will draw three souls out of one weaver !" What can be
better than Sir Toby's unanswerable answer to Malvolio,
"Dost thou think, because thou art virtuous, there shall
be no more cakes and ale ?" In a word, the best turn is
given to everything, instead of the worst. There is a
constant infusion of the romantic and enthusiastic, in
proportion as the characters are natural and sincere :

whereas, in the more artificial style of comedy, everything gives way to ridicule and indifference, there being
nothing left but affectation on one side, and incredulity
on the other. Much as we like Shakespear's comedies,
we cannot agree with Dr. Johnson that they are better
than his tragedies; nor do we like them half so well.
If his inclination to comedy sometimes led him to trifle
with the seriousness of tragedy, the poetical and impassioned passages are the best parts of his comedies. The
great and secret charm of 'Twelfth Night' is the
character of Viola. Much as we like catches and cakes
and ale, there is something that we like better. We have
a friendship for Sir Toby; we patronise Sir Andrew;
we have an understanding with the Clown, a sneaking
kindness for Maria and her rogueries; we feel a regard
for Malvolio, and sympathise with his gravity, his smiles,
his cross garters, his yellow stockings, and imprisonment
in the stocks. But there is something that excites in us
a stronger feeling than all this—it is Viola's confession
of her love.

> " *Duke.* And what's her history?
> *Viola.* A blank, my lord ; she never told her love :
> She let concealment, like a worm i' th' bud,
> Feed on her damask cheek : she pin'd in thought,
> And with a green and yellow melancholy,
> She sat like Patience on a monument,
> Smiling at grief. *Was not this love indeed?*
> We men may say more, swear more : but indeed,
> Our shows are more than will ; for still we prove
> Much in our vows, but little in our love.
> *Duke.* But died thy sister of her love, my boy?
> *Viola.* I am all the daughters of my father's house,
> And all the brothers too ;—and yet I know not."—[1]

Shakespear alone could describe the effect of his own
poetry.

> " O, it came o'er my ear like the sweet south

---

[1] Act ii., sc. 4.]

That breathes upon a bank of violets,
Stealing and giving odour."[1]

What we so much admire here is not the image of Patience
on a monument. which has been generally quoted, but the
lines before and after it.   They "give a very echo to the
seat where love is throned."   How long ago it is since
we first learnt to repeat them; and still, still they vibrate
on the heart, like the sounds which the passing wind
draws from the trembling strings of a harp left on some
desert shore!   There are other passages of not less impassioned sweetness.   Such is Olivia's address to Sebastian, whom she supposes to have already deceived her in a
promise of marriage:

" Blame not this haste of mine.   If you mean well,
Now go with me and with this holy man
Into the chantry by: there, before him,
And underneath that consecrated roof,
Plight me the full assurance of your faith,
*That my most jealous and too doubtful soul
May live at peace.*"[2]

We have already said something of Shakespear's songs
One of the most beautiful of them occurs in this play,
with a preface of his own to it:

" *Duke.* O fellow, come, the song we had last night.
Mark it, Cesario, it is old and plain:
The spinsters and the knitters in the sun,
And the free maids that weave their thread with bones,
Do use to chaunt it : it is silly sooth,
And dallies with the innocence of love.
Like the old age.
    Clo. Are you ready, sir?
    Duke. Ay: prithee sing.
                    SONG.
Clo. Come away, come away, death,
And in sad cypress let me be laid;
    Fly away, fly away, breath;
I am slain by a fair cruel maid.

[1 Act i., sc. 1.]   [2 Act iv., sc. 3.]

My shroud of white, stuck all with yew,
 O, prepare it;
My part of death no one so true
 Did share it.

Not a flower, not a flower sweet,
On my black coffin let there be strown;
 Not a friend, not a friend greet
My poor corpse, where my bones shall be thrown
A thousand thousand sighs to save,
 Lay me, O! where
Sad true-love never find my grave,
 To weep there."[1]

Who, after this, will say that Shakespear's genius was
only fitted for comedy? Yet after reading other parts of
this play, and particularly the garden-scene where Malvolio picks up the letter, if we were to say that his genius
for comedy was less than his genius for tragedy, it would
perhaps only prove that our own taste in such matters is
more saturnine than mercurial :—

" *Sir Toby.* Here comes the little villain :—*Enter Maria.* How
now, my metal of India?
 Maria. Get ye all three into the box-tree: Malvolio's coming
down this walk : he has been yonder i' the sun, practising behaviour
to his own shadow this half hour: observe him, for the love of
mockery ; for I know this letter will make a contemplative idiot of
him. Close, in the name of jesting ! [*The others hide themselves.*]
Lie thou there—[*Throws down a letter*] for here comes the trout
that must be caught with tickling. [*Exit.*

Enter MALVOLIO.

 Malvolio. 'Tis but fortune; all is fortune. Maria once told me,
she did affect me; and I have heard herself come thus near, that,
should she fancy, it should be one of my complexion. Besides, she
uses me with a more exalted respect than any one else that follows
her. What should I think on't?
 Sir Toby. Here's an over-weening rogue !
 Fabian. O, peace ! Contemplation makes a rare turkey-cock of
him ; how he jets under his advanced plumes !
 Sir Andrew. 'Slight, I could so beat the rogue !
 Sir Toby. Peace, I say.

[1 Act ii., sc. 4.]

Malvolio. To be Count Malvolio;—

Sir Toby. Ah, rogue!

Sir Andrew. Pistol him, pistol him.

Sir Toby. Peace, peace!

Malvolio. There is example for't; the lady of the Strachy married the yeoman of the wardrobe.

Sir Andrew. Fie on him, Jezebel!

Fabian. O, peace! now he's deeply in; look, how imagination blows him.

Malvolio. Having been three months married to her, sitting in my state,——

Sir Toby. O for a stone bow, to hit him in the eye!

Malvolio. Calling my officers about me, in my branched velvet gown; having come from a day-bed, where I have left Olivia sleeping:—

Sir Toby. Fire and brimstone!

Fabian. O, peace, peace!

Malvolio. And then to have the humour of state: and after a demure travel of regard,——telling them, I know my place, as I would they should do theirs,—to ask for my kinsman Toby.——

Sir Toby. Bolts and shackles!

Fabian. O, peace, peace, peace! now, now.

Malvolio. Seven of my people, with an obedient start, make out for him; I frown the while; and, perchance, wind up my watch, or play with some rich jewel. Toby approaches; courtsies there to me.

Sir Toby. Shall this fellow live?

Fabian. Though our silence be drawn from us by th' ears, yet peace.

Malvolio. I extend my hand to him thus, quenching my familiar smile with an austere regard of control.

Sir Toby. And does not Toby take you a blow o' the lips then?

Malvolio. Saying, Cousin Toby, my fortunes having cast me on your niece, give me this prerogative of speech;—

Sir Toby. What, what?

Malvolio. You must amend your drunkenness.

Fabian. Nay, patience, or we break the sinews of our plot.

Malvolio. Besides, you waste the treasure of your time with a foolish knight —

Sir Andrew. That's me, I warrant you.

Malvolio. One Sir Andrew——

Sir Andrew. I knew, 'twas I; for many do call me fool.

Malvolio. What employment have we here?

[*Taking up the letter.*"

The letter and his comments on it are equally good. If poor Malvolio's treatment afterwards is a little hard, poetical justice is done in the uneasiness which Olivia suffers on account of her mistaken attachment to Cesario, as her insensibility to the violence of the Duke's passion is atoned for by the discovery of Viola's concealed love of him.

THE TWO GENTLEMEN OF VERONA.[1]

THIS is little more than the first outline of a comedy loosely sketched in. It is the story of a novel dramatised with very little labour or pretension; yet there are passages of high poetical spirit, and of inimitable quaintness of humour, which are undoubtedly Shakespear's, and there is throughout the conduct of the fable a careless grace and felicity which marks it for his. One of the editors (we believe Mr. Pope) remarks in a marginal note to the ' Two Gentlemen of Verona '—" It is observable (I know not for what cause) that the style of this comedy is less figurative, and more natural and unaffected than the greater part of this author's, though supposed to be one of the first he wrote." Yet so little does the editor appear to have made up his mind upon this subject, that we find the following note to the very next (the second) scene. " This whole scene, like many others in these plays (some of which I believe were written by Shakespear, and others interpolated by the players) is composed of the lowest and most trifling conceits, to be accounted for only by the gross taste of the age he lived in ; *Populo*

---

[1] First printed in 1623; but, as it is mentioned by Meres in his ' Palladis Tamia,' as an extant drama in 1598, it is usually regarded as one of the poet's earliest original productions for the stage. See Dyce's Shakespear, 2nd edit., i., 261, and Collier's ' Shakespear's Library,' ii.—ED

ut placerent. I wish I had authority to leave them out,
but I have done all I could, set a mark of reprobation
upon them, throughout this edition." It is strange that
our fastidious critic should fall so soon from praising to
reprobating. The style of the familiar parts of this
comedy is indeed made up of conceits—low they may be
for what we know, but then they are not poor, but rich
ones. The scene of Launce with his dog (not that in the
second, but that in the fourth act) is a perfect treat in the
way of farcical drollery and invention ; nor do we think
Speed's manner of proving his master to be in love deficient
in wit or sense, though the style may be criticised as not
simple enough for the modern taste :

" *Valentine.* Why, how know you that I am in love?

Speed. Marry, by these special marks : first, you have learned,
like Sir Proteus, to wreathe your arms like a malcontent; to relish
a love-song like a robin-redbreast; to walk alone like one that had
the pestilence ; to sigh like a school-boy that had lost his ABC; to
weep like a young wench that had buried her grandam; to fast like
one that takes diet; to watch like one that fears robbing; to speak
puling like a beggar at Hallowmas. You were wont, when you
laughed, to crow like a cock; when you walked, to walk like one
of the lions; when you fasted, it was presently after dinner; when
you looked sadly, it was for want of money: and now you are
metamorphosed with a mistress, that when I look on you, I car
hardly think you my master."[1]

The tender scenes in this play, though not so highly
wrought as in some others, have often much sweetness of
sentiment and expression. There is something pretty
and playful in the conversation of Julia with her maid,
when she shows such a disposition to coquetry about receiving the letter from Proteus, and her behaviour afterwards, and her disappointment, when she finds him
faithless to his vows, remind us at a distance of Imogen's
tender constancy. Her answer to Lucetta, who advises
her against following her lover in disguise, is a beautiful
piece of poetry :

[1 Act ii., sc. 1.]

" *Lucetta.* I do not seek to quench your love's hot fire,
But qualify the fire's extreme rage,
Lest it should burn above the bounds of reason.
   Julia. The more thou damm'st it up, the more it burns;
The current that with gentle murmur glides,
Thou know'st, being stopp'd, impatiently doth rage;
But when his fair course is not hindered,
He makes sweet music with th' enamell'd stones
Giving a gentle kiss to every sedge
He overtaketh in his pilgrimage:
And so by many winding nooks he strays,
With willing sport, to the wild ocean.[1]
Then let me go, and hinder not my course;
I'll be as patient as a gentle stream,
And make a pastime of each weary step,
Till the last step have brought me to my love;
And there I'll rest, as after much turmoil,
A blessed soul doth in Elysium."[2]

If Shakespear indeed had written only this and other passages in the 'Two Gentlemen of Verona,' he would *almost* have deserved Milton's praise of him,—

" And sweetest Shakespear, Fancy's child,
Warbles his native wood-notes wild."

But as it is, he deserves rather more praise than this.

THE MERCHANT OF VENICE.[3]

THIS is a play that in spite of the change of manners and prejudices still holds undisputed possession of the stage.

---

[1] The river wanders at its own sweet will.—WORDSWORTH.

[2 Act iv., sc. 7.]

[3] This is supposed by Malone to be the 'Venetian Comedy mentioned by Henslowe under date of 1594. In 1598, it is enumerated by Meres among Shakespear's then extant productions, and in the same year it was entered at Stationers' Hall. It was not printed, however, till 1600, when two editions of it appeared. The story, on which it is mainly founded, is one which, in slightly varied forms, occurs in several collections of tales.—ED.

Shakespear's malignant has outlived Mr. Cumberland's benevolent Jew. In proportion as Shylock has ceased to be a popular bugbear, "baited with the rabble's curse," he becomes a half-favourite with the philosophical part of the audience, who are disposed to think that Jewish revenge is at least as good as Christian injuries. Shylock is *a good hater;* "a man no less sinned against than sinning." If he carries his revenge too far, yet he has strong grounds for "the lodged hate he bears Antonio," which he explains with equal force of eloquence and reason. He seems the depositary of the vengeance of his race; and though the long habit of brooding over daily insults and injuries has crusted over his temper with inveterate misanthropy, and hardened him against the contempt of mankind, this adds but little to the triumphant pretensions of his enemies. There is a strong, quick, and deep sense of justice mixed up with the gall and bitterness of his resentment. The constant apprehension of being burnt alive, plundered, banished, reviled, and trampled on, might be supposed to sour the most forbearing nature, and to take something from that "milk of human kindness," with which his persecutors contemplated his indignities. The desire of revenge is almost inseparable from the sense of wrong; and we can hardly help sympathising with the proud spirit, hid beneath his "Jewish gaberdine," stung to madness by repeated undeserved provocations, and labouring to throw off the load of obloquy and oppression heaped upon him and all his tribe by one desperate act of "lawful" revenge, till the ferociousness of the means by which he is to execute his purpose, and the pertinacity with which he adheres to it, turn us against him; but even at last, when disappointed of the sanguinary revenge with which he had glutted his hopes, and exposed to beggary and contempt by the letter of the law on which he had insisted with so little remorse, we pity him, and think him hardly dealt with by his judges. In all his answers and retorts upon his adversaries, he has the best not only of the argument but of the question, reasoning on their own principles and practice. They are so far from allowing of any measure of equal dealing, of common justice or humanity between themselves and the Jew, that even when they come to ask a favour of him, and Shylock reminds them that on such a day they spit upon him, another spurned him, another called him dog, and for these curtesies they request he'll lend them so much money,[1] Antonio, his old enemy, instead of any acknow-ledgment of the shrewdness and justice of his remon-strance, which would have been preposterous in a respect-able Catholic merchant in those times, threatens him with a repetition of the same treatment—

> " I am as like to call thee so again,
> To spit on thee again, to spurn thee too."[2]

After this, the appeal to the Jew's mercy, as if there were any common principle of right and wrong between them, is the rankest hypocrisy or the blindest prejudice; and the Jew's answer to one of Antonio's friends, who asks him what his pound of forfeit flesh is good for, is irresistible—

" To bait fish withal; if it will feed nothing else, it will feed my revenge. He hath disgrac'd me, and hindered me of half a million, laughed at my losses, mocked at my gains, scorn'd my nation, thwarted my bargains, cooled my friends, heated mine enemies : and what's his reason? I am a Jew. Hath not a Jew eyes; hath not a Jew hands, organs, dimensions, senses, affections, passions; fed with the same food, hurt with the same weapons, subject to the same diseases, healed by the same means, warmed and cooled by the same winter and summer that a Christian is? If you prick us, do we not bleed? If you tickle us, do we not laugh? If you poison us, do we not die? And if you wrong us, shall we not revenge? If we are like you in the rest, we will resemble you in that. If a Jew wrong a Christian, what is his humility? revenge. If a Christian wrong a Jew, what should his sufferance be by

---

[1 Act i., sc. 3.]　　　　　[2 *Ibid.*]

Christian example? why, revenge. The villainy you teach me I will execute, and it shall go hard but I will better the instruction."[1]

The whole of the trial-scene, both before and after the entrance of Portia, is a master-piece of dramatic skill. The legal acuteness, the passionate declamations, the sound maxims of jurisprudence, the wit and irony interspersed in it, the fluctuations of hope and fear in the different persons, and the completeness and suddenness of the catastrophe, cannot be surpassed. Shylock, who is his own counsel, defends himself well, and is triumphant on all the general topics that are urged against him, and only fails through a legal flaw. Take the following as an instance :—

> " *Shylock.* What judgment shall I dread, doing no wrong?
> You have among you many a purchas'd slave,
> Which like your asses, and your dogs, and mules,
> You use in abject and in slavish parts,
> Because you bought them :—shall I say to you,
> Let them be free, marry them to your heirs?
> Why sweat they under burdens? let their beds
> Be made as soft as yours, and let their palates
> Be season'd with such viands? You will answer,
> The slaves are ours :—so do I answer you:
> The pound of flesh, which I demand of him,
> Is dearly bought, 'tis mine, and I will have it:
> If you deny me, fie upon your law!
> There is no force in the decrees of Venice:
> I stand for judgment: answer,—shall I have it?"[2]

The keenness of his revenge awakes all his faculties; and he beats back all opposition to his purpose, whether grave or gay, whether of wit or argument, with an equal degree of earnestness and self-possession. His character is displayed as distinctly in other less prominent parts of the play, and we may collect from a few sentences the history of his life—his descent and origin, his thrift and domestic economy, his affection for his daughter, whom he loves next to his wealth, his courtship and his first

[1 Act iii., sc. 1.]   [2 Act iv., sc. 1.]

present to Leah his wife! "I would not have given it'
(the ring which he first gave her) "for a wilderness of
monkeys!"[1] What a fine Hebraism is implied in this
expression!

Portia is not a very great favourite with us; neither are
we in love with her maid, Nerissa. Portia has a certain
degree of affectation and pedantry about her, which is
very unusual in Shakespear's women, but which perhaps
was a proper qualification for the office of a "civil doctor,"
which she undertakes and executes so successfully. The
speech about Mercy is very well; but there are a thousand
finer ones in Shakespear. We do not admire the scene of
the caskets : and object entirely to the Black Prince,
Morocchius. We should like Jessica better if she had
not deceived and robbed her father, and Lorenzo, if he
had not married a Jewess, though he thinks he has a right
to wrong a Jew. The dialogue between this newly-
married couple by moonlight, beginning "On such a
night," &c., is a collection of classical elegancies.
Launcelot, the Jew's man, is an honest fellow. The
dilemma in which he describes himself placed between
his "conscience and the fiend," the one of which advises
him to run away from his master's service and the other
to stay in it, is exquisitely humorous.

Gratiano is a very admirable subordinate character.
He is the jester of the piece : yet one speech of his, in
his own defence, contains a whole volume of wisdom.

" *Antonio.* I hold the world but as the world, Gratiano,
A stage, where every man must play his part;
And mine a sad one.
    Gratiano.   Let me play the fool.
With mirth and laughter let old wrinkles come ;
And let my liver rather heat with wine,
Than my heart cool with mortifying groans.
Why should a man, whose blood is warm within,
Sit like his grandsire cut in alabaster?

[¹ Act iii., sc. 1]

Sleep when he wakes? and creep into the jaundice
By being peevish? I tell thee what, Antonio—
I love thee, and it is my love that speaks;—
There are a sort of men, whose visages
Do cream and mantle like a standing pond:
And do a wilful stillness entertain,
With purpose to be dress'd in an opinion
Of wisdom, gravity, profound conceit;
As who should say, *I am Sir Oracle,*
And when I ope my lips, let no dog bark!
O my Antonio, I do know of these,
That therefore only are reputed wise,
For saying nothing; when, I'm very sure,
If they should speak, would almost damn those ears,
Which hearing them, would call their brothers fools.
I'll tell thee more of this another time:
But fish not with this melancholy bait,
For this fool-gudgeon, this opinion." [1]

Gratiano's speech on the philosophy of love, and the effect of habit in taking off the force of passion, is as full of spirit and good sense. The graceful winding-up of this play in the fifth act, after the tragic business is despatched, is one of the happiest instances of Shakespear's knowledge of the principles of the drama. We do not mean the pretended quarrel between Portia and Nerissa and their husbands about the rings, which is amusing enough, but the conversation just before and after the return of Portia to her own house, beginning, "How sweet the moonlight sleeps upon this bank," and ending, 'Peace! how the moon sleeps with Endymion, and would not be awaked." There is a number of beautiful thoughts crowded into that short space, and linked together by the most natural transitions.

When we first went to see Mr. Kean in Shylock, we expected to see, what we had been used to see, a decrepit old man, bent with age and ugly with mental deformity, grinning with deadly malice, with the venom of his heart congealed in the expression of his countenance, sullen,

[1 Act i., sc. 1.]

morose, gloomy, inflexible, brooding over one idea, that of his hatred, and fixed on one unalterable purpose, that of his revenge. We were disappointed, because we had taken our idea from other actors, not from the play. There is no proof there that Shylock is old, but a single line, "Bassanio and *old* Shylock, both stand forth,"—which does not imply that he is infirm with age—and the circumstance that he has a daughter marriageable, which does not imply that he is old at all. It would be too much to say that his body should be made crooked and deformed to answer to his mind, which is bowed down and warped with prejudices and passion. That he has but one idea, is not true; he has more ideas than any other person in the piece ; and if he is intense and inveterate in the pursuit of his purpose, he shows the utmost elasticity, vigour, and presence of mind, in the means of attaining it. But so rooted was our habitual impression of the part from seeing it caricatured in the representation, that it was only from a careful perusal of the play itself that we saw our error. The stage is not in general the best place to study our author's characters in. It is too often filled with traditional common-place conceptions of the part, handed down from sire to son, and suited to the taste of *the great vulgar and the small.*—" 'Tis an unweeded garden · things rank and gross do merely gender in it !" If a man of genius comes once in an age to clear away the rubbish, to make it fruitful and wholesome, they cry, " 'Tis a bad school: it may be like nature, it may be like Shakespear, but it is not like us." Admirable critics ![1]

[1] Edmund Kean it was who, to the complete astonishment of the rest of the company with which he was acting at Drury-lane, first discarded the traditional red beard, in which Shylock had from time immemorial appeared on the boards, and substituted a black beard. —ED.

THE WINTER'S TALE.[1]

WE wonder that Mr. Pope should have entertained doubts
of the genuineness of this play. He was, we suppose,
shocked (as a certain critic suggests) at the Chorus, Time,
leaping over sixteen years with his crutch between the
third and fourth act, and at Antigonus's landing with the
infant Perdita on the sea-coast of Bohemia. These slips
or blemishes however do not prove it not to be Shakespear's;
for he was as likely to fall into them as anybody; but we
do not know anybody but himself who could produce the
beauties. The *stuff* of which the tragic passion is composed, the romantic sweetness, the comic humour, are
evidently his. Even the crabbed and tortuous style of
the speeches of Leontes, reasoning on his own jealousy,
beset with doubts and fears, and entangled more and more
in the thorny labyrinth, bears every mark of Shakespear's
peculiar manner of conveying the painful struggle of
different thoughts and feelings, labouring for utterance,
and almost strangled in the birth. For instance :—

> —————— " Ha' not you seen, Camillo ?
> But that's past doubt; you have, or your eyeglass
> Is thicker than a cuckold's horn, or heard,—
> For to a vision so apparent, rumour
> Cannot be mute; or thought—for cogitation
> Resides not within that man that does not think 't—
> My wife is slippery ? If thou wilt confess,

---

[1] First printed in 1623. The earliest record of its existence seems
to be the entry in the diary of Dr. Forman, under the date of
May 15, 1611, from which it is to be seen that the drama was
performed on that day at the Globe Theatre, Forman being present.
—ED.

Or else be impudently negative,
To have nor eyes, nor ears, nor thought." [1]

Here Leontes is confounded with his passion, and does not know which way to turn himself, to give words to the anguish, rage, and apprehension, which tug at his breast. It is only as he is worked up into a clearer conviction of his wrongs by insisting on the grounds of his unjust suspicions to Camillo, who irritates him by his opposition, that he bursts out into the following vehement strain of bitter indignation: yet even here his passion staggers, and is as it were oppressed with its own intensity :

　　　　　　　　" Is whispering nothing?
Is leaning cheek to cheek ? is meeting noses?
Kissing with inside lip? stopping the career
Of laughter with a sigh ?—a note infallible
Of breaking honesty !—horsing foot on foot ?
Skulking in corners? wishing clocks more swift ?
Hours, minutes? the noon, midnight? and all eyes
Blind with the pin-and-web, but theirs; theirs only,
That would unseen be wicked ? is this nothing?
Why then the world, and all that's in't is nothing,
The covering sky is nothing, Bohemia nothing,
My wife is nothing—" [2]

The character of Hermione is as much distinguished by its saint-like resignation and patient forbearance, as that of Paulina is by her zealous and spirited remonstrances against the injustice done to the queen, and by her devoted attachment to her misfortunes. Hermione's restoration to her husband and her child, after her long separation from them, is as affecting in itself as it is striking in the representation. Camillo, and the old shepherd and his son, are subordinate but not uninteresting instruments in the development of the plot, and though last, not least, comes Autolycus, a very pleasant, thriving rogue ; and (what is the best feather in the cap of all knavery) he escapes with impunity in the end.

The 'Winter's Tale' is one of the best acting of our

[1 Act i. sc. 2.]　　　　　　　[2 *Ibid.*]

author's plays. We remember seeing it with great
pleasure many years ago.[1] It was on the night that King
took leave of the stage, when he and Mrs. Jordan played
together in the after-piece of the 'Wedding-day.' Nothing
could go off with more *éclat*, with more spirit, and grandeur
of effect. Mrs. Siddons played Hermione, and in the last
scene acted the painted statue to the life—with true
monumental dignity and noble passion; Mr. Kemble, in
Leontes, worked himself up into a very fine classical
phrensy; and Bannister,[2] as Autolycus, roared as loud for
pity as a sturdy beggar could do who felt none of the pain
he counterfeited, and was sound of wind and limb. We
shall never see these parts so acted again; or if we did, it
would be in vain. Actors grow old, or no longer surprise
us by their novelty. But true poetry, like nature, is
always young; and we still read the courtship of Florizel
and Perdita, as we welcome the return of spring, with the
same feelings as ever:

> " *Florizel.* Thou dearest Perdita,
> With these forc'd thoughts, I prithee, darken not
> The mirth o' the feast: or, I'll be thine, my fair,
> Or not my father's: for I cannot be
> Mine own, nor anything to any, if
> I be not thine: to this I am most constant,
> Tho' destiny say no. Be merry, gentle;
> Strangle such thoughts as these with anything
> That you behold the while. Your guests are coming
> Lift up your countenance, as it were the day
> Of celebration of that nuptial, which
> We two have sworn shall come.
>   *Perdita.*   O Lady Fortune,
> Stand you auspicious!
>   *Florizel.*   See, your guests approach.
> Address yourself to entertain them sprightly,
> And let's be red with mirth.

---

[1] Nov. 28, 1811, at Covent Garden.—ED.

[2] Geneste (viii., 286) says that *Fawcett* filled the part of
Autolycus.—ED.

Enter SHEPHERD, *with* POLIXENES *and* CAMILLO *disguised;* CLOWN,
MOPSA, DORCAS, *and other Shepherds and Shepherdesses.*

Shepherd. Fie, daughter! when my old wife liv'd, upon
This day, she was both pantler, butler, cook;
Both dame and servant: welcom'd all, serv'd all:
Would sing her song and dance her turn: now here
At upper end o' the table, now i' the middle:
On his shoulder, and his: her face o' fire
With labour; and the thing she took to quench it
She would to each one sip.   You are retir'd,
As if you were a feasted one, and not
The hostess of the meeting: pray you, bid
These unknown friends to 's welcome; for it is
A way to make us better friends, more known.
Come, quench your blushes, and present yourself
That which you are, mistress o' the feast; come on,
And bid us welcome to your sheep-shearing,
As your good flock shall prosper.
 Perdita. [*To Pol.*] Sir, welcome!
It is my father's will I should take on me
The hostess-ship o' the day: [*To Cam.*] you're welcome, sir!
Give me those flowers there, Dorcas.—Reverend sirs,
For you there's rosemary and rue; these keep
Seeming and savour all the winter long:
Grace and remembrance be to you both,
And welcome to our shearing!
 Polixenes.   Shepherdess
(A fair one are you), well you fit our ages
With flowers of winter.
 Perdita.   Sir, the year growing ancient,—
Not yet on summer's death, nor on the birth
Of trembling winter, the fair'st flowers o' the season
Are our carnations, and streak'd gillyflowers,
Which some call nature's bastards: of that kind
Our rustic garden's barren; and I care not
To get slips of them.
 Polixenes.   Wherefore, gentle maiden,
Do you neglect them?
 Perdita.   For I have heard it said
There is an art which, in their piedness, shares
With great creating nature.
 Polixenes.   Say, there be:
Yet nature is made better by no mean,
But nature makes that mean: so, o'er that art

Which you say adds to nature, is an art
That nature makes. You see, sweet maid, we marry
A gentler scion to the wildest stock;
And make conceive a bark of baser kind
By bud of nobler race: this is an art
Which does mend nature,—change it rather: but
The art itself is nature.

 Perdita.   So it is.[1]

 Polixenes. Then make your garden rich in gillyflowers
And do not call them bastards.

 Perdita.   I'll not put
The dibble in earth, to set one slip of them;
No more than, were I painted, I would wish
This youth should say, 'twere well; and only therefore
Desire to breed by me.—Here's flowers for you;
Hot lavender, mints, savoury, marjoram;
The marigold, that goes to bed wi' the sun,
And with him rises weeping: these are flowers
Of middle summer, and, I think, they're given
To men of middle age. You are very welcome.

 Camillo. I should leave grazing, were I of your flock,
And only live by gazing.

 Perdita.   Out, alas!
You'd be so lean, that blasts of January
Would blow you through and through. Now my fair'st friends
I would I had some flowers o' the spring, that might
Become your time of day; and yours, and yours,
That wear upon your virgin branches yet
Your maidenheads growing:—O Proserpina,
For the flowers now, that, frighted, thou let'st fall
From Dis's waggon! daffodils,
That come before the swallow dares, and take
The winds of March with beauty: violets dim,
But sweeter than the lids of Juno's eyes,
Or Cytherea's breath; pale primroses,
That die unmarried, ere they can behold
Bright Phœbus in his strength (a malady
Most incident to maids); bold oxlips, and
The crown-imperial; lilies of all kinds,
The fleur-de-luce being one! O, these I lack
To make you garlands of; and my sweet friend

———————————————

[1] The lady, we here see, gives up the argument, but keeps her mind.

To strew him o'er and o'er.
   Florizel.   What, like a corse?
   Perdita. No, like a bank for love to lie and play on;
Not like a corse; or if—not to be buried,
But quick, and in mine arms. Come take your flowers:
Methinks, I play as I have seen them do
In Whitsun pastorals: sure this robe of mine
Does change my disposition.
   Florizel.   What you do,
Still betters what is done. When you speak, sweet,
I'd have you do it ever: when you sing,
I'd have you buy and sell so; so give alms;
Pray so; and for the ordering your affairs,
To sing them too; when you do dance, I wish you
A wave o' the sea, that you might ever do
Nothing but that: move still, still so,
And own no other function. Each your doing,
So singular in each particular.
Crowns what you're doing in the present deeds,
That all your acts are queens.
   Perdita.   O Doricles,
Your praises are too large; but that your youth
And the true blood, which peeps forth fairly through 't,
Do plainly give you out an unstain'd shepherd,
With wisdom I might fear, my Doricles,
You woo'd me the false way.
   Florizel.   I think you have
As little skill to fear, as I have purpose
To put you to't. But, come; our dance, I pray:
Your hand, my Perdita: so turtles pair,
That never mean to part.
   Perdita.   I'll swear for 'em.
   Polixenes. This is the prettiest low-born lass that ever
Ran on the green-sward; nothing she does, or seems,
But smacks of something greater than herself,
Too noble for this place.
   Camillo.   He tells her something
That makes her blood look out: good sooth she is
The queen of curds and cream." [1]

This delicious scene is interrupted by the father of the
prince discovering himself to Florizel, and haughtily

[1 Act iv., sc. 3.]

breaking off the intended match between his son and Perdita. When Polixenes goes out, Perdita says,

> " Even here undone :
> I was not much afeard ; for once or twice
> I was about to speak ; and tell him plainly,
> The self-same sun that shines upon his court,
> Hides not his visage from our cottage, but
> Looks on alike. [*To Florizel.*] Wilt please you, sir, be gone ?
> I told you what would come of this. Beseech you,
> Of your own state take care : this dream of mine,
> Being now awake, I'll queen it no inch farther,
> But milk my ewes and weep." [1]

As Perdita, the supposed shepherdess, turns out to be the daughter of Hermione, and a princess in disguise, both feelings of the pride of birth and the claims of nature are satisfied by the fortunate event of the story, and the fine romance of poetry is reconciled to the strictest court-etiquette.

ALL'S WELL THAT ENDS WELL.[2]

' ALL'S WELL THAT ENDS WELL ' is one of the most pleasing of our author's comedies. The interest is however more of a serious than of a comic nature. The character of Helen is one of great sweetness and delicacy. She is placed in circumstances of the most critical kind, and has to court her husband both as a virgin and a wife : yet the most scrupulous nicety of female modesty is not once violated. There is not one thought or action that ought to bring a blush into her cheeks, or that for a moment lessens her in our esteem. Perhaps the romantic attach-

[1 Act iv., sc. 3.]
[2] First printed in 1623. The composition is supposed to have been divided between two distinct periods of the author's life, the play having been laid aside unfinished, and then subsequently resumed and completed. It is thought to be the piece mentioned by Meres under the title of ' Love's Labours Won,' in 1598.—ED.

ment of a beautiful and virtuous girl to one placed above
her hopes by the circumstances of birth and fortune, was
never so exquisitely expressed as in the reflections which
she utters when young Rousillon leaves his mother's
house, under whose protection she has been brought up
with him, to repair to the French king's court:

> ' *Helena.* O, were that all—I think not on my father,
> And these great tears grace his remembrance more
> Than those I shed for him.   What was he like?
> I have forgot him : my imagination
> Carries no favour in it but Bertram's.
> I am undone, there is no living, none,
> If Bertram be away.   It were all one
> That I should love a bright particular star,
> And think to wed it, he is so above me :
> In his bright radiance and collateral light
> Must I be comforted, not in his sphere.
> Th' ambition in my love thus plagues itself;
> The hind that would be mated by the lion,
> Must die for love.   'Twas pretty, though a plague,
> To see him every hour, to sit and draw
> His arched brows, his hawking eye, his curls
> In our heart's table : heart too capable
> Of every line and trick of his sweet favour.
> But now he's gone, and my idolatrous fancy
> Must sanctify his relics."[1]

The interest excited by this beautiful picture of a fond
and innocent heart is kept up afterwards by her resolution
to follow him to France, the success of her experiment in
restoring the king's health, her demanding Bertram in
marriage as a recompense, his leaving her in disdain, her
interview with him afterwards disguised as Diana, a
young lady whom he importunes with his secret addresses,
and their final reconciliation when the consequences of
her stratagem and the proofs of her love are fully made
known.   The persevering gratitude of the French king to
his benefactress, who cures him of a languishing dis-
temper by a prescription hereditary in her family, the

[1 Act i., sc. 1.]

indulgent kindness of the Countess, whose pride of birth
yields, almost without a struggle, to her affection for
Helen, the honesty and uprightness of the good old lord
Lafeu, make very interesting parts of the picture. The
wilful stubbornness and youthful petulance of Bertram
are also very admirably described. The comic part of
the play turns on the folly, boasting, and cowardice of
Parolles, a parasite and hanger-on of Bertram's, the
detection of whose false pretensions to bravery and honour
forms a very amusing episode. He is first found out by
the old lord Lafeu, who says, "The soul of this man is
his clothes;" and it is proved afterwards that his heart is
in his tongue, and that both are false and hollow. The
adventure of "the bringing off of his drum" has become
proverbial as a satire on all ridiculous and blustering
undertakings which the person never means to perform:
nor can anything be more severe than what one of the
bystanders [the *First Lord*] remarks upon what Parolles
says of himself, "Is it possible he should know what he
is, and be that he is?"[1] Yet Parolles himself gives the
best solution of the difficulty afterwards when he is
thankful to escape with his life and the loss of character;
for, so that he can live on, he is by no means squeamish
about the loss of pretensions, to which he had sense
enough to know he had no real claim, and which he had
assumed only as a means to live.

> "*Parolles.* Yet am I thankful : if my heart were great,
> 'Twould burst at this. Captain I'll be no more,
> But I will eat and drink, and sleep as soft
> As captain shall : simply the thing I am
> Shall make me live. Who knows himself a braggart,
> Let him fear this; for it shall come to pass,
> That every braggart shall be found an ass.
> Rust, sword ! cool, blushes ! and, Parolles, live
> Safest in shame ! being fool'd, by foolery thrive !
> There's place and means for every man alive.
> I'll after them."

[1 Act iv., sc. 1.]

The story of 'All's Well that Ends Well,' and of several others of Shakespear's plays, is taken from Boccacio. The poet has dramatised the original novel with great skill and comic spirit, and has preserved all the beauty of character and sentiment without *improving upon* it, which was impossible. There is indeed in Boccacio's serious pieces a truth, a pathos, and an exquisite refinement of sentiment, which is hardly to be met with in any other prose writer whatever. Justice has not been done him by the world. He has in general passed for a mere narrator of lascivious tales or idle jests. This character probably originated in his obnoxious attacks on the monks, and has been kept up by the grossness of mankind, who revenged their own want of refinement on Boccacio, and only saw in his writings what suited the coarseness of their own tastes. But the truth is, that he has carried sentiment of every kind to its very highest purity and perfection. By sentiment we would here understand the habitual workings of some one powerful feeling, where the heart reposes almost entirely upon itself, without the violent excitement of opposing duties or untoward circumstances. In this way, nothing ever came up to the story of Frederigo Alberigi and his Falcon. The perseverance in attachment, the spirit of gallantry and generosity displayed in it, has no parallel in the history of heroical sacrifices. The feeling is so unconscious too, and involuntary, is brought out in such small, unlooked-for, and unostentatious circumstances, as to show it to have been woven into the very nature and soul of the author. The story of Isabella is scarcely less fine, and is more affecting in the circumstances and in the catastrophe. Dryden has done justice to the impassioned eloquence of the Tancred and Sigismunda; but has not given an adequate idea of the wild preternatural interest of the story of Honoria. Cimon and Iphigene is by no means one of the best, notwithstanding the popularity of the subject. The proof of unalterable affection given in the story of Jeronymo, and the simple touches of nature and picturesque beauty in the story of the two holiday lovers, who were poisoned by tasting of a leaf in the garden at Florence, are perfect master-pieces. The epithet of Divine was well bestowed on this great painter of the human heart. The invention implied in his different tales is immense : but we are not to infer that it is all his own. He probably availed himself of all the common traditions which were floating in his time, and which he was the first to appropriate. Homer appears the most original of all authors—probably for no other reason than that we can trace the plagiarism no farther. Boccacio has furnished subjects to numberless writers since his time, both dramatic and narrative. The story of Griselda is borrowed from his Decameron by Chaucer; as is the Knight's Tale (Palamon and Arcite) from his poem of the Theseid.

----◆----

LOVE'S LABOUR'S LOST.[1]

If we were to part with any of the author's comedies, it should be this. Yet we should be loth to part with Don Adriano de Armado, that mighty potentate of nonsense, or his page, that handful of wit; with Nathaniel the curate, or Holofernes the schoolmaster, and their dispute after dinner on " the golden cadences of poesy;" with Costard the clown, or Dull the constable. Biron is too accomplished a character to be lost to the world, and yet he could not appear without his fellow-courtiers and the

---

[1] This is believed to have been one of Shakespear's earliest dramatic efforts, if not *the* earliest one, in which he did not work on materials ready to his hand, as in the three parts of the 'Contention.' It was printed, *with corrections,* in 1598, but the date of the first edition is not known.—ED.

king: and if we were to leave out the ladies, the gentlemen would have no mistresses. So that we believe we
may let the whole play stand as it is, and we shall hardly
venture to "set a mark of reprobation on it." Still we
have some objections to the style, which we think savours
more of the pedantic spirit of Shakespear's time than of
his own genius; more of controversial divinity, and the
logic of Peter Lombard, than of the inspiration of the
Muse. It transports us quite as much to the manners of
the court, and the quirks of courts of law, as to the scenes
of nature or the fairy-land of his own imagination. Shakespear has set himself to imitate the tone of polite conversation then prevailing among the fair, the witty, and
the learned, and he has imitated it but too faithfully. It
is as if the hand of Titian had been employed to give
grace to the curls of a full-bottomed periwig, or Raphael
had attempted to give expression to the tapestry figures
in the House of Lords. Shakespear has put an excellent
description of this fashionable jargon into the mouth of
the critical Holofernes "as too picked, too spruce, too
affected, too odd, as it were, too peregrinate, as I may call
it;" and nothing can be more marked than the difference
when he breaks loose from the trammels he had imposed
on himself, "as light as bird from brake," and speaks in
his own person. We think, for instance, that in the
following soliloquy the poet has fairly got the start of
Queen Elizabeth and her maids of honour :—

> "*Biron.* O! and I, forsooth, in love,
> I that have been love's whip;
> A very beadle to a humorous sigh :
> A critic, nay, a night-watch constable,
> A domineering pedant o'er the boy,
> Than whom no mortal so magnificent.
> This wimpled, whining, purblind, wayward boy,
> This signior Junio, giant-dwarf, Dan Cupid,
> Regent of love-rhymes, lord of folded arms,
> Th' anointed sovereign of sighs and groans :
> Liege of all loiterers and malcontents,

> Dread prince of plackets, king of codpieces,
> Sole imperator, and great general
> Of trotting paritors:—O my little heart!—
> And I to be a corporal of his field,
> And wear his colours like a tumbler's hoop!
> What, what! I love! I sue! I seek a wife!
> A woman, that is like a German clock,
> Still a-repairing; ever out of frame;
> And never going aright, being a watch,
> But being watch'd, that it may still go right?
> Nay, to be perjur'd, which is worst of all:
> And among three to love the worst of all,
> A whitely wanton with a velvet brow,
> With two pitch balls stuck in her face for eyes,
> Ay, and by heav'n, one that will do the deed,
> Though Argus were her eunuch and her guard;
> And I to sigh for her! to watch for her!
> To pray for her! Go to; it is a plague
> That Cupid will impose for my neglect
> Of his almighty dreadful little might.
> Well, I will love, write, sigh, pray, sue, and groan:
> Some men must love my lady, and some Joan."[1]

The character of Biron drawn by Rosaline, and that which Biron gives of Boyet are equally happy. The observations on the use and abuse of study, and on the power of beauty to quicken the understanding as well as the senses, are excellent. The scene which has the greatest dramatic effect is that in which Biron, the king, Longaville, and Dumain, successively detect each other and are detected in their breach of their vow and in their profession of attachment to their several mistresses, in which they suppose themselves to be overheard by no one. The reconciliation between these lovers and their sweethearts is also very good, and the penance which Rosaline imposes on Biron, before he can expect to gain her consent to marry him, full of propriety and beauty:

> " *Rosaline.* Oft have I heard of you, my Lord Biron,
> Before I saw you: and the world's large tongue
> Proclaims you for a man replete with mocks;

[1 Act iii., sc. 1.]

Full of comparisons and wounding flouts;
Which you on all estates will execute,
That lie within the mercy of your wit.
To weed this wormwood from your faithful brain;
And therewithal to win me, if you please
('Without the which I am not to be won),
You shall this twelvemonth term from day to day
Visit the speechless sick, and still converse
With groaning wretches; and your task shall be,
With all the fierce endeavour of your wit,
T' enforce the pained impotent to smile.
 Biron. To move wild laughter in the throat of death?
It cannot be: it is impossible:
Mirth cannot move a soul in agony.
 Rosaline. Why, that's the way to choke a gibing spirit,
Whose influence is begot of that loose grace,
Which shallow-laughing hearers give to fools:
A jest's prosperity lies in the ear
Of him that hears it; never in the tongue
Of him that makes it: then, if sickly ears,
Deaf'd with the clamours of their own dear groans,
Will hear your idle scorns, continue them,
And I will have you, and that fault withal;
But, if they will not, throw away that spirit,
And I shall find you empty of that fault,
Right joyful of your reformation.
 Biron. A twelvemonth? Well, befall what will befall,
I ll jest a twelvemonth in an hospital." [1]

The famous cuckoo-song closes the play: but we shall add no more criticisms: "the words of Mercury are harsh after the songs of Apollo."

[[1] Act 7., sc. 2.]

MUCH ADO ABOUT NOTHING.[1]

THIS admirable comedy used to be frequently acted till of late years.[2] Mr. Garrick's Benedick was one of his most celebrated characters; and Mrs. Jordan, we have understood, played Beatrice very delightfully. The serious part is still the most prominent here. as in other instances that we have noticed. Hero is the principal figure in the piece, and leaves an indelible impression on the mind by her beauty, her tenderness, and the hard trial of her love. The passage in which Claudio first makes a confession of his affection towards her, conveys as pleasing an image of the entrance of love into a youthful bosom as can well be imagined :

> ————— " O, my lord,
> When you went onward on this ended action,
> I look'd upon her with a soldier's eye,
> That lik'd, but had a rougher task in hand
> Than to drive liking to the name of love;
> But now I am return'd, and that war-thoughts
> Have left their places vacant, in their rooms
> Come thronging soft and delicate desires,
> All prompting me how fair young Hero is,
> Saying, I lik'd her ere I went to wars." [3]

In the scene at the altar, when Claudio, urged on by the villain Don John, brings the charge of incontinence against her, and as it were divorces her in the very marriage-

---

[1] Printed in 1600, and in the folio of 1623. Shakespear seems here to have resorted to Ariosto's tale of ' Ariodanto and Genevra, which was extant in his time in at least two English translations, those by Harington and Beverley. But the former says that George Turbervile had also translated the story, which Harington calls " a pretty comical matter."—ED.

[2] It is still occasionally put on the stage (1869).—ED.

[3] Act i., sc. 1]

ceremony, her appeals to her own conscious innocence and honour are made with the most affecting simplicity.

" *Claudio.* No, Leonato,
I never tempted her with word too large,
But, as a brother to his sister, show'd
Bashful sincerity and comely love.
   Hero. And seem'd I ever otherwise to you?
   Claudio. Out on thy seeming! I will write against it:
You seem'd to me as Dian in her orb,
As chaste as is the bud ere it be blown;
But you are more intemperate in your blood
Than Venus, or those pamper'd animals
That rage in savage sensuality.
   Hero. Is my lord well, that he doth speak so wide? .
   Leonato. Are these things spoken, or do I but dream?
   John. Sir, they are spoken, and these things are true.
   Benedick. This looks not like a nuptial.
   Hero.   True! O God!" [1]

The justification of Hero in the end, and her restoration to the confidence and arms of her lover, is brought about by one of those temporary consignments to the grave of which Shakespear seems to have been fond. He has perhaps explained the theory of this predilection in the following lines:—

" *Friar.* She dying, as it must be so maintain'd,
Upon the instant that she was accus'd,
Shall be lamented, pitied, and excus'd,
Of every hearer: for it so falls out,
That what we have we prize not to the worth,
While we enjoy it; but being lack'd and lost,
Why then we rack the value; then we find
The virtue, that possession would not show us
Whilst it was ours. So will it fare with Claudio;
When he shall hear she died upon his words,
The idea of her love shall sweetly creep
Into his study of imagination;
And every lovely organ of her life
Shall come apparel'd in more precious habit,
More moving, delicate, and full of life,

[1 Act iv., sc. 1.]

I ito the eye and prospect of his soul,
Than when she liv'd indeed." ·

The principal comic characters in ' Much Ado about
Nothing,' Benedick and Beatrice, are both essences in
their kind. His character as a woman-hater is admirably
supported, and his conversion to matrimony is no less
happily effected by the pretended story of Beatrice's love
for him. It is hard to say which of the two scenes is the
best, that of the trick which is thus practised on Benedick,
or that in which Beatrice is prevailed on to take pity on
him by overhearing her cousin and her maid declare
(which they do on purpose) that he is dying of love for
her. There is something delightfully picturesque in the
manner in which Beatrice is described as coming to hear
the plot which is contrived against herself :

"For look where Beatrice, like a lapwing, runs
Close by the ground, to hear our conference." [2]

In consequence of what she hears (not a word of which is
true) she exclaims when these good-natured informants
are gone :

" What fire is in mine ears ? Can this be true ?
    Stand I condemn'd for pride and scorn so much ?
Contempt, farewell ! and maiden pride, adieu !
    No glory lives behind the back of such.
And, Benedick, love on, I will requite thee,
    Taming my wild heart to thy loving hand ;
If thou dost love, my kindness shall incite thee
    To bind our loves up in an holy band :
For others say thou dost deserve ; and I
Believe it better than reportingly." [3]

And Benedick, on his part, is equally sincere in his
repentance with equal reason, after he has heard the grey-
beard, Leonato, and his friend, " Monsieur Love," discourse
of the desperate state of his supposed inamorata.

" This can be no trick ; the conference was sadly [4] borne. They
aave the truth of this from Hero. They seem to pity the

---

[1] Act iv., sc. 1.]   [2] Act iii., sc. 1.]   [3] *Ibid.*]
        [4] *i. e.* seriously, in earnest.— ED.

lady; it seems her affections have their full bent. Love me! why, it must be requited. I hear how I am censur'd: they say, I will bear myself proudly, if I perceive the love come from her, they say too, that she will rather die than give any sign of affection.—I did never think to marry: I must not seem proud:—happy are they that hear their detractions, and can put them to mending. They say, the lady is fair; 'tis a truth, I can bear them witness: and virtuous;—'tis so, I cannot reprove it: and wise—but for loving me :—by my troth it is no addition to her wit;—nor no great argument of her folly, for I will be horribly in love with her.—I may chance have some odd quirks and remnants of wit broken on me, because I have rail'd so long against marriage : but doth not the appetite alter ?—a man loves the meat in his youth, that he cannot endure in his age. Shall quips and sentences, and these paper-bullets of the brain, awe a man from the career of his humour ?—no: the world must be peopled. When I said, I would die a bachelor, I did not think I should live till I were married.—Here comes Beatrice : by this day, she's a fair lady : I do spy some marks of love in her."[1]

The beauty of all this arises from the characters of the persons so entrapped. Benedick is a professed and stanch enemy to marriage, and gives very plausible reasons for the faith that is in him. And as to Beatrice, she persecutes him all day with her jests (so that he could hardly think of being troubled with them at night), she not only turns him but all other things into jest, and is proof against everything serious.

" *Hero.* Disdain and scorn ride sparkling in her eyes,
Misprising what they look on ; and her wit
Values itself so highly, that to her
All matter else seems weak: she cannot love,
Nor take no shape nor project of affection,
She is so self-endear'd.
    Ursula.   Sure I think so;
And therefore, certainly, it were not good
She knew his love, lest she make sport at it.
    Hero. Why, you speak truth : I never yet saw man,
How wise, how noble, young, how rarely featur'd,
But she would spell him backward : if fair-fac'd,
She'd swear the gentleman should be her sister;

[1 Act ii., sc. 2.]

> If black, why, nature, drawing of an antick,
> Made a foul blot : if tall, a lance ill-headed;
> If low, an agate very vilely cut:
> If speaking, why, a vane blown with all winds;
> If silent, why, a block moved with none.
> So turns she every man the wrong side out;
> And never gives to truth and virtue that
> Which simpleness and merit purchaseth." [1]

These were happy materials for Shakespear to work on, and he has made a happy use of them. Perhaps that middle point of comedy was never more nicely hit in which the ludicrous blends with the tender, and our follies, turning round against themselves in support of our affections, retain nothing but their humanity.

Dogberry and Verges in this play are inimitable specimens of quaint blundering and misprisions of meaning; and are a standing record of that formal gravity of pretension and total want of common understanding, which Shakespear no doubt copied from real life, and which in the course of two hundred years appear to have ascended from the lowest to the highest offices in the state.

AS YOU LIKE IT. [2]

SHAKESPEAR has here converted the forest of Arden into another Arcadia, where they " fleet the time carelessly, as they did in the golden world." [3] It is the most ideal

[1] Act ii., sc. 2.]

[2] First printed, so far as existing information goes, in the folio of 1623 ; but on the 4th of August, no year mentioned [? 1600] was entered, *inter alia*, ' As You Like Yt, a book.' The other articles, all by " Mr. Shakespear," were published; but of a quarto of ' As You Like It,' no trace has at present been found. Shakespear has here made good use of a novel by his contemporary Lodge, entitled ' Rosalynd, Euphues' Golden Legacie,' first published in 1590, and often reprinted.—ED.

[3] Act i., sc. 1.]

of any of this author's plays. It is a pastoral drama, in which the interest arises more out of the sentiments and characters than out of the actions or situations. It is not what is done, but what is said, that claims our attention. Nursed in solitude, "under the shade of melancholy boughs,"[1] the imagination grows soft and delicate, and the wit runs riot in idleness, like a spoiled child, that is never sent to school. Caprice and fancy reign and revel here, and stern necessity is banished to the court. The mild sentiments of humanity are strengthened with thought and leisure; the echo of the cares and noise of the world strikes upon the ear of those "who have felt them knowingly,"[2] softened by time and distance. "They hear the tumult, and are still." The very air of the place seems to breathe a spirit of philosophical poetry : to stir the thoughts, to touch the heart with pity, as the drowsy forest rustles to the sighing gale. Never was there such beautiful moralising, equally free from pedantry or petulance :

> " And this our life, exempt from public haunt,
> Finds tongues in trees, books in the running brooks,
> Sermons in stones, and good in everything."[3]

Jaques is the only purely contemplative character in Shakespear. He thinks, and does nothing. His whole occupation is to amuse his mind, and he is totally regardless of his body and his fortunes. He is the prince of philosophical idlers; his only passion is thought; he sets no value upon anything but as it serves as food for reflection. He can "suck melancholy out of a song, as a weasel sucks eggs;"[4] the motley fool, "who morals on the time,"[5] is the greatest prize he meets with in the forest. He resents Orlando's passion for Rosalind as some disparagement of his own passion for abstract truth; and leaves the Duke, as soon as he is restored to

[1 Act ii., sc. 7.]   [2 'Cymbeline,' act iii., sc. 3.]
[3 'As You Like It,' act ii., sc. 1.] [4 Act ii., sc. 5.] [5 *Ibid.* sc. 7.]

his sovereignty, to seek his brother out who has quitted it, and turned hermit.

> " Out of these convertites
> There is much matter to be heard and learn'd."

Within the sequestered and romantic glades of the forest of Arden, they find leisure to be good and wise, or to play the fool and fall in love. Rosalind's character is made up of sportive gaiety and natural tenderness : her tongue runs the faster to conceal the pressure at her heart. She talks herself out of breath, only to get deeper in love. The coquetry with which she plays with her lover in the double character which she has to support is managed with the nicest address. How full of voluble, laughing grace is all her conversation with Orlando :

> " In heedless mazes running
> With wanton haste and giddy cunning."

How full of real fondness and pretended cruelty is her answer to him when he promises to love her " For ever and a day !"

> " Say a day without the ever : no, no, Orlando ; men are April when they woo, December when they wed : maids are May when they are maids ; but the sky changes when they are wives. I will be more jealous of thee than a Barbary cock-pigeon over his hen ; more clamorous than a parrot against rain ; more new-fangled than an ape ; more giddy in my desires than a monkey ; I will weep for nothing, like Diana in the fountain, and I will do that, when you are disposed to be merry ; I will laugh like a hyen, and that when you are inclined to sleep.
> *Orlando.* But will my Rosalind do so ?
> *Rosalind.* By my life she will do as I do."[2]

The silent and retired character of Celia is a necessary relief to the provoking loquacity of Rosalind, nor can anything be better conceived or more beautifully described than the mutual affection between the two cousins :

[¹ Act v., sc. 4.]   [² Act iv., sc. 1.]

" We still have slept together,
Rose at an instant, learn'd, play'd, eat together.
And wheresoe'er we went, like Juno's swans,
Still we went coupled and inseparable." [1]

The unrequited love of Silvius for Phebe shows the perversity of this passion in the commonest scenes of life, and the rubs and stops which nature throws in its way, where fortune has placed none. Touchstone is not in love, but he will have a mistress as a subject for the exercise of his grotesque humour, and to show his contempt for the passion, by his indifference about the person. He is a rare fellow. He is a mixture of the ancient cynic philosopher with the modern buffoon, and turns folly into wit, and wit into folly, just as the fit takes him. His courtship of Audrey not only throws a degree of ridicule on the state of wedlock itself, but he is equally an enemy to the prejudices of opinion in other respects. The lofty tone of enthusiasm, which the Duke and his companions in exile spread over the stillness and solitude of a country life, receives a pleasant shock from Touchstone's sceptical determination of the question :

" *Corin.* And how like you this shepherd's life, Master Touchstone ?
Clown. Truly, shepherd, in respect of itself, it is a good life ; but in respect that it is a shepherd's life, it is naught. In respect that it is solitary, I like it very well ; but in respect that it is private, it is a very vile life. Now in respect it is in the fields, it pleaseth me well ; but in respect it is not in the court, it is tedious. As it is a spare life, look you, it fits my humour ; but as there is no more plenty in it, it goes much against my stomach." [2]

Zimmerman's celebrated work on Solitude discovers only *half* the sense of this passage.

There is hardly any of Shakespear's plays that contains a greater number of passages that have been quoted in books of extracts, or a greater number of phrases that

[1 Act i., sc. 3.]   [2 Act iii., sc. 2.]

have become in a manner proverbial. If we were to give all the striking passages, we should give half the play. We will only recall a few of the most delightful to the reader's recollection. Such are the meeting between Orlando and Adam, the exquisite appeal of Orlando to the humanity of the Duke and his company to supply him with food for the old man, and their answer, the Duke's description of a country life, and the account of Jaques moralising on the wounded deer, his meeting with Touchstone in the forest, his apology for his own melancholy and his satirical vein, and the well-known speech on the stages of human life, the old song of " Blow, blow, thou winter's wind," Rosalind's description of the marks of a lover and of the progress of time with different persons, the picture of the snake wreathed round Oliver's neck while the lioness watches her sleeping prey, and Touchstone's lecture to the shepherd, his defence of cuckolds, and panegyric on the virtues of " an If."—All of these are familiar to the reader : there is one passage of equal delicacy and beauty which may have escaped him, and with it we shall close our account of ' As You Like It.' It is Phebe's description of Ganimed, at the end of the third act.

> " Think not I love him, tho' I ask for him ;
> 'Tis but a peevish boy, yet he talks well ;—
> But what care I for words ! yet words do well,
> When he that speaks them pleases those that hear :
> It is a pretty youth—not very pretty—
> But sure he's proud, and yet his pride becomes him ;
> He'll make a proper man ; the best thing in him
> Is his complexion ; and faster than his tongue
> Did make offence, his eye did heal it up :
> He is not very tall, yet for his years he's tall ;
> His leg is but so so, and yet 'tis well ;
> There was a pretty redness in his lip,
> A little riper and more lusty red
> Than that mixed in his cheek ; 'twas just the difference
> Betwixt the constant red and mingled damask.
> There be some women. Silvius, had they mark'd him

In parcels as I did, would have gone near
To fall in love with him : but for my part
I love him not, nor hate him not; and yet
I have more cause to hate him than to love him ;
For what had he to do to chide at me ?"

THE TAMING OF THE SHREW.[1]

' THE TAMING OF THE SHREW ' is almost the only one of Shakespear's comedies that has a regular plot, and downright moral. It is full of bustle, animation, and rapidity of action. It shows admirably how self-will is only to be got the better of by stronger will, and how one degree of ridiculous perversity is only to be driven out by another still greater. Petruchio is a madman in his senses ; a very honest fellow, who hardly speaks a word of truth, and succeeds in all his tricks and impostures. He acts his assumed character to the life, with the most fantastical extravagance, with complete presence of mind, with untired animal spirits, and without a particle of ill-humour from beginning to end.—The situation of poor Katherine, worn out by his incessant persecutions, becomes at last almost as pitiable as it is ludicrous, and it is difficult to say which to admire most, the unaccountableness of his actions, or the unalterableness of his resolutions. It is a character which most husbands ought to study, unless perhaps the very audacity of Petruchio's attempt might alarm them more than his success would encourage them. What a sound must the following speech carry to some married ears !

---

[1] Only known to us in the folio of 1623, and in a subsequent quarto impression of 1631. There was an anterior drama, printed in 1594, 1596, and 1607, in which the incidents and general structure of the story are similar, and in which Shakespear has even been thought (probably in error) to have had a hand.—ED

> " Think you a little din can daunt my ears?
> Have I not in my time heard lions roar?
> Have I not heard the sea, puff'd up with winds,
> Rage like an angry boar, chafed with sweat?
> Have I not heard great ordnance in the field?
> And heav'n's artillery thunder in the skies?
> Have I not in a pitched battle heard
> Loud larums, neighing steeds, and trumpets clang?
> And do you tell me of a woman's tongue,
> That gives not half so great a blow to hear,
> As will a chesnut in a farmer's fire?"[1]

Not all Petruchio's rhetoric would persuade more than " some dozen followers " to be of this heretical way of thinking. He unfolds his scheme for the 'Taming of the Shrew,' on a principle of contradiction, thus:—

> " I will attend her here,
> And woo her with some spirit when she comes.
> Say that she rail; why then I'll tell her plain,
> She sings as sweetly as a nightingale;
> Say that she frown; I'll say she looks as clear
> As morning roses newly wash'd with dew;
> Say she be mute, and will not speak a word;
> Then I'll commend her volubility,
> And say she uttereth piercing eloquence:
> If she do bid me pack, I'll give her thanks,
> As though she bid me stay by her a week;
> If she deny to wed, I'll crave the day,
> When I shall ask the banns, and when be married?"[2]

He accordingly gains her consent to the match, by telling her father that he has got it; disappoints her by not returning at the time he has promised to wed her, and when he returns, creates no small consternation by the oddity of his dress and equipage. This, however, is nothing to the astonishment excited by his mad-brained behaviour at the marriage. Here is the account of it by an eye-witness:—

" *Gremio.* Tut, she's a lamb, a dove, a fool to him: I'll tell you, Sir Lucentio: when the priest

[1 Act i., sc. 2.]   [2 Act ii., sc. 1.]

Should ask if Katherine should be his wife?
Ay, by gogs wouns, quoth he; and swore so loud,
That, all amaz'd, the priest let fall the book ;
And as he stooped again to take it up,
This mad-brain'd bridegroom took him such a cuff,
That down fell priest and book, and book and priest.
Now take them up, quoth he, if any list.
 Tranio. What said the wench when he rose up again ?
 Gremio. Trembled and shook; for why he stamp'd and swore,
As if the vicar meant to cozen him.
But after many ceremonies done,
He calls for wine; a health ! quoth he ; as if
He'd been aboard, carousing with his mates
After a storm ; quaff'd off the muscadel,
And threw the sops all in the sexton's face ;
Having no other reason,
But that his beard grew thin and hungerly,
And seem'd to ask him sops, as he was drinking.
This done, he took the bride about the neck,
And kiss'd her lips with such a clamorous smack,
That at the parting all the church did echo :
And I, seeing this, came thence for very shame ;
And after me, I know, the rout is coming.
Such a mad marriage never was before." [1]

The most striking and at the same time laughable feature in the character of Petruchio throughout, is the studied approximation to the intractable character of real madness, his apparent insensibility to all external considerations, and utter indifference to everything but the wild and extravagant freaks of his own self-will. There is no contending with a person on whom nothing makes any impression but his own purposes, and who is bent on his own whims just in proportion as they seem to want common sense. With him a thing's being plain and reasonable is a reason against it. The airs he gives himself are infinite, and his caprices as sudden as they are groundless. The whole of his treatment of his wife at home is in the same spirit of ironical attention and inverted gallantry. Everything flies before his will, like a

[1 Act iii., sc. 2.]

conjuror's wand, and he only metamorphoses his wife's
temper by metamorphosing her senses and all the objects
she sees, at a word's speaking. Such are his insisting
that it is the moon and not the sun which they see, &c.
This extravagance reaches its most pleasant and poetical
height in the scene where, on their return to her father's,
they meet old Vincentio, whom Petruchio immediately
addresses as a young lady :—

" *Petruchio.* Good morrow, gentle mistress, where away?
Tell me, sweet Kate, and tell me truly too,
Hast thou beheld a fresher gentlewoman?
Such war of white and red within her cheeks ;
What stars do spangle heaven with such beauty,
As those two eyes become that heav'nly face ?
Fair lovely maid, once more good day to thee :
Sweet Kate, embrace her for her beauty's sake.
   Hortensio. 'A will make the man mad to make a woman of him.
   Katherine. Young budding virgin, fair and fresh and sweet,
Whither away, or where is thy abode?
Happy the parents of so fair a child ;
Happier the man whom favourable stars
Allot thee for his lovely bed-fellow.
   Petruchio. Why, how now, Kate, I hope thou art not mad:
This is a man, old, wrinkled, faded, wither'd,
And not a maiden, as thou say'st he is.
   Katherine. Pardon, old father, my mistaking eyes
That have been so bedazzled with the sun
That everything I look on seemeth green.
Now I perceive thou art a reverend father."[1]

The whole is carried off with equal spirit, as if the
poet's comic Muse had wings of fire. It is strange how
one man could be so many things; but so it is. The
concluding scene, in which trial is made of the obedience
of the new-married wives (so triumphantly for Petruchio)
is a very happy one.—In some parts of this play there is
a little too much about music-masters and masters of
philosophy. They were things of greater rarity in those
days than they are now. Nothing however can be better

[1 Act iv., sc. 6.]

than the advice which Tranio gives his master for the
prosecution of his studies :—

> " The mathematics, and the metaphysics,
> Fall to them as you find your stomach serves you :
> No profit grows where is no pleasure ta'en :
> In brief, sir, study what you most affect." [1]

We have heard the ' Honeymoon' called " an elegant
Katherine and Petruchio." We suspect we do not understand this word *elegant* in the sense that many people do.
But in our sense of the word, we should call Lucentio's
description of his mistress elegant :

> " Tranio, I saw her coral lips to move,
> And with her breath she did perfume the air :
> Sacred and sweet was all I saw in her." [2]

When Biondello tells the same Lucentio for his encouragement, " I knew a wench married in an afternoon as she
went to the garden for parsley to stuff a rabbit, and so
may you, sir "—there is nothing elegant in this, and yet
we hardly know which of the two passages is the best.

' The Taming of the Shrew' is a play within a play.
It is supposed to be a play acted for the benefit of Sly
the tinker, who is made to believe himself a lord, when
he wakes after a drunken brawl. The character of Sly
and the remarks with which he accompanies the play are
as good as the play itself. His answer when he is asked
how he likes it, " Indifferent well ; 'tis a good piece of
work, would 'twere done," is in good keeping, as if he
were thinking of his Saturday night's job. Sly does not
change his tastes with his new situation, but in the midst
of splendour and luxury still calls out lustily and re-
peatedly " for a pot o' small ale." He is very slow in
giving up his personal identity in his sudden advancement—

> " I am Christophero Sly ; call me not honour nor lordship. I ne'er
> drank sack in my life : and if you give me any conserves, give me

---

[1] Act. i., sc. 1.]   [2] *Ibid.*]

conserves of beef: ne'er ask me what raiment I'll wear, for I have no more doublets than backs, no more stockings than legs, nor no more shoes than feet, nay, sometimes more feet than shoes, or such shoes as my toes look through the over-leather.—What, would you make me mad? Am not I Christophero Sly, old Sly's son of Burton-heath, by birth a pedlar, by education a card-maker, by transmutation a bear-herd, and now by present profession a tinker? Ask Marian Hacket, the fat alewife of Wincot, if she know me not; if she say I am not fourteen-pence on the score for sheer ale, score me up for the lying'st knave in Christendom." [1]

This is honest. "The Slys are no rogues," as he says of himself. We have a great predilection for this representative of the family; and what makes us like him the better is, that we take him to be of kin (not many degrees removed) to Sancho Panza.

MEASURE FOR MEASURE. [2]

This is a play as full of genius as it is of wisdom. Yet there is an original sin in the nature of the subject, which prevents us from taking a cordial interest in it. "The height of moral argument" which the author has maintained in the intervals of passion or blended with the more powerful impulses of nature, is hardly surpassed in any of his plays. But there is in general a want of passion; the affections are at a stand; our sympathies are repulsed and defeated in all directions. The only passion which influences the story is that of Angelo; and yet he seems to have a much greater passion for hypocrisy than for his mistress. Neither are we greatly enamoured of Isabella's rigid chastity, though she could not act other-

[1 'Induction,' sc. 2.]
[2] First printed in the folio of 1623. It appears to have been written early in 1604. Shakespear found his material chiefly in an old drama by George Whetstone, entitled 'Promos and Cassandra,' 1578, or in Whetstone's own prose version of that story in the Heptameron of Civil Discourses,' 1582.—Ed.

wise than she did. We do not feel the same confidence
in the virtue that is "sublimely good" at another's
expense, as if it had been put to some less disinterested
trial. As to the Duke, who makes a very imposing and
mysterious stage-character, he is more absorbed in his own
plots and gravity than anxious for the welfare of the state;
more tenacious of his own character than attentive to the
feelings and apprehensions of others. Claudio is the
only person who feels naturally; and yet he is placed in
circumstances of distress which almost preclude the wish
for his deliverance. Mariana is also in love with Angelo,
whom we hate. In this respect, there may be said to be
a general system of cross-purposes between the feelings of
the different characters and the sympathy of the reader or
the audience. This principle of repugnance seems to have
reached its height in the character of Master Barnardine,
who not only sets at defiance the opinions of others, but
has even thrown off all self-regard,—" a man that appre-
hends death no more dreadfully but as a drunken sleep;
careless, reckless, and fearless of what's past, present, or
to come."[1] He is a fine antithesis to the morality and the
hypocrisy of the other characters of the play. Barnardine
is Caliban transported from Prospero's wizard island to
the forests of Bohemia or the prisons of Vienna. He is
the creature of bad habits as Caliban is of gross instincts.
He has however a strong notion of the natural fitness of
things, according to his own sensations—" He has been
drinking hard all night, and he will not be hanged that
day "—and Shakespear has let him off at last. We do
not understand why the philosophical German critic,
Schlegel, should be so severe on those pleasant persons,
Lucio, Pompey, and Master Froth, as to call them
" wretches." They appear all mighty comfortable in
their occupations, and determined to pursue them, " as
the flesh and fortune should serve." A very good exposure

[1 Act iv., sc. 2.]

of the want of self-knowledge and contempt for others, which is so common in the world, is put into the mouth of Abhorson, the jailer, when the Provost proposes to associate Pompey with him in his office—"A bawd, sir? Fie upon him, he will discredit our mystery." And the same answer will serve in nine instances out of ten to the same kind of remark, "Go to, sir, you weigh equally ; a feather will turn the scale." Shakespear was in one sense the least moral of all writers ; for morality (commonly so called) is made up of antipathies; and his talent consisted in sympathy with human nature, in all its shapes, degrees, depressions, and elevations. The object of the pedantic moralist is to find out the bad in everything : his was to show that "there is some soul of goodness in things evil." Even Master Barnardine is not left to the mercy of what others think of him; but when he comes in, speaks for himself, and pleads his own cause, as well as if counsel had been assigned him. In one sense, Shakespear was no moralist at all : in another, he was the greatest of all moralists. He was a moralist in the same sense in which nature is one. He taught what he had learnt from her. He showed the greatest knowledge of humanity with the greatest fellow-feeling for it.

One of the most dramatic passages in the present play is the interview between Claudio and his sister, when she comes to inform him of the conditions on which Angelo will spare his life.

> "*Claudio.* Let me know the point.
> *Isabella.* O, I do fear thee, Claudio : and I quake,
> Lest thou a feverous life should'st entertain,
> And six or seven winters more respect
> Than a perpetual honour. Dar'st thou die ?
> The sense of death is most in apprehension ;
> And the poor beetle, that we tread upon,
> In corporal sufferance finds a pang as great
> As when a giant dies.
> *Claudio.*   Why give you me this shame ?

Think you I can a resolution fetch
From flowery tenderness? If I must die,
I will encounter darkness as a bride,
And hug it in mine arms.

 Isabella. There spake my brother! there my father's grave
Did utter forth a voice! Yes, thou must die:
Thou art too noble to conserve a life
In base appliances. This outward-sainted deputy—
Whose settled visage and deliberate word
Nips youth i' the head, and follies doth emmew,
As falcon doth the fowl—is yet a devil.
His filth within being cast, he would appear
A pond as deep as hell.

 Claudio.   The priestly Angelo?

 Isabella O, 'tis the cunning livery of hell,
The damned'st body to invest and cover
In priestly guards! Dost thou think, Claudio,—
If I would yield him my virginity,
Thou mightst be freed?

 Claudio.   O, heavens! it cannot be.

 Isabella. Yes, he would give 't thee, from this rank offence,
So to offend him still. This night's the time
That I should do what I abhor to name,
Or else thou diest to-morrow.

 Claudio.   Thou shalt not do 't.

 Isabella. O, were it but my life,
I'd throw it down for your deliverance
As frankly as a pin.

 Claudio. Thanks, dear Isabel.

 Isabella. Be ready, Claudio, for your death to-morrow

 Claudio. Yes.—Has he affections in him,
That thus can make him bite the law by the nose,
When he would force it? Sure it is no sin,
Or of the deadly seven it is the least.

 Isabella.   Which is the least?

 Claudio. If it were damnable, he being so wise,
Why should he for the momentary trick
Be perdurably fin'd? O, Isabel!

 Isabella. What says my brother?

 Claudio.   Death's a fearful thing

 Isabella. And shamed life a hateful.

 Claudio. Ay, but to die, and go we know not where;
To lie in cold obstruction, and to rot;
This sensible warm motion to become

A kneaded clod ; and the delighted spirit
To bathe in fiery floods, or to reside
In thrilling regions of thick-ribbed ice ;
To be imprison'd in the viewless winds,
And blown with restless violence round about
The pendent world ; or to be worse than worst
Of those that lawless and incertain thoughts
Imagine howling !—'tis too horrible !
The weariest and most loathed worldly life,
That age, ache, penury, and imprisonment
Can lay on nature, is a paradiso
To what we fear of death.
   Isabella.   Alas ! alas !
   Claudio.   Sweet sister, let me live :
What sin you do to save a brother's life,
Nature dispenses with the deed so far,
That it becomes a virtue." [1]

What adds to the dramatic beauty of this scene and
the effect of Claudio's passionate attachment to life is, that
it immediately follows the Duke's lecture to him, in the
character of the Friar, recommending an absolute indifference to it :

   " Reason thus with life,—
If I do lose thee, I do lose a thing
That none but fools would keep : a breath thou art,
Servile to all the skyey influences
That do this habitation, where thou keep'st,
Hourly afflict : merely, thou art death's fool ;
For him thou labour'st by thy flight to shun,
And yet runn'st toward him still. Thou art not noble ;
For all th' accommodations that thou bear'st
Are nurs'd by baseness. Thou'rt by no means valiant ;
For thou dost fear the soft and tender fork
Of a poor worm. Thy best of rest is sleep,
And that thou oft provok'st ; yet grossly fear'st
Thy death, which is no more. Thou art not thyself ;
For thou exist'st on many a thousand grains
That issue out of dust. Happy thou art not ;
For what thou hast not, still thou striv'st to get ;
And what thou hast, forgett'st. Thou art not certain ;

[1 Act iii., sc. 1.]

For thy complexion shifts to strange effects,
After the moon. If thou art rich thou'rt poor ;
For, like an ass whose back with ingots bows
Thou bear'st thy heavy riches but a journey,
And death unloads thee. Friend thou hast none ;
For thy own bowels, which do call thee sire,
The mere effusion of thy proper loins,
Do curse the gout, serpigo, and the rheum,
For ending thee no sooner. Thou'st nor youth, nor age
But, as it were, an after-dinner's sleep,
Dreaming on both : for all thy blessed youth
Becomes as aged, and doth beg the alms
Of palsied eld ; and when thou art old, and rich,
Thou hast neither heat, affection, limb, nor beauty,
To make thy riches pleasant. What's yet in this,
That bears the name of life ? Yet in this life
Lie hid more thousand deaths ; yet death we fear,
That makes these odds all even." [1]

THE MERRY WIVES OF WINDSOR. [2]

The 'Merry Wives of Windsor' is no doubt a very
amusing play, with a great deal of humour, character, and
nature in it : but we should have liked it much better if
any one else had been the hero of it, instead of Falstaff.
We could have been contented if Shakespear had not
been " commanded to show the knight in love." Wits
and philosophers, for the most part, do not shine in that
character ; and Sir John himself by no means comes off
with flying colours. Many people complain of the
degradation and insults to which Don Quixote is so
frequently exposed in his various adventures. But what
are the unconscious indignities which he suffers, com-

[1 Act iii., sc. 1.]
[2] First printed (imperfectly) in 1602 ; the earliest genuine text is
in the folio of 1623. The more or less probable sources of Shakespear's drama are collected in the Appendix to the Shakespear
Society's reprint of edit. 1602.—Ed.

pared with the sensible mortifications which Falstaff is made to bring upon himself? What are the blows and buffettings which the Don receives from the staves of the Yanguesian carriers or from Sancho Panza's more hard-hearted hands, compared with the contamination of the buck-basket, the disguise of the fat woman of Brentford, and the horns of Herne the hunter, which are discovered on Sir John's head? In reading the play, we indeed wish him well through all these discomfitures, but it would have been as well if he had not got into them. Falstaff in the 'Merry Wives of Windsor' is not the man he was in the two parts of 'Henry IV.' His wit and eloquence have left him. Instead of making a butt of others, he is made a butt of by them. Neither is there a single particle of love in him to excuse his follies: he is merely a designing bare-faced knave, and an unsuccessful one. The scene with Ford as Master Brook, and that with Simple, Slender's man, who comes to ask after the Wise Woman, are almost the only ones in which his old intellectual ascendency appears. He is like a person recalled to the stage to perform an unaccustomed and un-gracious part; and in which we perceive only "some faint sparks of those flashes of merriment that were wont to set the hearers in a roar." But the single scene with Doll Tearsheet, or Mrs. Quickly's account of his desiring "to eat some of housewife Keach's prawns," and telling her "to be no more so familiarity with such people," is worth the whole of the 'Merry Wives of Windsor' put together. Ford's jealousy, which is the mainspring of the comic incidents, is certainly very well managed. Page, on the contrary, appears to be somewhat uxorious in his disposition; and we have pretty plain indications of the effect of the characters of the husbands on the different degrees of fidelity in their wives. Mrs. Quickly makes a very lively go-between, both between Falstaff and his Dulcineas, and Anne Page and her lovers, and seems in the latter case so intent on her own interest as totally to overlook the intentions of her employers. Her master, Doctor Caius, the Frenchman, and her fellow-servant, Jack Rugby, are very completely described. This last-mentioned person is rather quaintly commended by Mrs. Quickly as " an honest, willing, kind fellow, as ever servant shall come in house withal, and I warrant you, no tell-tale, nor no breed-bate; his worst fault is, that he is given to prayer; he is something peevish that way; but nobody but has his fault." [1] The Welch Parson, Sir Hugh Evans (a title which in those days was given to the clergy) is an excellent character in all respects. He is as respectable as he is laughable. He has " very good discretions and very odd humours." The duel-scene with Caius gives him an opportunity to show his "cholers and his tremblings of mind," his valour and his melancholy, in an irresistible manner. In the dialogue which at his mother's request he holds with his pupil, William Page, to show his progress in learning, it is hard to say whether the simplicity of the master or the scholar is the greatest. Nym, Bardolph, and Pistol are but the shadows of what they were; and Justice Shallow himself has little of his consequence left. But his cousin, Slender, makes up for the deficiency. He is a very potent piece of imbecility. In him the pretensions of the worthy Gloucestershire family are well kept up, and immortalised. He and his friend Sackerson and his book of songs and his love of Anne Page and his having nothing to say to her can never be forgotten. It is the only first-rate character in the play: but it is in that class. Shakespear is the only writer who was as great in describing weakness as strength.

[1 Act I., sc. 4.]

THE COMEDY OF ERRORS.[1]

THIS comedy is taken very much from the Menæchmi of Plautus, and is not an improvement on it. Shakespear appears to have bestowed no great pains on it, and there are but a few passages which bear the decided stamp of his genius. He seems to have relied on his author, and on the interest arising out of the intricacy of the plot. The curiosity excited is certainly very considerable, though not of the most pleasing kind. We are teazed as with a riddle, which notwithstanding we try to solve. In reading the play, from the sameness of the names of the two Antipholises and the two Dromios, as well from their being constantly taken for each other by those who see them, it is difficult, without a painful effort of attention, to keep the characters distinct in the mind. And again, on the stage, either the complete similarity of their persons and dress must produce the same perplexity whenever they first enter, or the identity of appearance which the story supposes will be destroyed. We still, however, having a clue to the difficulty, can tell which is which, merely from the practical contradictions which arise as soon as the different parties begin to speak; and we are indemnified for the perplexity and blunders into which we are thrown by seeing others thrown into greater and almost inextricable ones. This play (among other

[1] This was one of Shakespear's earliest dramatic productions; it is supposed, with some reason, to be the same play which was performed at Gray's Inn in 1594. There is no edition of it, however, prior to that contained in the first folio. The author resorted to the 'Menæchmi' of Plautus, of which no English translation is at present known earlier than that by W. W[arner], 1595, 4to.—ED.

considerations) leads us not to feel much regret that
Shakespear was not what is called a classical scholar.
We do not think his *forte* would ever have lain in imi-
tating or improving on what others invented, so much
as in inventing for himself, and perfecting what he
invented,—not perhaps by the omission of faults, but by
the addition of the highest excellences. His own genius
was strong enough to bear him up, and he soared longest
and best on unborrowed plumes. The only passage of a
very Shakespearian cast in this comedy is the one in
which the Abbess, with admirable characteristic artifice,
makes Adriana confess her own misconduct in driving her
husband mad :

" *Abbess.* How long hath this possession held the man ?
  Adriana. This week he hath been heavy, sour, sad,
And much, much different from the man he was ;
But, till this afternoon, his passion
Ne'er brake into extremity of rage.
  Abbess. Hath he not lost much wealth by wreck of sea ?
Buried some dear friend ? Hath not else his eye
Stray'd his affection in unlawful love ?
A sin prevailing much in youthful men,
Who give their eyes the liberty of gazing.
Which of these sorrows is he subject to ?
  Adriana. To none of these, except it be the last :
Namely, some love that drew him oft from home.
  Abbess. You should for that have reprehended him.
  Adriana. Why, so I did.
  Abbess.   Ay, but not rough enough.
  Adriana. As roughly as my modesty would let me.
  Abbess. Haply, in private ?
  Adriana.   And in assemblies too.
  Abbess. Ay, but not enough.
  Adriana. It was the copy of our conference :
In bed, he slept not for my urging it ;
At board, he fed not for my urging it ;
Alone it was the subject of my theme ;
In company, I often glanc'd at it ;
Still did I tell him it was vile and bad.
  Abbess. And therefore came it that the man was mad :
The venom'd clamours of a jealous woman

Poison more deadly than a mad dog's tooth.
It seems, his sleeps were hinder'd by thy railing :
And therefore comes it that his head is light.
Thou says't his meat was sauc'd with thy upbraidings ;
Unquiet meals make ill digestions,
Therefore the raging fire of fever bred :
And what's a fever but a fit of madness ?
Thou says't his sports were hinder'd by thy brawls ;
Sweet recreation barr'd, what doth ensue
But moody and dull melancholy,
Kinsman to grim and comfortless despair
And at her heels a huge infectious troop
Of pale distemperatures and foes to life ?
In food, in sport, and life-preserving rest
To be disturb'd, would mad or man or beast ;
The consequence is, then, thy jealous fits
Have scar'd thy husband from the use of wits.
 Luciana. She never reprehended him but mildly,
When he demeaned himself rough-rude, and wildly.—
Why bear you these rebukes, and answer not ?
 Adriana. She did betray me to my own reproof." [1]

Pinch the conjuror is also an excrescence not to be found in Plautus. He is indeed a very formidable anachronism :

 " They brought one Pinch, a hungry lean-fac'd villain,
A mere anatomy, a mountebank,
A thread-bare juggler and a fortune-teller ;
A needy, hollow-ey'd, sharp-looking wretch,
A living-dead man." [2]

This is exactly like some of the Puritanical portraits to be met with in Hogarth.

———◆◇◆———

DOUBTFUL PLAYS OF SHAKESPEAR.

WE shall give for the satisfaction of the reader what the celebrated German critic, Schlegel, says on this subject, and then add a very few remarks of our own.

  [1 Act v., sc. 1.]   [2 *Ibid.*]

"All the editors, with the exception of Capell, are unanimous in rejecting 'Titus Adronicus' as unworthy of Shakespear, though they always allow it to be printed with the other pieces, as the scape-goat, as it were, of their abusive criticism. The correct method in such an investigation is first to examine into the external grounds, evidences, &c., and to weigh their worth; and then to adduce the internal reasons derived from the quality of the work. The critics of Shakespear follow a course directly the reverse of this; they set out with a preconceived opinion against a piece, and seek, in justification of this opinion, to render the historical grounds suspicious, and to set them aside. 'Titus Andronicus' is to be found in the first folio edition of Shakespear's works, which it was known was conducted by Heminge and Condell, for many years his friends and fellow-managers of the same theatre. Is it possible to persuade ourselves that they would not have known if a piece in their repertory did or did not actually belong to Shakespear? And are we to lay to the charge of these honourable men a designed fraud in this single case, when we know that they did not show themselves so very desirous of scraping everything together which went by the name of Shakespear, but, as it appears, merely gave those plays of which they had manuscripts in hand? Yet the following circumstance is still stronger: George Meres, a contemporary and admirer of Shakespear, mentions 'Titus Andronicus' in an enumeration of his works, in the year 1598. Meres was personally acquainted with the poet, and so very intimately, that the latter read over to him his Sonnets before they were printed. I cannot conceive that all the critical scepticism in the world would be sufficient to get over such a testimony.

"This tragedy, it is true, is framed according to a false idea of the tragic, which by an accumulation of cruelties and enormities degenerates into the horrible, and yet leaves no deep impression behind: the story of Tereus and Philomela is heightened and overcharged under other names, and mixed up with the repast of Atreus and Thyestes, and many other incidents. In detail there is no want of beautiful lines, bold images, nay, even features which betray the peculiar conception of Shakespear. Among these we may reckon the joy of the treacherous Moor at the blackness and ugliness of his child begot in adultery; and in the compassion of Titus Andronicus, grown childish through grief, for a fly which had been struck dead, and his rage afterwards when he imagines he discovers in it his black enemy, we recognise the future poet of 'Lear.' Are the critics afraid that Shakespear's fame would be injured, were it established that in his early youth he ushered into the world a feeble and immature work? Was Rome the less the conqueror of the world because Remus could leap over its first walls? Let any one place himself in Shakespear's situation at the commencement of his career. He found only a few indifferent models, and yet these met with the most favourable reception, because men are never difficult to please in the novelty of an art before their taste has become fastidious from choice and abundance. Must not this situation have had its influence on him before he learned to make higher demands on himself, and by digging deeper in his own mind, discovered the richest veins of a noble metal? It is even highly probable that he must have made several failures before getting into the right path. Genius is in a certain sense infallible, and has nothing to learn; but art is to be learned, and must be acquired by practice and experience. In Shakespear's acknowledged works we find hardly any traces of his apprenticeship, and yet an apprenticeship he certainly had. This every artist must have, and especially in a period where he has not before him the example of a school already formed. I consider it as extremely probable, that Shakespear began to write for the theatre at a

much earlier period than the one which is generally
stated, namely, not till after the year 1590. It appears
that, as early as the year 1584, when only twenty years
of age, he had left his paternal home and repaired to
London. Can we imagine that such an active head
would remain idle for six whole years without making
any attempt to emerge by his talents from an uncongenial
situation ? That in the dedication of the poem of Venus
and Adonis he calls it, "the first heir of his invention,"
proves nothing against the supposition. It was the first
which he printed; he might have composed it at an
earlier period ; perhaps, also, he did not include theatrical labours, as they then possessed but little literary
dignity. The earlier Shakespear began to compose for
the theatre, the less are we enabled to consider the im-
maturity and imperfection of a work as a proof of its
spuriousness in opposition to historical evidence, if we
only find in it prominent features of his mind. Several
of the works rejected as spurious may still have been
produced in the period betwixt 'Titus Andronicus' and
the earliest of the acknowledged pieces.

"At last, Steevens published seven pieces ascribed to
Shakespear in two supplementary volumes. It is to be
remarked, that they all appeared in print in Shakespear's
life-time, with his name prefixed at full length.[1] They
are the following :—

"1. 'Locrine.'[2] The proofs of the genuineness of this
piece are not altogether unambiguous; the grounds for
doubt, on the other hand, are entitled to attention. However, this question is immediately connected with that
respecting 'Titus Andronicus,' and must be at the same
time resolved in the affirmative or negative.

[1] This is not the case.—Ed.

[2] By Charles Tylney, 1595, 4to. It has the initials *W. S.* on the
title; but in an extant copy it is assigned in a MS. note by Sir
George Buc, Master of the Revels under James I., to Tylney.—Ed.

"2. 'Pericles, Prince of Tyre.'[1] This piece was acknowledged by Dryden, but as a youthful work of Shakespear. It is most undoubtedly his, and it has been admitted into several of the late editions. The supposed imperfections originate in the circumstance that Shakespear here handled a childish and extravagant romance of the old poet Gower, and was unwilling to drag the subject out of its proper sphere. Hence he even introduces Gower himself, and makes him deliver a prologue entirely in his antiquated language and versification. This power of assuming so foreign a manner is at least no proof of helplessness.

"3. 'The London Prodigal.'[2] If we are not mistaken, Lessing pronounced this piece to be Shakespear's, and wished to bring it on the German stage.

"4. 'The Puritan; or, the Widow of Watling Street.' One of my literary friends, intimately acquainted with Shakespear, was of opinion that the poet must have wished to write a play for once in the style of Ben Jonson, and that in this way we must account for the difference between the present piece and his usual manner. To follow out this idea however would lead to a very nice critical investigation.[3]

"5. 'Thomas, Lord Cromwell.'[4]

[1] This drama is included by Mr. Dyce in his 2nd edit.; he recognises Shakespear's hand in the later portions, assigning the principal share of the production to a very inferior pen. The materials employed in its composition are reprinted in 'Shakespear's Library.' But the most curious circumstance connected with 'Pericles' is, perhaps, the prose novel which was formed from it by some one who witnessed its performance, and was printed in 1608, a year prior to any known impression of the play.—ED.

[2] Both this and the following were published in 1607.—ED.

[3] Some of the incidents in this play, clearly not Shakespear's, appear to have been founded on real events on the life of George Peele the dramatist, the George Pyeboard of the piece. See 'Old English Jest Books,' 1864, ii. 262, *et seqq.*—ED.

[4] Printed in 1602, and again in 1613.—ED.

"6. 'Sir John Oldcastle—First Part.[1]

"7. 'A Yorkshire Tragedy.'[2]

"The three last pieces are not only unquestionably Shakespear's, but in my opinion they deserve to be classed among his best and maturest works.[3] Steevens admits at last, in some degree, that they are Shakespear's, as well as the others, excepting 'Locrine,' but he speaks of all of them with great contempt, as quite worthless productions. This condemnatory sentence is not however in the slightest degree convincing, nor is it supported by critical acumen. I should like to see how such a critic would, of his own natural suggestion, have decided on Shakespear's acknowledged master-pieces, and what he would have thought of praising in them, had the public opinion not imposed on him the duty of admiration. 'Thomas, Lord Cromwell,' and 'Sir John Oldcastle,' are biographical dramas, and models in this species: the first is linked, from its subject, to 'Henry the Eighth,' and the second to 'Henry the Fifth.' The second part of 'Oldcastle' is wanting; I know not whether a copy of the old edition has been discovered in England, or whether it is lost.[4] 'The Yorkshire Tragedy' is a tragedy in one act, a dramatised tale of murder: the tragical effect is overpowering, and it is extremely important to see how poetically Shakespear could handle such a subject.

"There have been still farther ascribed to him:—1st. 'The Merry Devil of Edmonton,' a comedy in one act, printed in Dodsley's old plays.[5] This has certainly some

[1] No more was ever printed. This drama was a sort of joint compilation by Munday, Drayton, Wilson, and Hathaway; but to what extent each was concerned does not appear.—ED.

[2] First printed in 1608.—ED.

[3] *Chacun à son goût!*—ED.

[4] The 'First Part' is one of the least rare of the old quartos; no copy of the 'Second Part' has been found, and, it is believed, for the good reason that it was never written.—ED.

[5] Printed in 1608; there are later editions. The author is not known.—ED.

appearances in its favour. It contains a merry landlord, who bears a great similarity to the one in the 'Merry Wives of Windsor.' However, at all events, though an ingenious, it is but a hasty sketch. 2nd. 'The Arraignment of Paris.'[1] 3rd. 'The Birth of Merlin.'[2] 4th. 'Edward the Third.'[3] 5th. 'Fair Em.'[4] 6th. 'Mucedorus.'[5] 7th. 'Arden of Feversham.'[6] I have never seen any of these, and cannot therefore say anything respecting them. From the passages cited, I am led to conjecture that the subject of 'Mucedorus' is the popular story of Valentine and Orson; a beautiful subject which Lope de Vega has also taken for a play. 'Arden of Feversham' is said to be a tragedy on the story of a man, from whom the poet was descended by the mother's side. If the quality of the piece is not too directly at variance with this claim, the circumstance would afford an additional probability in its favour. For such motives were not foreign to Shakespear: he treated Henry the Seventh, who bestowed lands on his forefathers for services performed by them, with a visible partiality.

" Whoever takes from Shakespear a play early ascribed to him, and confessedly belonging to his time, is unquestionably bound to answer, with some degree of

[1] By George Peele. It is in Mr. Dyce's edition of his works, 1828, 1829, 1861.—ED.

[2] This drama purports to have been written by William Shakespear and William Rowley as a joint production; it was first printed, so far as can be now ascertained, in 1662. Shakespear's concern in its execution is extremely doubtful.—ED.

[3] 'The Raigne of Edward the Third,' a well-written play, but not Shakespear's, was printed in 1596 and 1599.—ED.

[4] Printed in 1631, unless an undated 4to. is (which I think likely) earlier.—ED.

[5] Printed in 1598; there are later editions.—ED.

[6] Printed in 1592, 1599, 1633. In 1770 the play was republished by Mr. Jacob of Feversham as Shakespear's; but the opinion has not obtained many converts. There is a later drama by Lillo, founded on this tragical occurrence.—ED.

probability, **this** question : who has then written it ? Shakespear's competitors in the dramatic walk are pretty well known, and if those of them who have even acquired a considerable name, a Lilly, a Marlow, a Heywood, are still so very far below him, we can hardly imagine that the author of a work, which rises so high beyond theirs, would have remained unknown." [1]

We agree to the truth of this last observation, but not to the justice of its application to some of the plays here mentioned. It is true that Shakespear's best works are very superior to those of Marlow, or Heywood, but it is not true that the best of the doubtful plays above enu-merated are superior or even equal to the best of theirs. ' The Yorkshire Tragedy,' which Schlegel speaks of as an undoubted production of our author's, is much more in the manner of Heywood than of Shakespear. The effect is indeed overpowering, but the mode of producing it is by no means poetical. The praise which Schlegel gives to ' Thomas, Lord Cromwell,' and to ' Sir John Oldcastle.' is altogether exaggerated. They are very indifferent compositions, which have not the slightest pretensions to rank with ' Henry V.' or ' Henry VIII.' We suspect that the German critic was not very well acquainted with the dramatic contemporaries of Shakespear, or aware of their general merits; and that he accordingly mistakes a resemblance in style and manner for an equal degree of excellence. Shakespear differed from the other writers of his age not in the mode of treating his subjects, but in the grace and power which he displayed in them. The reason assigned by a literary friend of Schlegel's for supposing ' The Puritan ; or, the Widow of Watling Street,' to be Shakespear's, viz., that it is in the style of Ben Jonson, that is to say, in a style just the reverse of his own, is not very satisfactory to a plain English understanding. ' Locrine,' and ' The London Prodigal,' if they were

Shakespear's at all, must have been among the sins of his youth. 'Arden of Feversham' contains several striking passages, but the passion which they express is rather that of a sanguine temperament than of a lofty imagination; and in this respect they approximate more nearly to the style of other writers of the time than to Shakespear's. 'Titus Andronicus' is certainly as unlike Shakespear's usual style as it is possible. It is an accumulation of vulgar physical horrors, in which the power exercised by the poet bears no proportion to the repugnance excited by the subject. The character of Aaron the Moor is the only thing which shows any originality of conception; and the scene in which he expresses his joy "at the blackness and ugliness of his child begot in adultery," the only one worthy of Shakespear. Even this is worthy of him only in the display of power, for it gives no pleasure. Shakespear managed these things differently. Nor do we think it a sufficient answer to say that this was an embryo or crude production of the author. In its kind it is full grown, and its features decided and overcharged. It is not like a first imperfect essay, but shows a confirmed habit, a systematic preference of violent effect to everything else. There are occasional detached images of great beauty and delicacy, but these were not beyond the powers of other writers then living. The circumstance which inclines us to reject the external evidence in favour of this play being Shakespear's is, that the grammatical construction is constantly false and mixed up with vulgar abbreviations, a fault that never occurs in any of his genuine plays. A similar defect, and the halting measure of the verse are the chief objections to 'Pericles of Tyre,' if we except the far-fetched and complicated absurdity of the story. The movement of the thoughts and passions has something in it not unlike Shakespear, and several of the descriptions are either the original hints of passages which Shakespear has engrafted on his other plays, or are imitations of them by some contemporary poet. The most memorable idea in it is in Marina's speech, where she compares the world to "a lasting storm, hurrying her from her friends."

POEMS AND SONNETS.

OUR idolatry of Shakespear (not to say our admiration) ceases with his plays. In his other productions, he was a mere author, though not a common author. It was only by representing others that he became himself. He could go out of himself, and express the soul of Cleopatra; but in his own person he appeared to be always waiting for the prompter's cue. In expressing the thoughts of others, he seemed inspired; in expressing his own, he was a mechanic. The licence of an assumed character was necessary to restore his genius to the privileges of nature, and to give him courage to break through the tyranny of fashion, the trammels of custom. In his plays, he was "as broad and casing as the general air:" in his poems, on the contrary, he appears to be "cooped, and cabined in" by all the technicalities of art, by all the petty intricacies of thought and language, which poetry had learned from the controversial jargon of the schools, where words had been made a substitute for things. There was, if we mistake not, something of modesty, and a painful sense of personal propriety at the bottom of this. Shakespear's imagination, by identifying itself with the strongest characters in the most trying circumstances, grappled at once with nature, and trampled the littleness of art under his feet: the rapid changes of situation, the wide range of the universe, gave him life and spirit, and afforded full scope to his genius; but returned into his closet again, and having assumed the badge of his profession, he could only labour in his vocation, and conform himself to existing models. The thoughts, the passions, the words which the poet's pen, " glancing from heaven to earth, from earth to heaven," lent to others, shook off the fetters of pedantry and affectation ; while his own thoughts and feelings, standing by themselves, were seized upon as lawful prey, and tortured to death according to the established rules and practice of the day. In a word, we do not like Shakespear's poems, because we like his plays : the one, in all their excellences, are just the reverse of the other. It has been the fashion of late to cry up our author's poems, as equal to his plays : this is the desperate cant of modern criticism. We would ask, was there the slightest comparison between Shakespear, and either Chaucer or Spenser, as mere poets ? Not any. The two poems of Venus and Adonis and of Tarquin and Lucrece appear to us like a couple of ice-houses. They are about as hard, as glittering, and as cold. The author seems all the time to be thinking of his verses, and not of his subject,—not of what his characters would feel, but of what he shall say ; and as it must happen in all such cases, he always puts into their mouths those things which they would be the last to think of, and which it shows the greatest ingenuity in him to find out. The whole is laboured, up-hill work. The poet is perpetually singling out the difficulties of the art to make an ex- hibition of his strength and skill in wrestling with them. He is making perpetual trials of them, as if his mastery over them were doubted. The images, which are often striking, are generally applied to things which they are the least like : so that they do not blend with the poem, but seem stuck upon it, like splendid patch-work, or remain quite distinct from it, like detached substances, painted and varnished over. A beautiful thought is sure to be lost in an endless commentary upon it. The speakers are like persons who have both leisure and inclination to make riddles on their own situation, and to twist and turn every object or incident into acrostics and anagrams. Everything is spun out into allegory; and a digression is always preferred to the main story. Sentiment is built up upon plays of words; the hero or heroine feels, not from the impulse of passion, but from the force of dialectics. There is besides a strange attempt to substitute the language of painting for that of poetry to make us *see* their feelings in the faces of the persons and again, consistently with this, in the description of the picture in Tarquin and Lucrece, those circumstances are chiefly insisted on which it would be impossible to convey except by words. The invocation to opportunity in the Tarquin and Lucrece is full of thoughts and images, but at the same time it is overloaded by them. The concluding[1] stanza expresses all our objections to this kind of poetry :—

> " Out, idle words, servants to shallow fools ;
> Unprofitable sounds, weak arbitrators !
> Busy yourselves in skill-contending schools :
> Debate where leisure serves with dull debaters ;
> To trembling clients be you mediators :
> For me I force not argument a straw,
> Since that my case is past the help of law."

The description of the horse in Venus and Adonis has been particularly admired, and not without reason : —

> " Round-hoof'd, short-jointed, fetlocks shag and long,
> Broad breast, full eye, small head, and nostril wide,
> High crest, short ears, straight legs, and passing strong,
> Thin mane, thick tail, broad buttock, tender hide ;
> Look, what a horse should have, he did not lack,
> Save a proud rider on so proud a back."

Now this inventory of perfections shows great knowledge of the horse ; and is good matter-of-fact poetry. Let the reader but compare it with a speech in the ' Midsummer Night's Dream,' where Theseus describes his hounds—-

---

[1] It is not the *concluding* stanza. See Dyce's 2nd edit., viii 316.—Ed.

" And their heads are hung
With ears that sweep away the morning dew "—

and he will perceive at once what we mean by the difference between Shakespear's own poetry, and that of his
plays. We prefer the Passionate Pilgrim very much to
the Lover's Complaint. It has been doubted whether the
latter poem is Shakespear's.[1]

Of the Sonnets we do not well know what to say. The
subject of them seems to be somewhat equivocal; but
many of them are highly beautiful in themselves, and
interesting as they relate to the state of the personal
feelings of the author. The following are some of the
most striking :—

[CONSTANCY.]

" Let those who are in favour with their stars,
　Of public honour and proud titles boast,
　Whilst I, whom fortune of such triumph bars,
　Unlook'd-for joy in that I honour most.
　Great princes' favourites their fair leaves spread
　But as the marigold in the sun's eye;
　And in themselves their pride lies buried,
　For at a frown they in their glory die.
　The painful warrior famoused for fight,
　After a thousand victories once foil'd,
　Is from the book of honour razed quite,
　And all the rest forgot for which he toil'd :
　　Then happy I, that love and am belov'd,
　　Where I may not remove nor be remov'd."

[LOVE'S CONSOLATION.]

' When in disgrace with fortune and men's eyes,
　I all alone beweep my outcast state,
　And trouble deaf heaven with my bootless cries,
　And look upon myself, and curse my fate,
　Wishing me like to one more rich in hope,
　Featur'd like him, like him with friends possess'd,
　Desiring this man's art, and that man's scope,
　With what I most enjoy contented least :
　Yet in these thoughts myself almost despising,

---

[1] Without any substantial reason.—ED.

Haply I think on thee,—and then my state
(Like to the lark at break of day arising
From sullen earth) sings hymns at heaven's gate;
  For thy sweet love remember'd, such wealth brings,
  That then I scorn to change my state with kings."

[NOVELTY.]

" My love is strengthen'd, though more weak in seeming;
I love not less, though less the show appear:
That love is merchandis'd, whose rich esteeming
The owner's tongue doth publish everywhere.
Our love was new, and then but in the spring,
When I was wont to greet it with my lays:
As Philomel in summer's front doth sing,
And stops his pipe in growth of riper days:
Not that the summer is less pleasant now
Than when her mournful hymns did hush the night,
But that wild music burdens every bough,
And sweets grown common lose their dear delight.
  Therefore, like her, I sometime hold my tongue,
  Because I would not dull you with my song."

[LIFE'S DECAY.]

" That time of year thou may'st in me behold
When yellow leaves, or none, or few, do hang
Upon those boughs which shake against the cold,
Bare ruin'd choirs, where late the sweet birds sang.
In me thou seest the twilight of such day,
As after sunset fadeth in the west,
Which by and by black night doth take away,
Death's second self, that seals up all in rest.
In me thou seest the glowing of such fire,
That on the ashes of his youth doth lie,
As the death-bed whereon it must expire,
Consum'd with that which it was nourish'd by.
  This thou perceiv'st, which makes thy love more strong,
  To love that well which thou must leave ere long."

In all these, as well as in many others, there is a mild
tone of sentiment, deep, mellow, and sustained, very
different from the crudeness of his earlier poems.

THE END